International Perspectives on Special Educational Needs

Edited by
Colin Brock and Rosarii Griffin

John Catt Educational Limited

First Published 2000
by John Catt Educational Ltd,
Great Glemham, Saxmundham, Suffolk IP17 2DH
Tel: 01728 663666 Fax: 01728 663415
E-mail: enq@johncatt.co.uk

Managing Director: Jonathan Evans. Editor-in-Chief: Derek Bingham

ISBN: 0 901577 45 6

Set and designed by
John Catt Educational Limited

Printed and bound in Great Britain by
Bell & Bain Ltd, Glasgow, Scotland

Contents

continued overleaf

Contents (continued)

Notes on Contributors

Colin Brock is a Lecturer in Comparative and International Education at the University of Oxford, an international educational consultant and a former chair of the British Association of International and Comparative Education. He has worked extensively in Africa, Asia, Europe the Americas and the tropical island zones. A former editor of *Compare*, he has published widely and is currently series editor for *Frontiers of International Education* (Cassell) and *Monographs in International Education* (Symposium Books). Over the past three years, he has worked with John Catt Educational Limited on their annual National Conference for Special Educational Needs.

Rosarii Griffin is a researcher, a teacher and an international educational consultant and is currently engaged on a transatlantic comparative research project between England, Ireland and the USA towards her doctoral research at the University of Oxford. She has both researched and lectured at various universities in North America and Europe. Her research interests include how policy issues translate into practice; third world development issues; and the theory of Multiple Intelligences and how it relates to special educational needs. She has also been involved with John Catt Educational Limited and their National Conference for Special Educational Needs.

Harvey B Adams worked in an advisory capacity in the UK where he developed curricula for problem-solving in science and technology. From here, he went to the University of Natal developing new courses in cognitive psychology for undergraduates and Master's students. As Professor and Head of the Department of Educational Psychology, he developed a new approach for the training of educational psychologists which emphasised the importance of cognitive psychology. He has also written extensively in the field.

Pilar Arnaiz is a full time Lecturer in Special Educational Needs at the University of Murcia, Spain. She is Head of the Research Group of 'Special Educational Needs - Psychology Educational' at the University and is currently developing a UNESCO project on 'Effective Schools for All'.

Dan G Bachor is a Professor in the Department of Educational Psychology and Leadership Studies, Faculty of Education, University of Victoria, Canada. He teaches courses in assessment and instruction for students with learning problems, current issues in special education, research design and developmental psychology. His research interests are in classroom assessment practices, individualised diagnostic assessment and instruction for children with special educational needs.

Markus Baer is a graduate student studying in the Department of Educational Psychology and Leadership Studies, Faculty of Education, University of Victoria, Canada. He has taught students with special educational needs in Canada and worked as an English as a Second Language teacher in Japan.

Maria Báez is a Lecturer in Education and active researcher at the Special Needs Research Centre, Educational Department, University of Newcastle-upon-Tyne. She received a PhD in Special Education from Brunel University, London. Her research interests are international issues on Special Needs Education and Comparative Special Education. Dr Báez has extensive experience on education systems of Latin America. She is a member of the British Association of International and Comparative Education.

Robert Barratt is a Lecturer in the Department of Educational Studies at the University of Oxford. He is involved in initial teacher education, educational research, consultancy and in service training in the UK and abroad. He has a particular research interest in how children with emotional and behavioural difficulties make sense of large scale environments. His previous career has included senior management, teaching and advisory roles in special education. He has worked in primary, secondary and further education contexts, including both mainstream and special education.

Elisabeth Barratt Hacking is a Lecturer in Education at the University of Bath. She is involved in initial and experienced teacher education and educational research. Elisabeth co-ordinates the Post-Graduate

Certificate of Education Programme and Professional Studies Programme at the University of Bath and is also a PGCE subject tutor. She has a particular research interest in novice teachers' professional training.

Edward Casey is a senior manager at the National Rehabilitation Board in Dublin, Ireland. He is responsible for the computer service, projects and Foreign Consultancies. From 1982 - 1990 he was National Manager, Vocational Services, which was responsible for vocational assessment, counselling, training and job replacement of persons with disabilities, including special educational needs.

Jennifer Evans has worked in the field of special needs research and policy analysis since 1983, at the Institute of Education, London University and currently at the National Foundation for Educational Research. Her publications include *Managing Special Education: Codes, Charters and Competition*, Open University Press (with John Fish) and *Reflecting on School Management*, Falmer Press 1999, (with Anne Gold).

Philip Garner is a Professor of Education (Special Educational Needs) at Nottingham Trent University. He was formerly Reader in Education at Brunel University. He has authored a number of books on SEN, including *What Teachers Do* (1995) and *Pupils with Problems: Rational Fears and Radical Solutions* (1999).

Dale Goldhaber is currently Director of Early Childhood Education Programmes at the University of Vermont, Burlington, USA. He is the author of *Life-Span Human Development* and *Theories of Human Development: Integrative Perspectives*. His major scholarly interests are theories of human development, early childhood education and early childhood teacher education.

Jeanne Goldhaber is currently Associate Professor of Early Childhood Education at the University of Vermont, Burlington, USA. She has written extensively on early childhood teacher education, the documentation of children's' learning and the development of early literacy skills in young children.

Winnifred M Hall has taught children with and without special needs at the secondary level. Currently a Senior Lecturer in the School of Education at the University of the West Indies, Jamaica, teaching and supervising undergraduate and graduate students, she is also co-ordinator of the School's graduate studies programme. She has also published on aspects of Caribbean special educational needs.

Gary Hornby is a Senior Lecturer in Special Education at the University of Hull. He previously worked as a mainstream and special class teacher, educational psychologist and Teachers College Lecturer. He has published several books and articles in the field of special education and counselling. He has recently spent two years developing training for teachers of children with special needs in Barbados.

Dorothy Howie is a Senior Lecturer in the Centre for Educational Studies within the Institute for Learning at the University of Hull. She is Course Leader for the Special Educational Needs postgraduate Certificate and Diploma course offered by the University of Hull, and also directs the taught Master's Programmes in Education. She was previously at the University of Auckland, New Zealand, where she carried out research on both special educational needs and the teaching of thinking.

Tetsuya Munekata is a Senior Research Scientist of the National Institute of Special Education, Japan. His speciality is Special Education Technology and his related publications range from nation-wide surveys to development of educational materials using virtual reality technology. Mr Munekata has recently served as a member of the Advisory Panel on Information Education, the Ministry of Education, Science, Sports and Culture as well as being a member of the Research Committee of the Japanese Society for Educational Technology as the representative of the field of Special Needs Education.

Toshiro Ochiai is Chief of the Section of Education for Children with Severe Intellectual Disabilities at the National Institute of Special Education, Kanagawa, Japan. His publications in English include 'History, Issues and Trends of Japanese Special Education', *International*

Journal of Special Education, 9(2), 1992 and 'Why We Need A New Paradigm of Special Teacher Education: The Japanese Experience', in *Partnerships in Teacher Development for a New Asia*, Report of the International Conference by UNESCO-ACEID and UNICEF, 1995.

Christine O'Hanlon is presently a Senior Lecturer in Education at the University of Birmingham. She has worked extensively in Europe on the topic of 'inclusive practice' and has published a number of books and articles on 'European Inclusion' in education. She has written a number of texts about teacher education in Europe and has recently completed a teacher development programme for inclusive practice supported by the EU. Her main professional focus is teacher development through practitioner research.

Marva L Ribeiro PhD has been a secondary school teacher for the past 26 years. She is also a part-time Lecturer in Remedial Mathematics at the University of the West Indies, St Augustine, Trinidad. Dr Ribeiro is the mother of four children, the eldest a girl of 21 years, who is an oral/aural severely hearing-impaired student at the University.

Shimpei Takuma is a Full Professor at Kawasaki University of Medical Welfare, Okayama, Japan, as well as an Emeritus Researcher, the National Institute of Special Education. He holds the Medal of Educational Achievement issued by the Ministry of Education, Science, Sports and Culture, and is President of the Japanese Society of Child Safety Studies and Vice President of the Japan Stanford Association. In 1993, he served as the President of the National Convention of Japanese School Health Association. Dr Takuma has contributed to many publications as a writer or an editor, including *New Century Cyclopedia for Education and Welfare of Disabled Persons*, Do-bun Shoin, Tokyo, 1989.

Max Timmerman is a visual artist, consultant on Art and Handicap and Division Manager for ABRONA, Institute for the Care of People with a Mental Handicap, Utrecht in the Netherlands. He is also a board member of Very Special Arts (VSA NL) and a member of INSEA (International Society for Education through Art). He is author of the book *I am an artist: original Art for people with mental disabilities*, based on his 24-

year experience in this field. He has organised successful museological exhibitions and is a staunch advocate of the integration into our social and cultural society of artistically gifted people with mental disabilities.

Diana Tzokova is currently an Associate Research Fellow at Brunel University School of Education, where she teaches on Master's programmes in Severe Learning Difficulties. She holds a doctorate from Sofia University, Bulgaria, and has written extensively on SEN issues in Eastern Europe. She was co-ordinator of an EU TEMPUS Programme in Special Education, involving universities in Bulgaria, England, Ireland and Greece.

Belle Wallace developed curricula in relation to developing problem-solving in learners in the UK before moving to South Africa to the University of Natal where she continued this work in relation to severely disadvantaged students oppressed by apartheid. She is Co-Director of the Curriculum Development Unit in the Faculty of Education teaching Master's students in Curriculum as well as working extensively within African communities. She has also written a considerable amount in relation to thinking skills and problem-solving.

Introduction

Colin Brock and Rosarii Griffin

Providing the appropriate educational opportunities for learners with special educational needs is a universal concern. It applies to all-age groups and spans sectoral divisions such as between formal and non-formal, and public and private. The literature is beginning to accommodate a more international approach to the discussion of issues relating to special educational needs as exemplified by *From Them to Us* (1998) and *Inclusive Education* (1999), the latter being the World Yearbook of Education for 1999. In assembling this collection of chapters, we aim to contribute to this international approach.

Viewed historically, we may see an immense progression from extremes of exclusion, through forms of seclusion and separation to the current trend towards inclusion. This has led, especially in Western Europe, North America and Australasia, not only to the increasing accommodation of special needs students in mainstream classes, but also the recognition that many in the majority have some kind of special need in terms of learning difficulties. This is reflected in a profound change of attitude from finding ways of coping with disabilities to maximising the potential of all students from pre-school to university.

In many developing countries, and also in areas experiencing situations of conflict, entire communities have special educational needs, often of a scale and complexity that is difficult to comprehend from the outside. Such extreme variants of special needs lie beyond the scope of this book, but should not be forgotten. They are well identified and discussed in *Education as a Humanitarian Response* (1998).

In this collection of chapters are assembled commentaries and discussions from a wide range of countries, though with some emphasis on cases from Europe and North America whence the main trends towards provision for learners with special educational needs have emerged. In general, we are concerned with policies and patterns rather than the technical discussion of particular forms of disadvantage and detailed pedagogical responses to the challenges they present. However, the chapters by Max Timmerman on 'Original Powers of Expression' and by Belle Wallace and Harvey B Adams on 'The Enhancement of Cognitive Development in

Disadvantaged Communities' do have respective concerns with particular forms and approaches in terms of providing opportunities for expression and for learning. Even so, the messages from both are near universally relevant.

The bulk of the chapters illustrate, in different ways and to different degrees, how policies and provision in respect of special educational needs are affected by the globalisation/localisation relationship. All are clearly on the move towards integration and inclusion, as promoted by the global discourse and increasing international interaction. This has been reinforced by the Salamanca Statement of 1994. At the national and local levels, different social and cultural contexts, informed by particular histories of political and educational development, make for diversity as well as different forms of inertia.

Nonetheless, there is a widespread trend towards both integration and inclusion deriving from Scandinavia in the 1960s, with most West European countries having specific initiatives to reform the approach to the provision of special educational needs in the 1970s and 1980s. As O'Hanlon describes, the European Union and Commission have provided frameworks through which the sharing of policy and practice has been enhanced, including working networks, funded collaborative programmes and other forms of co-operation. This has engendered a degree of convergence in approaches to meeting special educational needs, towards inclusion, but as the author notes: 'countries with relatively advanced special school systems find it most difficult to move away from it'.

In most of the national cases under consideration here, such special school systems derive from the 'medical model' of recognising certain disabilities and providing specific provision to address the needs arising. Such approaches seem to have developed significantly in the late nineteenth century with provision for each form of disadvantage being related to private, charitable and philanthropic sources. As systems of public education developed, they did not necessarily include either structural or economic support for special needs, but as they did begin to meet this challenge, it was normally with a segregated approach. In Eastern Europe, as exemplified by the chapter on Bulgaria, the impact of Communism was to centralise existing provisions under the psycho-medical paradigm. As Garner and Tzokova describe, there was an 'ideological notion of separateness', which is well illustrated by the establishments of the field of 'Defectology' and the exclusion of emotional and behavioural difficulties from its parameters. However, the polytechnic dimension of communist education did lead to some vocational provision for people with special needs. As schemes like TEMPUS begin to support east-west links across Europe, the beginnings of movement toward more integrative approaches may be enhanced.

Outside Europe, the same general movement from segregation through separation and integration to exclusion is clear from the chapters on Canada, the USA and New Zealand, with contextual and residual factors again having a significant influence. In both Canada and the USA, different degrees of provincial/state and local control make for considerable disparity, as do population distribution and multiculturalism. The advent of 'free and appropriate education' for all with special educational needs in the USA in 1975 was a watershed in that country, while in Canada, the 'Canadian Charter of Rights and Freedoms' of 1982 was likewise of real significance. In both countries, but especially in the USA, the fragmentation of funding sources constrains the quality of systems delivery and the realisation of objectives such as integration and inclusion. However, both have strong research profiles in this area which are highlighting the importance of a number of issues including the importance of achieving greater degrees of inclusion to the benefit of all; the enhancement of the professional skills and status of all teachers in respect of responding to special educational needs; the role of quality assurance in the raising of standards; and the provision of appropriate environments for learning. Ideally, as Dale and Jeanne Goldhaber point out, these are the 'least restricted environments', and they believe that integration and inclusion have to begin in the early childhood stage where there is least resistance from residual factors.

In all countries, there exist problems of connecting an expanding special needs dimension with mechanisms for the provision of mainstream schooling, which are also subject to reform. In some countries, this is exemplified in conflict between policy and legislation, where the latter does not allow for the implementation of the former as intended. This is discussed by Howie in respect of New Zealand where the adoption of market-oriented policies of public schooling provision may also work to restrict rather than enhance the realisation of inclusive objects for those with special needs. The market issue is clearly of significance in England and Wales, as Evans illustrates in her chapter. Indeed the foundation legislation providing for the market-oriented approach, the Education Act of 1988, failed to address the issue of special educational needs. A number of subsequent researches in this country have illustrated the adverse effect of keen competition on provision for relatively expensive students who may not be likely to contribute strongly to the enhancement of the academic profile of the school. In those States of the USA where such policies are also in operation, the same reaction is becoming evident.

Another widespread concern in meeting the challenges of the more inclusive and integrated approaches is the training and professional development of teachers in respect of special educational needs. This is commented on in a number of chapters, and especially in respect of the implications of integrated and inclusive policies (for special needs). Specialist training for teaching in relation to specific disadvantages has long been available in most of the countries represented here, but inclusion and integration require a thorough preparation of all teachers for a wide variety of special needs techniques and support.

In a climate of priority for the raising of academic standards across the subjects of the curriculum, increasing emphasis may be placed on teaching methods related to each subject rather than to the range of students likely to be found in the inclusive classroom. The shorter the programme, the more difficult it will be to accommodate all that is necessary in the thorough training of a teacher. This is well illustrated with specific reference to special needs in the chapter by Barratt and Barratt-Hacking in which they examine five one-year full-time graduate initial training courses in England. They find minimal reference to this dimension of training in these courses and call for an alignment of teacher preparation with a thoroughgoing policy of inclusive education.

It is clear from the various country and regional studies included here that considerable progress has been made in recent decades to enhance the recognition and status of special educational needs in terms of being a mainstream rather than a minority issue. There have also been specific measures enacted in many of the countries, especially since the 1970s, to support the enhancement of this field, including through legislation. Opportunities for global discourse and international interaction have assisted this development, and in the case of the countries of the European Union, mutual benefits have been gained from their involvement in cross-national projects.

In general, the movement towards integration and inclusion has received widespread support, but has been significantly constrained by a number of key factors including residual systems of funding and administration that affect delivery services; concurrent policies and regulations that apply to the mainstream and conflict with those for special needs; the current inadequacy of teacher training and professional development programmes to prepare teachers for the classroom realities of inclusion.

Striking an effective balance between the wider benefits of inclusion and the necessity for some separation is difficult to achieve, but the objective is well put by Casey in his chapter on Ireland, which is to have 'as much integration as is appropriate and feasible, with as little segregation as possible'. Ireland has the lowest percentage of its school age population in special schools of all EU countries. According to Casey, this is due to the prioritisation long given to 'Special Needs' by the Department of Education, the high quality of the teaching force and the training received, the support of the religious orders and opportunities for parental involvement. There are of course downsides too, but something may be gained from international comparison so that successful structures and operations can be fully understood.

Throughout this book, we have accepted the terminology used by contributors in respect of special educational needs, since this reflects the practice in their respective countries. In a book of this size, it is obviously not possible to include all countries. We have therefore chosen a cross-section of countries which highlights both global trends and different local situations.

We would like to thank all the contributors to this book, also Shirley Brock for compiling the index, and the staff of John Catt Educational Limited for their support and technical advice.

References

Booth, T and Ainscow, M (1998), *From Them to Us: An International Study of Inclusion in Education*, London, Routledge

Daniels, H and Garner, P (Eds) (1999), *Inclusive Education*, World Yearbook of Education, London, Kogan Page

Retamal, G and Aedo-Richmond, R (Eds) (1998), *Education as a Humanitarian Response*, London, Cassell

Chapter 1

From Warnock to the market place: the development of Special Education Policy in England and Wales: 1978-1998

Jennifer Evans

Introduction

In England and Wales, the 1981 Education Act represented the culmination of a series of changes in the dominant conceptualisation of special educational needs and provision which had taken place during the 1960s and 1970s. These changes had been documented and discussed by a Committee of Enquiry, set up in 1973 and chaired by Mary Warnock, at the instigation of the then Secretary of State for Education, Margaret Thatcher and which reported in 1978 (DES 1978).

Prior to the implementation of the 1981 Act in March 1983, special education had been organised around a number of categories of handicap and provided, for the most part, in separate segregated institutions which were, themselves, categorised in terms of distinct disabilities. The development of the use of these categories and the system of education which grew up around them has been documented by (among others) Tomlinson (1982) and Norwich (1990). Their creation had been part of the 1944 Education Act, the underlying premise of which was that children should be classified and differentiated according to their 'age, ability and aptitude' (Heward and Lloyd-Smith, 1990) and which had established 12 categories of handicap (or 'defects of body or mind') for which provision had to be made.

One group, the 'severely sub-normal' were deemed to be the responsibility of the health rather than the education authorities but, for the rest, provision was to be made in special schools. The categories corresponded to sensory and physical handicaps and intellectual and emotional difficulties. The emphasis in assessment was on deficits within the individual child and a medical model of diagnosis and treatment reflected the dominance of the medical profession in decision-making about this group of children.

At the time, the education system of England and Wales was highly differentiated in terms of measured intellectual ability, with an examination, for children in ordinary schools, at the age of 11, to classify them into groups suitable for one of three main types of secondary school: academic, technical or 'modern'. It is not surprising, then, that the special education system reflected the dominance of selection, categorisation and segregation on the basis of ability and disability. The emergence of educational psychologists as a powerful professional group within this sorting process is one of the features of the development of the education system during the immediate post-war years (*ibid*).

During the 1960s and 1970s, parents and others interested in the education and welfare of children with disabilities campaigned for a change in approach (Peter 1995). There was concern that a significant proportion of children (those deemed to be severely sub-normal) were the responsibility of the health authorities rather than the education authorities and were being provided for in 'junior training centres' rather than in schools. This was felt to be unacceptable and, in 1971, after a long campaign, the responsibility for the education of 'educationally sub-normal (severe)' children was transferred to local education authorities. Thus, the right of all children to some form of education was established.

This was part of a wider movement in education towards 'comprehensivisation', and the abolition of selection at 11 years old in many local education authorities (LEAs). There had been a sustained critique of the rigid categorisation of children into 'academic' and 'non-academic' at this early age, and a concern that many children were not realising their potential. The work of educational sociologists in the 1960s and 1970s had drawn attention to the social class bias within the system (*eg* Jackson and Marsden 1962; Jackson 1964; Bernstein 1977; Willis 1977) and it was argued that the abolition of selection at 11 would eliminate the worst effects of this, although later experience has shown this to be an over-optimistic aspiration (Hargreaves 1989).

A second concern of many parents, educators and other professionals was the system of categorisation that appeared to be both rigid and arbitrary, and relied upon a medical model in which the emphasis was on a child's deficits and did not take into account compensating strengths or the interaction between the child and his or her environment in creating or ameliorating educational difficulties. It was also seen as simplistic, because it did not acknowledge the complexity of children's problems and that a child might have a number of areas of difficulty, some of which might be ignored if he or she were categorised by a single handicap. During the 1970s, increasing numbers of children were being placed in special schools, and 'ascertainment' of a child as 'handicapped' became increasingly seen as having the consequence of marginalisation in respect of a child's peers and opportunities within the labour market (Coard 1971; Tomlinson 1982).

The 1981 Education Act

The 1981 Education Act can be seen as the legislative embodiment of the key recommendations of the Warnock Report. It was described by the Minister of the time as the embodiment of good practice (Goacher, Evans *et al* 1988). It was part of a shift in ideas and policies about special education which was taking place in many other western states, including the United States of America, which passed similar legislation in 1975, and Italy which brought about a radical change, requiring the integration of all but the most severely handicapped children, by legislation passed in 1971.

Many of these legislative changes resulted from a wider political and societal emancipation which embodied ideas about democracy, equity and human rights. The 1981 Act can be seen therefore as... 'just one event in the general process of policy and service development' (Goacher, Evans *et al, op cit*) which was subject to many influences both within Great Britain and beyond.

The particular manifestation of these ideas within the British context has, however, been the subject of both positive and negative evaluation by commentators. Kirp (1982) described the British government's response as 'professional-centred' in contrast to the American approach, which he described as 'rights-centred'. American welfare legislation stresses 'individual entitlement to governmentally subsidised benefits' and a perception of clients as active participants in decisions about their needs and the services they require.

The British system, by contrast, is seen by Kirp as 'enabling professionals, by the exercise of benign discretion, to offer the highest level of service on the least stigmatising terms possible, given available social resources.' (*ibid*, p 173). This has been described by Sally Tomlinson (Tomlinson *op cit*) as 'benevolent humanitarianism'. Kirp acknowledged, however, that the new emphasis on parental choice within Warnock and the 1980 White paper, and greater control over local expenditure by central government might challenge the professional hegemony.

19

However, as Welton and Evans (1986) note, the principles underlying the 1981 Act: 'were formed in a climate of educational thinking and government policies very different from those which prevailed at the time of its implementation' (p 210).

The 'fiscal crisis of the State' (O'Connor 1973) had resulted in a change of attitude in Government to the funding of the welfare state. The 1960s had been a period of expansion in welfare, and the Warnock Report had been conceived in a time when there was an expectation of continuing, or even expanding, support for children with learning difficulties. The 1981 Act was a strange mixture of vagueness and detailed prescription. On the one hand, it provided a tautological definition of special educational needs which linked them to the extent of special educational provision in schools, so there were no nationally applicable guidelines to help LEAs decide what level of learning difficulty constituted a special educational need. This neatly avoided the necessity for the government to make any estimate of the costs of implementation, or to provide any extra funding.

On the other hand it laid down, in minute detail, the procedures to be followed for the making of a statement of special educational needs which entailed an LEA making a formal commitment to provide extra resources for an individual child. Thus the responsibility for deciding to allocate extra funding would be at the local level, resting with education, social services and health authorities. Indeed, Goacher *et al* (*op cit*) found that most LEAs had increased spending on special education in the years following the implementation of the 1981 Act. However, there was no central government commitment of funding to support implementation, and, this, together with strict curbs on local authority and health authority spending, meant that an unofficial rationing of provision took place, as professionals and bureaucrats who acted as the gate-keepers made decisions at the 'street level' (Weatherley and Lipsky, 1977; Goacher *et al*, 1988) about who should have access to extra resources.

Fulcher (1989) has observed that the widening of the definition of special educational needs to include 20 percent of the school population was an attempt to de-stigmatise the notion of handicap. However, what it has succeeded in doing, in her view, is to legitimate the notion that up to 20 percent of the school population has needs which are outside the facilities which ordinary schools generally provide. As well as the implications of this for equality of opportunity (also dealt with by Tomlinson 1982, 1985), it set in motion a conflict between schools and LEAs about whose responsibility it was to provide resources for pupils with special educational needs.

More positive evaluations of the 1981 Act saw it as 'empowering parents' (Russell 1986), providing a means for open decision-making and account-ability for the use of resources (Wedell 1990), providing a stimulus to the development of a wide range of support for pupils with learning difficul-ties (Lunt and Evans 1994), and opening the way to greater integration of pupils with special educational needs into mainstream schools (Bennett and Cass 1989). However, these positive evaluations of the policy and practice implications of the Act have been tempered as examples of its implementation in LEAs have emerged.

The Definition of Special Educational Needs

The 1981 Act (and subsequently the 1993 and 1996 Acts) defined special educational needs and provision as follows:

1. A child has special educational needs if he has a learning difficulty which calls for special, educational provision to be made for him.

2. A child has a learning difficulty if:

    (a) he has significantly greater difficulty in learning than the majority of children of his age;

    (b) he has a disability which either prevents or hinders him from making use of educational facilities of a kind generally provided in schools within the area of the local authority concerned, for children of his age; or

    (c) he is under the age of five years and is, or would be if special educational provision were not made for him, likely to fall within paragraph (a) or (b) when over that age.

3. Special educational provision means:

    (a) in relation to a child who had attained the age of two years, educational provision which is additional to, or otherwise different from, the educational provision made generally for children of his age in schools maintained by the local education authority concerned;

    (b) in relation to children under that age, educational provision of any kind.

4. A child is not taken as having a learning difficulty solely because his language (or form of the language) in which he is, or will be, taught is different from a language (or form of a language) which has at any time been spoken in his home.

A major problem has been the difficulty of organising and funding an education system around the concept of 'need'. These difficulties have been explored in some depth by Lee (1996). He asserts that 'in reviewing the literature, one confronts a massive, diverse, sometimes confusing and often plain contradictory collection of theories, statements and uses of 'need' (p 23). He suggests that statements relating to needs are 'essentially triadic in form'. That is: A needs B in order to achieve C. In social welfare policy, generally, C could be defined as a minimum standard (such as the poverty line) or as an abstract optimal state such as 'well-being'. Thus, there is the potential for dispute over the desired ends of any social welfare intervention.

Current arguments about a minimum wage are a good example of this. There will also be differences of opinion about what is required at B to achieve C. For example, what do single mothers need to enable them to take up paid employment? Subsidised child care? Training opportunities? A flexible welfare system which allows them keep enough of their earnings to climb out of the poverty trap? Or, as in the USA, a threat to cut off their benefits if they have more children? The first part of the statement is also potentially (and actually in the case of children with learning difficulties) a matter for dispute. Who is to be included in the group that needs B to achieve C? Means-testing, in social welfare, is one way of deciding whether a particular individual is entitled to a particular welfare intervention.

After reviewing the general literature on need, Lee discusses the particular case of special educational needs. He argues that it is unusual in that it is defined by law; that there is a duty on local education authorities to identify, assess and provide for individual special education needs; and, that the concept of need is individualised – it cannot be inferred from aggregate data on group performance.

However, I would argue that the discourse around 'special educational needs' is very similar to that around other types of welfare or medical need. First, the optimal (or minimum) standards towards which any intervention is directed is defined by professionals and bureaucrats and not by recipients. Secondly, most interventions are allocated on an individualised basis, with the onus on the individual to demonstrate that he or she fits certain criteria. Thirdly, a 'deficit model' is employed, in that an individual is positioned as 'lacking' something and that the exposure of the lack is in some way stigmatising. Fourthly, as Norwich (1990) argues, there are both evaluative and descriptive elements involved in the use of the term, and these are often conflated. Thus, the outwardly rational and empirical process of ascertaining an individual's needs (which operates within the realm of professional expertise) disguises a normative and evaluative process about what intervention is most appropriate and what the outcome of the intervention should be. Thus, in the realm of special educational needs, parents often disagree with professionals about the best form of provision for their child.

It is not surprising, then, that research about the implementation of the 1981 Education Act found that, while the abolition of categories of handicap and their replacement with a more general concept of 'special educational needs' was generally welcomed by those working in the field and there was a recognition that the old system of categories did not adequately reflect the complexity of children's needs, nevertheless there were difficulties for professionals, bureaucrats and parents in working with the new definition (Sandow *et al*, 1987; Goacher *et al, op cit*).

For example, there was, and continues to be (see Audit Commission/HMI, 1992), a wide variation between LEAs in the proportions of children given statements in different LEAs and the types of need which were considered eligible for a statement. These differences stem from the definition of eligibility contained in the 1981 Act, which defined special educational provision as that which was 'additional to or otherwise different from' provision made generally in schools in the LEA. A statement was to be provided for those children for whom the LEA was 'to determine' the provision.

These two aspects of the definition of special educational needs have caused wide discrepancies in practice in LEAs across the UK. Since the 1981 Act, wide differences in statement rates have emerged. Some LEAs have fewer that one per cent of their pupils with statements, whereas others have almost four per cent. As the Audit Commission concluded, the differing level of statements was not due to differences in the level of need in the populations, but in LEAs' interpretation of the 1981 Act (Vevers 1992). There have been calls for national criteria for the threshold of need which would require a statement (Audit Commission/HMI, *op cit*) but given the further fragmentation of responsibilities for educational provision, this would seem to be impossible to accomplish.

Another problem, which still has resonance today, was that the concentration of resources on children with statements had diverted attention away from children with special educational needs who did not have statements (Goacher *et al, op cit*; Evans and Lunt, 1994). LEAs had begun to build up expertise among teachers and advisers for SEN during the 1980s and these were offering support to some children without statements. But increasingly, as education budgets were squeezed during the 1980s, and particularly more recently after the introduction of LMS, special needs resources became more and more tied to statements.

In the early 1980s, before LMS and the close monitoring of resources which that entailed, LEAs were finding planning for special educational provision difficult. 'Needs' is an open-ended concept, and estimating the size of demand was problematic. In practice, LEAs tended to be reactive rather than proactive, and this led to major difficulties in controlling expenditure and in rationalising resource allocation. Even with the current more detailed awareness of the impact of resource allocation decisions, LEAs are finding it difficult to control SEN expenditure (Lunt and Evans, *op cit*).

Integration

The inclusion of pupils with special educational needs within mainstream education was said to be a growing feature of a more comprehensive conceptualisation of education current in the late 1970s. This conceptualisation has been under threat since the 1980s and the inclusion of pupils with special educational needs has not shown a marked increase since the implementation of the 1981 Act (Swann 1991).

The 1981 Act was seen by many as promoting inclusion, since it stipulated that LEAs had a duty to ensure that children with special educational needs, including those with statements, were educated in ordinary schools if this is what their parents wanted. There were three provisos attached to this: that the child received the special education he or she required; that it was compatible with the efficient education of other children in the school; and that it was an efficient use of resources.

In practice this meant that the proportion of children being educated in special schools dropped by only 12.5% between 1983 and 1991 (Audit Commission/HMI, *op cit*). In some LEAs, the proportion of pupils in special schools had increased (Swann, 1988). The proportion of children with statements in mainstream schools has also increased but this is due, in most LEAs, to the overall increase in children with statements in the school population (Evans and Lunt, 1992). So the 1981 Act did not provide the basis for a revolution in the ways in which children with special educational needs were educated.

The Market and Special Education Policy

During the 1980s, the key discourses in education turned from being professionally dominated, with their philosophical basis within the social democratic post-war consensus and became a market-dominated one, with its philosophical bases within the anti-intellectual 'common-sense' of New Right libertarianism and the traditionalism of neo-conservatism. The 'rational' and 'humanistic' model of the 1960s and 1970s was subject to a sustained 'discourse of derision' (CCCS 1981; Ball 1990) and the new framework for education became 'the three Es: Efficiency, Economy, Effectiveness' (Simkins 1994). According to Simkins, a fourth E – Equity – was not part of the government's concerns when framing the legislation which set up the local management of schools.

A number of commentators: (Bowe, Ball *et al* 1992; Housden 1993; Evans and Lunt *op cit*; Gewirtz, Ball *et al* 1995; Lee 1996; Evans and Vincent 1997) have attempted to analyse the possible impact of a market within the education system. Their conclusions are that existing inequalities in access to education, which are related to class, 'race' and gender, as well as special educational needs, will be exacerbated by a market in which parental choice and schools responses to the possibilities of choice are the main organising principles.

Special education was virtually ignored by the policy-makers framing the 1988 Education Act. The delegation of budgets to schools under LMS and the opportunity to opt for grant-maintained status were not given to special schools under that Act. The opportunity to choose (or to 'express a preference' as it as later worded) was not given to parents of children with statements of special educational needs, who were still operating under the 1981 Education Act. Although there was energetic lobbying by the special needs lobby (Wedell 1988), special education was not high on the government's agenda and appeared to be seen as a separate issue, still somewhat within the remit of professionals. For example, a Circular on staffing for pupils with SEN was issued in 1990 (DES 1990). It uses the language of 'cost-effectiveness' and 'efficiency', but still gives LEAs a key role in reviewing and planning the balance of provision. The model employed to decide staffing levels is explicitly an educational one: 'The model derives from observations of classroom work seen to promote effective learning and care for various groups of pupils' (Para 6)

It is also a model which derives from practice in special schools, and although presented as equally suitable for supporting pupils in mainstream placements, does not take account of the extra resourcing needs of the placement of pupils with severe difficulties in mainstream settings. In fact, it does not explicitly discuss the issue of integration or refer to the Warnock levels and types of integration. Those working with the reality of supporting pupils with special educational needs in local authorities have produced much more sophisticated and workable models.

At the time this Circular was issued, the government was already considering the extension of LMS to special schools and had commissioned the management consultants Touche Ross to prepare a feasibility study (Touche-Ross 1990). The use of management consultants was a signal that the professional dominance over special education policy-making was under threat, just as the use of Coopers and Lybrand to prepare the initial recommendations on LMS had indicated that policy-making in this area was underpinned by the discourse of the private business sector.

The Touche Ross report concluded that the extension of LMS to special schools (to be known as local management of special schools (LMSS)) was both feasible and desirable. However, having considered a number of alternatives, the consultants felt that it was not desirable to introduce a competitive element into special schooling by funding schools on a pupil-led basis. Accordingly, they recommended that special schools should be funded according to the number of places they offered for different types of need.

The government accepted the case for this made out by Touche Ross, and in April 1991 they issued Circular 7/91(DES 1991), which, *inter alia*, laid out the framework for LMSS. As well as the place element, the formula for funding special schools would include an element per pupil on roll, to reflect the marginal costs of each pupil admitted. This was expected by the Secretary of State to be at a low level, to reflect the expected cost of consumables such as books, stationery and inexpensive equipment. There was also the opportunity for LEAs to include an 'outreach' element in the formula, to resource the work which many special schools undertake in collaboration with local mainstream schools. For example, this might include using the staff of a special school to support the integration of some of its pupils into the mainstream. Thus education in special schools was to be an excepted case; it was to be protected from the full rigours of the market place and the influence of the LEA in planning the number and types of special school places was still to be dominant. The discourse of benevolent humanitarianism was still prevalent in policy-making in this area.

However, Circular 7/91 was also designed to increase the extent of delegation to mainstream schools. It set out new rules about excepted items which LEAs must or could retain central funding for, and defined the remainder of the schools' budget as the 'potential schools budget' (PSB). LEAs would be required to delegate 85% of the PSB to schools. This would leave 15% of the PSB to fund, *inter alia*, central support teams for special educational needs, educational psychology services and funding for support in mainstream schools allocated through statements. There was also the option for LEAs to delegate Statement funding to schools.

As well as the new delegation requirements, Circular 7/91 also changed the balance of 'pupil-led funding' to require LEAs to raise the age-weighted element from 75% to 80% of the formula, but to include within this some weighting for pupils with special educational needs, whether or not these had statements (previously, weightings for SEN were calculated solely within the 25% non-age-weighted element). The thrust of these changes was, therefore, to increase the market-driven ethos within mainstream schools and to diminish the role of the LEA in such schools, thus leaving pupils with special educational needs in mainstream schools more vulnerable to schools' policies and practices.

Another indicator of this trend was the ordering of a review by the Audit Commission and HMI of the operation of the 1981 Act. This review, published in 1992, indicated that many of the initial problems of implementation were still prevalent. These were summarised by one of the authors of the report as: 'a lack of clarity, accountability and incentives'(Vevers *op cit*). In the same article, Paul Vevers writes: 'this lack of clarity has several consequences: First, parents are unclear when they are entitled to extra help for their child. Secondly, the respective roles of schools and LEAs have not been defined, leaving room for conflict over who is responsible in any given case. Thirdly, LEAs have an open-ended commitment to an ill-defined group at a time when their resources are limited'. This was an acknowledgement that the new organisation and governance of the education system had caused severe problems for the provision of special education.

The Report made a number of recommendations. At a national level, these included: DFE guidance as to the level of need which should 'trigger' a formal assessment *ie* the threshold of need which constitutes the '*prima facie*' case for full assessment; a framework for defining the responsibilities of ordinary schools, *ie* the generally available provision; a new type of statement, specifying objectives and resources; time limits to complete statements; the use of special needs performance indicators at school level; consideration of the use of financial incentives to implement the 1981 Act and publication of indicators of LEA performance in special needs.

At a local level the report recommended a clear distinction between the role of the purchaser of services (the local education authority) and provider of services (usually the school). Greater financial delegation by local education authorities is clearly a step in this direction.

Thus special education began to be discussed in the new language of the market.

The Code of Practice

Alongside new arrangements under the 1993 Act, the Government issued a Code of Practice on the Identification and Assessment of Special Educational Needs (DFE 1994). This volume, which runs to 134 A4 pages, plus 32 pages of appendices, is a detailed prescription for the identification and assessment of children with special educational needs. It was likened in the House of Lords to the Highway Code, in that it was not law, but that LEAs and schools would have to demonstrate that they 'had regard for' the Code in all their procedures.

The Code sets up a detailed system of surveillance and identification of children with special educational needs. It requires each school to have procedures in place and to keep a record of all children with special educational needs at one of five levels. Each child's progress must be reviewed regularly (the suggestion being that this should be on a termly basis), to see whether the child should be moved up or down a level, or removed from the SEN register.

Thus a huge bureaucracy has been set up, which entails a huge amount of record-keeping and, as Bines (1995) points out, is again processural, and does not guarantee that a child's needs will be met. Indeed, as Garner (1995) argues, the Code poses a number of dilemmas and tensions for schools about whether the special educational needs co-ordinators (SENCOs), who have to be appointed in every school, should use their time to support pupils with special needs, or as record-keepers and advisers to other staff. Bett (1996) has documented the huge range of tasks expected of SENCOs and has concluded that they are 'being put under enormous pressure from unrealistic demands that they cannot meet'(p 60).

Furthermore, as a consequence of the requirement to identify, more and more children as being found to have special educational needs, and the pressure on resources, is escalating as was predicted by Bibby (1994). Similarities to the 'At Risk' register mandated by the 1989 Children Act suggest themselves, in that a bureaucratic structure has been set up which consumes large amounts of professionals' time and energy, deflecting them away from preventative work with their clients.

Interestingly, at the time the Code of Practice was published, the Government also published a series of Circulars entitled *Pupils with Problems* (DFE 1994), which gave the government's views on how to deal with other groups of pupils whom the system finds it difficult to cope with. These include: children with emotional and behavioural difficulties;

children excluded from school; children being educated 'otherwise' than at school (*ie* in PRUs or by home tuition); sick children; and, children being 'looked after' by local authorities. There is also a circular in the pack entitled *Pupil Behaviour and Discipline*. Thus, by 1994, a whole apparatus was beginning to be set up to deal with growing numbers of children and their families who, for one reason or another, were causing problems for the mainstream system of schooling.

Foucault has suggested that a feature of modern societies has been the identification and registration of deviant groups. Professionals play a key role in these activities, as the state inserts its power into the private lives of its subjects (Allen 1994). Marshall (1990) has suggested that the family has become 'an instrument of government' through which the state exerts control over every aspect of people's lives.

The Green Paper and the Programme of Action

The incoming Labour Government in 1997 published a Green Paper (consultation document) on Special Education (DfEE, 1997). Entitled *Excellence for All Children: Meeting Special Educational Needs*, the document lays out the Government's approach to special education and presages legislation to take special education policy forward beyond the year 2000. It lays out a number of goals for achievement by 2002. Among these are:

- Better arrangements for early identification of SEN;

- Better support for parents whose children have SEN;

- A revised Code of Practice which will reduce paperwork;

- Reduction in the numbers of children being given statements of SEN;

- More inclusion of children with SEN in mainstream schools;

- More collaboration between special and mainstream schools for SEN;

- Regional planning for low incidence SEN;

- Better training for SEN teachers and learning support assistants;

- Better co-ordination between health, education and social services for meeting SEN;

- There will be a special focus on pupils with Emotional and Behavioural Difficulties (EBD), with support for teachers and more training.

The Green Paper has been followed up by a Programme of Action, which gives details of the specific initiatives the government is undertaking to achieve its objectives in relation to SEN.

Reflections on the changes in special education policy during the 1980s and 90s

The influence of Warnock and the 1981 Act on the conceptualisation of special educational needs appears to remain strong, even after the immense changes in the structure and governance of education which have taken place since 1988. Despite the difficulties with a relative definition of special educational needs and provision, these have been incorporated into a new system which stresses *national* norms of attainment and standards of provision. The difficulties and inconsistencies resulting from this have been acknowledged (for example in the Audit Commission/HMI 1992 Report) but, aside from exhortations to government and LEAs to provide clear and unambiguous criteria for deciding that a child has special educational needs, no solutions to these difficulties have been proposed.

The broad definition of special educational needs which the Warnock Report introduced, has been applied to a growing proportion of the school population with the result, as Fulcher (1989) has commented, that a growing number of children has been labelled as having special educational needs and teachers have seen themselves as responsible for a diminishing proportion of pupils – those *without* special educational needs. Research on the effects of Local Management of Schools (LMS) on special education (Evans and Lunt 1994) has indicated that more children are being given statements and more children are being excluded from school since the implementation of LMS and competition between schools for pupils was established. Skrtic (1991) has suggested that:

> 'the traditional bureaucratic configuration of schools is as a performance organisation, an inherently non-adaptable form that must screen out diversity by forcing students with special educational needs out of the system.'

He maintains that students with special educational needs are 'artefacts of the traditional curriculum'. Given the pressure to traditionalise and normalise the English school curriculum, and the devolution of responsibilities for provision for special education to schools who have a huge range of other responsibilities, it is likely that the lack of criteria for deciding on special educational needs will result with more pupils being included in this group.

The extended rights given to parents of pupils with special educational needs under the 1981 and 1993 Acts reflect the broader entitlements for parents given by the 1980 and 1988 Acts, and the Parent's Charters. However, rights for parents of children with SEN are still somewhat circumscribed, and partnership in terms of consultation and involvement in decision-making still seems to be limited. Indeed, one could argue that over-subscribed schools now have more power to select pupils and to reject those with special educational needs.

The 1981 Act, which was conceived in a time of a broadly-based commitment to a comprehensive, inclusive system of education, with a thrust towards social justice and equality of opportunity (Welton, 1989; Roaf and Bines 1989), has been superseded by legislation which places education within a market framework in which individual parents compete to claim the 'best' education for their child. Under such a system, it is difficult to envisage that the broad principles of the 1981 Act, which were to offer children with special needs the same range of opportunities as those without special educational needs, can be realised.

The abandonment of the social democratic project in the UK and elsewhere has led to a reappraisal of the role and purpose of state-managed welfare, and, for some, has called into question whether the State has any role at all (Chubb and Moe, 1990; Tooley, 1996; Lawlor, 1997). However the administration of welfare, far from becoming less bureaucratic, has become increasingly subject to centralised control in terms of the systems set up by government to ensure that public money delegated to individual institutions is properly spent (for instance the establishment of Ofsted in education, the extension of the powers of the Audit Commission, the production of league tables of schools and of hospitals). Thus, the power of the State has become diffused throughout the welfare system in a way that leaves it less accountable, but in a more powerful position *vis-à-vis* the individual. As Foucault (1984) has observed:

> Humanity does not gradually progress from combat to combat to combat until it arrives at universal reciprocity, where the rule of law finally replaces warfare; humanity installs each of its violences in a system of rules and thus proceeds from domination to domination.

Thus, the organisation of the welfare state along market principles, and the introduction of consumerism does not signify a move towards greater personal freedom. It is merely a more sophisticated way for the State to mask its role in the control of people's lives.

The role of special education within this 'marketisation project' is a crucial one. As Skrtic (*op cit*) has pointed out, special education serves to safeguard a system of education which is increasingly rigid in its frameworks and expectations. Tomlinson (*op cit*) analysed the role of special education in marginalising a proportion of pupils who caused problems for the system. This proportion has grown over the last decade. A greater number of pupils is being given Statements of special educational needs. More children are being identified and placed on special needs registers. More children are being excluded from school because of their troublesome behaviour.

The latest policy initiatives from the Labour Government seem designed to mitigate the worst effects of the market system and to provide more support for those pupils who have difficulties in fitting into the system. However, there is a dilemma at the heart of Government policy, which is that the emphasis on 'excellence' and 'standards' has created a climate where schools are in competition and want to attract the most able students in order to enhance their market position. Thus, it seems that pupils with special educational needs will continue to receive a less favourable education within the English and Welsh system.

References

Allen, J (1994), *Foucault and Special Educational Needs: developing a framework for analysing children's experiences of mainstreaming,* British Educational Research Association Annual Conference, Oxford, England

Audit Commission/HMI (1992), *Getting in on the Act,* London, HMSO

Ball, S (1990), Politics and Policy Making in Education, London, Routledge

Bernstein, B (1977), *Class, Codes and Control: Towards and Theory of Educational Transmissions,* London, Routledge

Bett, J (1996), Managing the Code of Practice: the role of the SEN co-ordinator, London University Institute of Education, unpublished Masters dissertation

Bibby, P (1994), 'Dreamland of special needs draft', *Times Educational Supplement,* London, 8

Bines, H (1995), 'Special educational needs in the market place', *Journal of Education Policy,* 10(2), (pp 157-171)

Bowe, R, Ball, S, *et al* (1992), *Reforming Education and Changing Schools,* London, Routledge

CCCS (1981), *Unpopular Education*, London, Hutchinson

Chubb, J and Moe, T (1990), *Politics, Markets and America's Schools,* Washington DC, The Brookings Institution

Coard, B (1971), *How the West Indian Child is Made Educationally Subnormal in the British School System: The Scandal of the Black child in Schools in Britain,* London, Beacon Press

DES (1978), *Special Educational Needs. Report of a Committee of Enquiry into the Education of Handicapped Children and Young People* (The Warnock Report) London: HMSO

DES (1990), *Staffing for Pupils with Special Educational Needs*, Circular 11/90, London, Department of Education and Science

DES (1991), *Local Management of Schools: Further Guidance*, Circular 7/91, London, DES

DES (1992), *Children with special needs: A guide for parents* London, HMSO

DES (1983). *Assessments and Statements of Special Educational Needs*, Circular 1/83, London, DES

DFE (1994). *A Code of Practice on the identification and assessment of special educational needs*, London, HMSO

DFE (1994), *Pupils with Problems. Pupil behaviour and discipline*, Circular 8/94, London, HMSO

Evans, J and Lunt, I (1992), *Developments in Special Education under LMS*, London, Institute of Education

Evans, J and Lunt, I (1994), *Markets, Competition and Vulnerability: Some effects of recent legislation on children with special educational needs*, London, Institute of Education and Tufnell Press

Evans, J and Vincent, C (1997), Parental Choice and Special Education, in R Glatter, P Woods and C Bagley (Eds) *Choice and Diversity in Schooling: Perspectives and Prospects,* London, Routledge

Foucault, M (1984), Neitzsche, genealogy and history, Rabinow (Ed) *The Foucault Reader*, London, Penguin

Fulcher, G (1989), *Disabling Policies? A comparative approach to education policy and disability*, London, Falmer Press

Garner, P (1995), 'Sense or Nonsense? Dilemmas in the SEN Code of Practice', *Support for Learning,* 10(1), (pp 3-7)

Gewirtz, S, Ball, S and Bowe, R (1995), *Markets Choice and Equity in Education,* Buckingham, Open University Press

Goacher, B, Evans, J, Welton, J and Wedell, K (1988), *Policy and Provision for Special Educational Needs,* London, Cassell

Hargreaves, A (1989), The crisis of motivation and assessment, A Hargreaves and D Reynolds (Eds) *Education Policies: Controversies and Critiques,* London, Falmer Press

Heward, C and Lloyd-Smith, M (1990), 'Assessing the impact of legislation on special education policy', *Journal of Education Policy,* 5(1), (pp 21-36)

Housden, P (1993), *Bucking the Market: LEAs and Special Needs,* Stafford, National Association for Special Education

Jackson, B (1964), *Streaming: an education system in miniature,* London, Routledge and Kegan Paul

Jackson, B and Marsden, D (1962), *Education and the Working Class,* London, Routledge and Kegan Paul

Kirp, D (1982), 'Professionalism as Policy Choice: British Special Education in Comparative Perspective', *World Politics,* XXXIV(2), (pp 137-174)

Lee, T (1996), *The Search for Equity: Funding Additional Educational Needs under LMS,* Aldershot, Avebury

Lunt, I and Evans, J (1994), *Allocating Resources for Special Educational Needs Provision,* Stafford, NASEN

Marshall, J (1990), Foucault and Educational Research, S Ball (Ed) *Foucault and Education. Disciplines and Knowledge,* London, Routledge

Norwich, B (1990), *Reappraising Special Needs Education,* London, Cassell

Norwich, B, (1992), *Time to Change the 1981 Education Act,* London, Institute of Education University of London

Norwich, B (1994), *Segregation and inclusion : English LEA statistics 1988-92,* Bristol, Centre for Studies on Inclusive Education

O'Connor, J (1973), *The Fiscal Crisis of the State,* New York, St Martin's Press

Peter, M (1995), Lobbying for Special Education, I Lunt, B Norwich and V Varma (Eds), *Psychology and Education for Special Needs,* Aldershot, Arena, (pp 193-210)

Roaf, C and Bines, H (1989), Needs, Rights and Opportunities in Special Education, in C Roaf and H Bines (Eds) *Needs, Rights and Opportunities: Developing Approaches to Special Education*, London, The Falmer Press. (pp 5-19)

Sandow, S, Stafford, D *et al* (1987), *An Agreed Understanding? Parent-Professional Communication and the 1981 Education Act*, Slough, NFER-Nelson

Simkins, T (1994), 'Efficiency, effectiveness and the local management of schools', *Journal of Education Policy*, 9(1) (pp 15-33)

Skrtic, T M (1991), Students with Special Educational Needs: Artifacts of the Traditional Curriculum, in M Ainscow (Ed) *Effective Schools for All*, London, David Fulton

Swann, W (1988), 'Trends in school placement to 1986. Measuring, assessing and explaining integration', *Oxford Review of Education*, 11(1)

Swann, W (1991), *Variations between LEAs in levels of segregation in special schools, 1982-90*, CSIE

Tomlinson, S (1982), *A Sociology of Special Education*, London, Routledge and Kegan Paul

Tomlinson, S (1985), 'The expansion of special education', *Oxford Review of Education*, 11(2), (pp 157-165)

Tooley, J (1996), *Education without the State*, London, Institute of Economic Affairs

Touche-Ross (1990), *Extending Local Management to Special Schools*, Touche Ross Management Consultants

Vevers, P (1992), 'Getting in on the Act', *British Journal of Special Education*, 19(3), (pp 88-91)

Weatherley, R and Lipsky,M (1977), 'Street-Level Bureaucrats and Institutional Innovation: Implementing Special-Education Reform', *Harvard Educational Review*, 47(2), (pp 171-197)

Wedell, K (1988), *The Education Reform Bill and provision for children and young people with special educational needs*, London University Institute of Education

Welton, J (1989), Incrementalism to Catastrophe Theory: Policy for Children with Special Educational Needs, C Roaf and H Bines (Eds) *Needs, Rights and*

Opportunities: Developing Approaches to Special Education, London, The Falmer Press, (pp 20-27)

Welton, J and Evans, J (1986), 'The development and implementation of special education policy: Where did the 1981 Act fit in?' *Public Administration,* 64 (Summer), (pp 209-227)

Willis, P (1977), *Learning to Labour*, Farnborough, Saxon House

Chapter 2

Initial teacher training and Special Educational Needs in England and Wales

Robert Barratt and Elisabeth Barratt Hacking

Introduction

This chapter explores how special educational needs (SEN) provision is developing within initial teacher training (ITT) in England and Wales. It focuses on the one-year Post Graduate Certificate in Education (PGCE) course for secondary subject teachers and discusses how provision is made for special educational needs in these programmes.

The PGCE is one of several training options available to new entrants to the teaching profession. Other routes to Qualified Teacher Status (QTS) include undergraduate bachelor status courses (BEd/BA QTS) and post-graduate school-centred initial teacher training programmes (SCITT). The following discussion is based on evidence from five secondary PGCE courses in higher education institutions (HEI) in England (see also, Mittler, 1992; Postlethwaite and Raban, 1990; Raban, 1989; Aubrey, 1994). Their current training provision is discussed in respect of SEN as defined by the National Standards for QTS (TTA, 1998). Recent developments in SEN at national, local and school level provide a background to these courses.

An agenda for Special Educational Needs

The last ten years have witnessed a concerted effort by the international community to raise the profile of SEN. A number of significant activities have supported this agenda, for example,

- 1989 UN Convention on the Rights of the Child

- 1994 World Conference on Special Needs Education and the genesis of the Salamanca Statement

- 1996 UNESCO survey of international laws relating to SEN.

Common to these activities has been the concern that the international community takes responsibility for addressing the educational needs of *all* young citizens. This encourages countries to invoke and/or reinstate their commitment to the educational rights of all. To this end communities are being encouraged to develop inclusive educational policies. In some countries this is being expressed through inclusive school settings which are open to and sensitive of the individual needs of all children.

Within England and Wales the spirit of this international agenda is reflected in the government's Green Paper *Excellence for All Children: Meeting Special Educational Needs* (DfEE, 1997). The Green Paper makes a commitment to raise standards for all children including those with SEN. It advocates the development of real partnerships between various community stake holders (education, welfare, social and health) by 2002. It also calls for more rigour in teacher training and raising the professional profile of teachers in respect of their SEN activities. This has particular significance in terms of developing SEN provision in ITT.

SEN Policy: the context for teacher training in England and Wales

Impact of the Green Paper

It is argued that government policy in England and Wales will reform the educational context within which teacher training takes place. The recent Green Paper (*ibid*) represents the government's vision for the 21st century and has stimulated a searching review of SEN policy and practice at all tiers. National bodies such as the National Advisory Group for Special Educational Needs (NAGSEN), Special Educational Needs Training Consortium (SENTC), British Educational Communications and Technology Agency (BECTa) and other groups are undertaking this review. Key areas for consideration include:

- legislation such as the Code of Practice;

- pre- and post-service SEN training provision within HEIs and other groups;

- local authority and school SEN practices;

- competence of those working in the field of SEN as expressed through the National Standards for SEN specialist teachers and co-ordinators;

- current SEN research activity.

Evolving SEN Policy and Practice

SEN policy and practice continues to evolve in response to national institutional development and the spirit of national policy. This is exemplified at school level as practitioners reconceptualise SEN provision and shape the nature of new inclusive school settings. It is further exemplified at local education authority level by the development and establishment of policy to support collaborative inter-agency, family and child-centred practices. Authorities are favourably continuing their shift from segregationist to integrationist (or inclusive) models for SEN provision.

Positively, these developments are challenging schools to develop new ways of working within and between themselves as they seek to improve their SEN effectiveness. For example, some schools are involved in cross phase consortia which are working together to develop their SEN practice.

SEN-related Teaching Standards

Alongside these developments the government's concern to develop professional profiles for SEN specialist teachers and co-ordinators is consolidating existing good practice in schools. This is reflected in the government's new standards for SEN Co-ordinators and Specialist Teachers of SEN (TTA, 1999). Both of these initiatives require HEIs and other training providers to consider their training and accreditation models.

Concurrently, the government has introduced National Standards for the Award of Qualified Teacher Status (QTS), (TTA, 1998) and newly qualified teachers (NQTs), (TTA, 1999). The former are being assessed within HEI partnerships and the latter within schools. These initiatives aim to raise the professional competence and status of new entrants into the profession.

Interestingly, within both QTS and NQT standards there are SEN-related competences. The relatively new National Standards for QTS (TTA, 1997) set out the minimum requirements for QTS. These are expressed as a set of expectations in relation to subject knowledge, planning, teaching and class management and other professional requirements (*ibid*).

Standards with SEN-related references include knowledge of the Code of Practice and the identification, assessment and support of SEN pupils.

Specifically, to be awarded QTS trainees must demonstrate that they:

- 'Are familiar with the Code of Practice on the identification and assessment of special educational needs and, as part of their responsibilities under the Code, implement and keep records on individual Education Plans (IEPs) for pupils at stage 2 of the Code and above'

- 'plan to achieve progression in pupils' learning through ... identifying pupils who :

  a) have special educational needs including specific learning difficulties;

  b) are very able;

  c) are not fluent in English

  and knowing where to get help in order to give positive and targeted support.'   TTA, (1997)

The inclusion of SEN-related competences within the Standards will ensure that new teachers are to some extent prepared to meet the individual needs of pupils. Further, the introduction of SEN-related competences require HEIs and schools to provide quality experiences which enable trainees and NQTs to achieve these competences. While this places a further expectation on an already full PGCE and induction year, this level of expertise will be required from trainees and NQTs working within inclusive school settings.

Summary

The dynamic picture described above highlights a changing national and local policy context which is shaping the development of inclusive school settings. The challenge for ITT courses is to interpret and respond to this complex policy context. It will be important for partnerships to provide appropriate experiences and examples of good SEN practice.

SEN provision in Initial Teacher Training (Secondary PGCE)

From our review of SEN provision in five institutions we have identified a number of ways in which SEN is integrated into PGCE courses. This review forms the basis of the following analysis of SEN provision in ITT.

An introduction to the PGCE Course

Secondary PGCE courses are subject-based (covering National Curriculum subjects in England and Wales) and trainees have usually undergone a period of undergraduate level study in their subject or a closely related field prior to enrolment. In some cases trainees have prior personal or professional special needs experience. This experience is not a prerequisite for recruitment but, interestingly, it is considered to be an advantage by many institutions.

Since 1992 all PGCE courses have been required to be organised within a partnership between HEIs and schools (DoE, 1992). The content of PGCE courses varies considerably between institutions, nevertheless there are some similarities. The majority of courses include both subject and professional development programmes. Subject programmes focus on the development of skills and understandings which are required of specialist subject teachers. Professional development programmes focus on the wider role of the teacher exploring issues of relevance to all teachers, regardless of their subject specialism. In both programmes trainees are involved in both HEI and school-based experiences working with a range of identified professionals. HEI experiences tend to involve seminar and workshop-style sessions with lecture programmes in some cases.

Schools and school teachers now take an active role in ITT (Garner, 1992), for example, by providing subject and professional development tutors to complement those in the HEI. The school-based elements of the PGCE are normally developed through a range of activities and meetings with school tutors. In most courses schools attempt to provide an experience which is directly related to that in the university programme. This enables trainees to explore both theoretical and school perspectives concurrently.

In all of the courses reviewed, responsibility for developing subject and professional development programmes lies with HEI and school tutors. This occurs within partnership arrangements and PGCE courses are internally moderated at least yearly. Subject programmes are inspected every three years by the Office for Standards in Education (OFSTED). This represents a key influence on the nature of PGCE courses. The inspection process includes a focus on the quality of the trainees' teaching in relation to the Standards and therefore to some extent the trainees' SEN-related competence is inspected.

SEN provision within the Subject Programme

SEN provision within Subject programmes tends to be within the context of theoretical and practical perspectives on meeting individual needs within mainstream classrooms. Typically, programmes consider four key issues:

* What is the nature and range of pupils' individual needs in the subject classroom and how can the subject teacher meet these needs?

* What difficult concepts and skills do pupils face when studying the subject and how can the subject teacher support the learning of all pupils in relation to these?

* What are pupils' common conceptions and misconceptions within the subject and how can misconceptions be rectified by the subject teacher?[1]

* What are the responsibilities of the subject teacher in implementing school and national SEN policy?

It is argued that the first of these areas is primarily pupil-centred, the second and third are primarily subject-centred, the fourth is teacher-centred. A key objective of the subject programme is to enable trainees to bring together these pupil, subject and teacher concerns when planning, teaching and evaluating their lessons.

The opportunity for a trainee teacher to develop subject-related SEN competence will, to some extent, depend on the nature of the schools involved in the training. For example, where a school lies along the segregation/inclusion continuum will be significant in providing experiences of a range of special needs (Ainscow,1998).

SEN provision within the Professional Development Programme

The professional development programme includes reference to SEN in all of the courses reviewed. This tends to focus on whole-school issues which are explored in both HEI and school contexts. Examples include issues relating to national policy, school policy and practice, equalising opportunities and types of SEN provision.

In all courses trainees are made aware of the school's SEN department. In the best examples trainees liaise with SEN teachers and learning support assistants. This involves trainees in working directly with an individual

---

[1] The National Standards for QTS make reference to pupils' misconceptions of subject knowledge.

education programme (IEP). Trainees may be introduced to the multi-professional agencies who work with the school and other external links. Examples include working with outside professionals and making visits to local feeder primary schools and special schools.

The experience of whole-school SEN issues will to some extent depend upon the particular context of the school, for example if it is a rural or an inner-city school, or if it is an inclusive or segregated needs setting. There will also be particular HEI institutional requirements in relation to the partnership for example, some HEIs require schools to provide a comprehensive experience.

There are other models of SEN provision within professional development programmes. For example, one PGCE course provides a complementary SEN programme. This explores a range of issues in more depth such as SEN legislation, identifying and meeting individual needs and behaviour management.

PGCE assessment

All courses include elements of continuous assessment throughout the year with a final summative assessment culminating in the award of QTS. Courses usually have two elements of assessment. The first element is assessment of the trainee's school-based performance. The second element is assessment of written and oral assignments in which trainee's discuss their theoretical and practical understandings of subject and professional issues. Together these assessments provide evidence of the achievement of QTS Standards.

Assessment of a trainee's school-based performance usually involves the judgements of school and HEI tutors in relation to the achievement of Standards. This will therefore include assessment of SEN competence. In addition, trainees are involved in self assessment. In some courses this takes the form of trainees gathering and recording evidence of their progress and achievement in respect of each Standard or groups of Standards.

A guiding philosophy of some courses is to develop teachers who are 'reflective practitioners'. A typical approach is for school or HEI tutors to undertake focused observation of the trainee's teaching with post-lesson reflections. This approach supports the trainee in undertaking a critical analysis of the lesson resulting in the trainee's identification of action and targets for their future teaching. As this process is set in the context of the

National Standards for QTS, SEN-related standards will be a focus of at least some of these reflections.

In most of the courses reviewed, PGCE assignments include both subject and professional development assignments. There are no cases where a SEN-related assignment is a course requirement for all trainees. Nevertheless, there may be SEN assignments for some trainees, for example, within specific subject programmes. Professional development assignments typically include a dissertation or extended essay. Dissertations normally focus on a whole school issue selected by the trainee in negotiation with their school and HEI tutors. Interestingly, in all courses a SEN focus appears to be a popular choice for dissertations. In our experience this reflects trainees' interest in this field and a concern to develop their understanding of SEN. Given that assignments require reference to academic literature and national policy alongside school-based evidence, they provide important vehicles for the development of trainees' educational and professional knowledge and understanding. It is clear that only some trainees have opportunities to develop their SEN-related professional understandings in this way.

Issues arising

Differences in provision

Given that the content of PGCE courses varies considerably between institutions it is to be expected that there will also be differences in SEN provision (Brayton and Dew-Hughes, 1997). Nevertheless, the extent of the differences has been greater than expected. The extent to which subject-based ITT courses are taking account of the changing training context, and particularly the SEN Standards for QTS, are peculiar to individual partnerships. It would appear that institutional interpretation and local school circumstances are dictating the nature of provision.

Our review suggests that there is a range of models of SEN provision in PGCE courses. These exist along a continuum from minimalist to evolving models. In the minimalist models SEN provision relates to traditional levels of need within subject classrooms in mainstream schools. By contrast, the evolving models challenge the notions of SEN represented by the Standards and explore critically the purposes of inclusive school settings. These models may also include multi-professional contributions delivered by professionals employed on a sessional basis from 'outside' the HEI. It is argued that the Standards are the driving force for current

SEN provision in PGCE courses. Therefore it may be that the minimal nature of the SEN-related Standards will do little to encourage the evolving model of SEN provision.

SEN expertise within HEIs

Evidence from our review suggests a number of other possible reasons for the different models of SEN provision in PGCE courses. The five institutions reviewed, like many HEI education departments, have been concerned traditionally with subject-based PGCE courses. Therefore many of their PGCE tutors are subject specialists who may or may not have an interest in SEN. SEN expertise and interest also varies between HEI education departments. Some departments have extensive SEN research and consultancy centres whilst others have little or no ongoing SEN research.

Nationally SEN training at both undergraduate and postgraduate level is found in only a limited number of institutions. Typically these institutions offer three-year undergraduate training programmes leading to bachelor degrees. At postgraduate level, courses have been restricted to qualified practitioners with at least one to three years mainstream school experience. These courses include one- to two-year specialist SEN diploma courses.

Despite these differences in SEN expertise all PGCE tutors are now expected to prepare subject teachers to work in inclusive school settings. However, these courses were primarily designed to prepare teachers to work in mainstream schools. Therefore courses are beginning to provide further opportunities for developing trainees' SEN understandings. Two of the courses reviewed now include contributions from outside SEN professionals. There may be further opportunities for these professionals to work directly with subject tutors to support the development of subject programmes.

There would appear to be a clear need for PGCE courses to consider how their SEN provision should be developed in response to the changing SEN context. This is particularly important given that there is not a tradition of preparation for SEN work within ITT. No evidence is available to suggest ways in which the subject tutors are being briefed on SEN developments as these relate to policy or evolving inclusive school settings. This would suggest the need for SEN working groups within partnerships to support the development of professional and subject programmes. Further, inter-institutional collaboration may be a useful way to share SEN expertise and support the development of PGCE courses in this area.

SEN research within HEIs

The courses reviewed suggest that SEN research in mainstream schools by PGCE tutors is limited. However, the majority of tutors hold extensive experience of supporting trainees in undertaking SEN research during school placements, for example, as part of dissertation research. Interestingly, SEN research at masters and doctoral level is being supervised within some HEIs. Examples include research in the fields of teachers' thinking, auditory capacities and classroom learning. Other SEN research activity has been reported in relation to European funded projects. This is concerned with developing city and regional educational infrastructures to support the inclusion of young citizens with differing needs into school settings (Sayer, 1999).

The extent to which research findings are being shared across PGCE, Continuing Professional Development, masters and doctoral level courses, PGCE partnership schools and other HEIs has not been established. Nevertheless, there are obvious opportunities to support the development of trainees' SEN understandings through the sharing of such knowledge.

SEN research in inclusive school settings has a central role to play in the development of schools and education departments. Given that research activity is a prime task of HEIs, as reflected in the national Research Assessment Exercise (RAE), PGCE courses are well placed to lead in this role. The future of such research will depend on national funding and institutions bidding for available funds. We would argue that SEN provision within PGCE courses is an appropriate and valuable avenue for research.

Standards for QTS

The National Standards for QTS represent a key influence on the development of courses since appropriate experiences are required to enable trainees to achieve the Standards. In addition OFSTED inspection gradings to some extent reflect the quality of trainees' teaching in relation to the Standards. Training quotas and therefore funding are dependent on good OFSTED gradings.

The Standards are not subject specific, therefore in some institutions derivative subject-based interpretations of Standards are being explored. These aim to support HEI and school subject tutors to develop common understandings of what the Standards require of the teacher of that particular subject. In our experience this process has proved to be problematic.

However, the subject tutors' interpretation of the SEN-related Standards has been less difficult. This may be because the SEN-related Standards refer to particular aspects of SEN responsibilities. We would argue that the SEN-related Standards are limited in breadth and depth. These Standards lack reference to a number of important aspects of SEN competence including understanding specific needs (for example, dyslexia, see Lepkowska, 1998), methods of identification and assessment, developing focused resources and ways of working with learning support assistants. Importantly, this raises the question of what is an appropriate SEN curriculum for trainee subject teachers? From our review there is little evidence to suggest that this question is being given emphasis in the development of PGCE courses.

An emerging picture and policy context

Inclusive schooling

As the national shift to inclusive school settings gains momentum there is greater pressure on PGCE courses to prepare teachers for the changing face of 21st century schools. There is a need for PGCE courses to take account of wider notions of inclusion (Gardiner, 1997) and the purposes of schooling. For example, there is a growing expectation that schools will serve the local, national and international community more effectively. Such ideas are reflected in the new Citizenship National Curriculum which is currently in a period of consultation (DfEE, 1999).

A further prospect is that schools and their teachers will be required to develop high expectations for all pupils (DfEE Green Paper: *Excellence for All Children: Meeting Special Educational Needs*, 1997). In response to such expectations one course is blurring its subject and professional development margins. Here greater emphasis is being placed on the role of the subject programme in preparing trainees for their wider professional role, including their role in meeting SEN.

Teachers' professional status

The government's concern to raise the professional status of teachers is central to the development of a General Teaching Council (GTC). Only one teacher from the field of SEN will be represented on this council. This is perhaps a missed opportunity to raise the profile of SEN, but time will tell. The need to raise the status of the teaching profession is reflected in the current crisis in national teacher recruitment (Millet, 1999). This crisis raises issues and questions about the image of teaching. Some have argued that the public image of teaching as expressed through competence-based training does little to encourage intellectual and creative thinkers to the profession (Pring, 1999). A further issue is that of the pay and conditions and career prospects of teachers which consistently compare unfavourably with other professions.

In an attempt to encourage teachers into the profession a number of different recruitment schemes are being trialled nationally. The success of such schemes, such as 'work release', are yet to be fully evaluated. However, these flexible models of training are popular for many prospective entrants to the profession. Flexible models have the advantage of encouraging mature entrants or those whose circumstances inhibit them from taking a one year full-time course. Such entrants may have had prior careers including valuable experience in special needs.

Developing SEN practice

It is anticipated that the outcomes of the national SEN review groups (in response to the government's Green Paper, DfEE, 1997) will create change in SEN practice at higher education, local authority and school level. PGCE courses will need to be responsive to these new practices. Certainly there is much scope for HEIs to develop courses to support the National Standards for the Award of Specialist SEN Teachers and Coordinators (DfEE, 1999, Farrell,1998). This raises a further question about quality assurance in terms of the suitability of training providers. This issue has already been raised by NAGSEN (1999) in terms of the lack of consistency across and between current SEN courses as illustrated by the TTA Survey of Special Educational Needs Training Provided by Higher Education August, 1997 (Thornton 1998).

Implications for PGCE courses

Given the dynamic context in which training is currently taking place it might be argued that PGCE courses are involved in a reactive, as opposed to a proactive, role in the development of SEN within ITT programmes. HEI partnerships play a primary role in raising standards in teaching, therefore it would seem reasonable that they should play a fundamental role in developing SEN provision that best meets the needs of training subject teachers. This raises a fundamental question about what we might expect of an NQT in relation to their SEN understandings and skills by the end of an ITT course? Given that SEN work will become central to the practices of newly-qualified teachers working within inclusive school settings there is a clear need for PGCE courses to develop a vision for their future SEN provision.

Final thoughts

In each academic year strategists within HEI education departments will continue their internal assessment of their work including PGCE activity. This means working within their ITT partnerships to evaluate existing practices and define initiatives for the next academic year. SEN initiatives may fall within this wider discussion. Inevitably these discussions will be strongly influenced by government proposals, TTA guidance and OFSTED inspection criteria, together with the considerable range of other internal and external influences and areas of work the department may wish to engage in (Clough 1998).

What is clear is that nationally HEI education departments are rationalising their activity, including PGCE work, as they look towards developing their research, regional roles and identities as centres of excellence. Given the changes in SEN policy and practice there is likely to be a significant training need. A case for committing to SEN training outside of PGCE will be argued by those departments who have access to SEN expertise. Certainly, this training opportunity will be attractive to providers outside of the higher education sector such as Local Education Authorities. Therefore, HEIs will be required to define their distinctive contribution in this field. If this stimulates greater SEN activity and interest it will clearly have a positive effect on all SEN training and hopefully an impact on the quality of SEN provision within the PGCE.

Authors' note

This chapter is based on a paper presented by Robert Barratt at the National Conference for Special Educational Needs, St Catherine's College, Oxford, 1999. We are grateful to those who participated in the workshop ITE and SEN at the National Conference on SEN for their stimulating discussion.

References

Ainscow, M (1998), Exploring Links Between Special Educational Needs and School Improvement, *Support for Learning*, 13, 2, May, (pp 70-75)

Aubrey, C (1994), Who Teaches the Teachers?, *Special Children*, 78, October, (pp 20-22)

Brayton, H and Dew-Hughes, K (1997), Initial Teacher Tarring and Pupils with Special Educational Needs, *Support for Learning*, 12, 4, November, (pp 175-179)

Clough, P (1998), Balancing Acts: Policy Agenda for Teacher Education and Meeting Special Educational Needs, *Journal of Education for Teaching*, 24, 1, April, (pp 63-710

DoE (1992) *Circular 9/92*, HMSO

DfEE (1999), *Citizenship. The National Curriculum*

Farrell, M (1998), The Role of the Special Educational Needs Co-ordinator: Looking Forward, *Support for Learning*, 13, 2, May, (pp 82-86)

Gardiner, J (1997), Inclusion on the Way in, *Times Educational Supplement*, October 24

Garner, P (1992), Special Educational Needs and Initial Teacher Education: a Recent PGCE Development, *Support for Learning*, 7, 3, August, (pp 125-129)

Lepkowska, D (1998), Concern at Poor Dyslexia Training, *Times Educational Supplement*, May 29

Millet, A (1999), Address to the Royal Geographical Society

Mittler, P (1992), Preparing all Initial Teacher Training Students to Teach Children with Special Educational Needs: a Case Study from England, *European Journal of Special Needs Education*, 7, 1, March, (pp 1-10)

National Association for SEN (1999), *Response to the DfEE White Paper Excellence for All Children*, National Association for SEN, Chapter 6. www.nasen.org.uk/consult

Postlethwaite, K and Raban, B (1990), Special Needs in Initial Teacher Training: Course Development and Evaluation in an English University, *Journal of Education for Teaching*, 16, 3, (pp 283-297)

Pring, R (1999), Personal comment

Raban, B (1989), Special Education Aspects of PGCE Courses in University Departments of Education: a Survey Report, *Journal of Further and Higher Education*, 13, 2, Summer, (pp 49-61)

Sayer, J (1999), *Opening Schools for All*, Garant

Teacher Training Agency (1997), *Survey of Special Educational Needs Training Provided by Higher Education*, TTA

TTA, (1998), *National Standards for the Award of Qualified Teacher Status*, TTA

Teacher Training Agency (1999), *Consultation on National Standards for Special Educational Needs (SEN) Specialist Teachers*, TTA

Teacher Training Agency (1999), *National Standards for Special Educational Needs Co-ordinators*, TTA, www.teach-tta.gov.uk/nssen.htm

Thornton, K (1998), Model for Special Needs Training, *Times Educational Supplement*, 4294, October 16, (p 19)

www.teach-tta.gov.uk/senconsu.htm

UNESCO, (1996), *Survey of Laws Relating to SEN*, UNESCO

United Nations (1989), *UN Convention on the Rights of the Child*, New York, UN

World Conference on Special Needs Education (1994), *Salamanca Statement*, Salamanca, World Conference on Special Needs Education

Chapter 3

Education in Ireland for persons with Special Education Needs

Edward J Casey

Introduction

The Irish system of education for persons with disabilities and those with special needs is in transition. Increasingly, parents are opting to seek education for their children in mainstream schools. As in many countries of the world, the thrust of educational policy in Ireland is towards the development of inclusive education systems, where the 'special' and the 'mainstream' blend, drawing on the skills and expertise of both, in support of all students.

In this paper, a brief overview of the Irish educational system is provided and some of the strengths and weaknesses of the system of educational provision for those with special needs are enumerated. Some of the key principles and recommendations in recent government reports are discussed.

An Irish Education Act was introduced in late 1998. It is far too early to expect substantial changes on the ground as a result of this Act. However, the government is actively working towards the implementation of its provisions.

Overview of the educational system in Ireland

The total population of the Republic is 3.6 million approximately. Compulsory education in Ireland extends from six to fifteen years of age. In practice, however, the majority of children between four and six years of age attend primary schools. The provision of pre-school education in Ireland is very limited.

In 1990/91, there were approximately 552,500 pupils attending first level schools. This figure includes almost 9000 in private, fee-paying schools and 8300 in Special Schools. There were about 3800 pupils in Special Classes.

Second-level education is provided in Secondary Schools which are privately owned but largely financed by the State and in Comprehensive, Community and Vocational Schools and Colleges. In general, pupils transfer to second-level education between the ages of 13 and 14. The junior second-level cycle lasts for three years, at the end of which pupils sit for the Junior Certificate. The great majority of students progress to the two-year senior cycle and complete the Leaving Certificate. About 6000 pupils complete a Transition Year before going on to complete their Leaving Certificate.

In 1990/91 there were 70,000 students in third-level education. Private third-level colleges provide a small but growing percentage of places. It is estimated that approximately 1000 students with disabilities attend third-level colleges.

Special education in Ireland

Provision is made for pupils with special needs in both ordinary and special schools. Approximately 3800 pupils with a variety of physical, sensory and mental handicaps and those with language disorders are enrolled in special classes in primary schools. There are 48 officially recognised special classes for pupils with learning difficulties in post-primary schools. Five post-primary schools are recognised as designated schools for the education of students with physical, hearing or visual impairment.

Currently, the proportion of the total population of compulsory school attendance age (6-15 years) enrolled in special schools is approximately 1.2%. The great majority are children with mild and moderate learning difficulties (mental handicap) but there are also significant numbers of children with visual or hearing impairment, physical handicap or emotional disturbance provided for in special schools.

This level of special school provision is low in comparison with other countries of the European Community. Nevertheless, a policy of integration will inevitably have impact on special schools, as students in these schools with less severe degrees of disability are able to be provided for in ordinary schools.

Special schools

About 8,000 pupils are enrolled in 114 special schools and some 3800 pupils with various disabilities are in special classes in primary schools. Special schools are national schools and can cater for pupils from four to 18 years of age. Of this total, 3300 pupils have a mild learning difficulty and attend 31 special schools and 2000 pupils with moderate learning difficulty attend 33 Special Schools. The remaining students attend a variety of schools which cater for students with physical, sensory and multiple disabilities, specific learning difficulties, emotional disturbance, children-at-risk and young offenders.

Strengths and weaknesses of the present system of educational provision for persons with special needs and disabilities

Strengths:

A major strength of the present system is evidenced by the fact that provision has already been made to cater, as a priority, for the largest groups of students with special educational needs. Various government partnership programmes have given commitments to increase the level of provision. As a result of capital investment by central government, most special school buildings are relatively new. The government has given a commitment to increase significantly the number of remedial teachers, as indicated below.

Another major strength of the Irish system of provision for students with special needs is the high calibre of teachers involved. Research has shown that Irish teachers, as a group, are drawn from a cohort of students, which is higher achieving by way of examination success than is the case for teachers in many other developed countries (Greaney *et al*, 1987). All teachers in Special Education have attended specific in-service training courses on special educational needs. Almost all teachers have taken one of a variety of Diploma Courses, *eg* Diploma in Special Education, Diploma in Compensatory and Remedial Education.

The powerful presence of religious orders and lay voluntary organisations represents a particular strength of the Irish system. At this time many of the religious orders have contracted due to falling numbers of religious staff but the orders are still large-scale service providers. Some of the lay voluntary organisations have grown and developed to become major service providers capable of providing life-long services for their clients. The vast bulk of their funding, in some cases up to 95%, now comes directly from various Departments of State.

The active involvement of parents in education at all levels for many years is also a positive factor. Their contributions were recognised in the White Paper on Education (Irish Department of Education, 1995) and given a statutory basis in the Education Act of 1998.

Weaknesses:

A major weakness of the Irish system up to 1998 had been the lack of legislation for most forms of education, including that for students with special needs, which meant that access to education was not statutorily guaranteed.

Apart from the Vocational Education Committees, which are responsible for the post-primary vocational schools, there is a lack of an intermediate administrative structure between the Department of Education and the schools. This is a particularly inefficient and inappropriate way to provide for the needs of the many small and widely scattered schools attempting to cater for special education needs.

Such schools would be better served by a local, flexible structure which could respond promptly and sensitively to individual needs. A locally-based structure is more likely to be better informed about local requirements and would, for instance, be likely to be more effective in channelling scarce resources to those with greatest need. To date, particular weaknesses of the Irish system have been about gaps in provision such as – the widespread lack of pre-school facilities for children with special needs, especially in small towns and rural areas and the shortage of remedial teachers.

Another major weakness of the Irish educational system, which has two parallel sub-systems of ordinary and special schools, is the lack of contact and interchange between both systems. This separation of the two sub-systems inhibits the realisation of the goal of enabling students with special educational needs to live, socialise and work in their communities.

A further weakness which should be mentioned is the less-than-adequate provision available for students with special educational needs in ordinary post-primary schools. While the majority of special classes in ordinary schools catering for those with mild mental handicaps are offering a multi-faceted curriculum, covering a broad variety of subjects and involving access to all the facilities and the specialist teachers of the school, a significant minority of special classes fail in this regard. In such instances students with mild mental handicap may spend all day in their special classrooms and do not have access to the range of facilities offered by the school or to teachers other than their own.

Report of the Special Education Review Committee

One the most significant developments in the field of educational provision for young people with special educational needs was the establishment of the Special Education Review Committee (SERC) in August 1991. This Committee reported in 1993 (Irish Department of Education, 1993). Its terms of reference were:

'To report and make recommendations on the educational provision for children with special needs in respect of:

a) the identification of children with special needs and their assessment with a view to determining the educational provision best suited to the needs of each child;

b) the arrangements which should be put in place in order to provide for the educational requirements of such children through complete or partial integration in ordinary schools, through special classes in ordinary schools or through special schools or other special arrangements, in accordance with the circumstances as assessed of each child;

c) the range of support services which may be required and in particular the future relationship between remedial teachers, visiting teachers, other support-teachers and ordinary class teachers;

d) the linkages which should exist with other Departments of State and service providers provided under their aegis'.

In charting the way forward the Review Committee proposed that the following seven principles should serve as guidelines for future development:

1 All children, including those with special needs, have a right to appropriate education.

2 The need of the individual child should be the paramount consideration when decisions are being made concerning the provision of special education for that child.

3 The child's parents are entitled, and should be enabled, to play an active part in the decision-making process: their wishes should be taken into consideration when recommendations on special education provision are being made.

4 A continuum of services should be provided for children with special educational needs ranging from full-time education in ordinary classes, with additional inputs as may be necessary, to full-time education in special schools.

5 Appropriate education for all children with special education needs should be provided in ordinary schools, except where individual circumstances make this impracticable.

6   Only in the most exceptional circumstances should it be necessary for a child to live away from home in order to avail of an appropriate education.

7   The State should provide adequate resources to ensure that children with special educational needs can have an education appropriate to those needs.

For the purpose of its report, the Review Committee defined *pupils with special needs* as:

'those whose disabilities and/or circumstances prevent or hinder them from benefiting adequately from the education which is normally provided for pupils of the same age, or for whom the education which can generally be provided in the ordinary classroom is not sufficiently challenging'.

Special education was defined as

'any educational provision which is designed to cater for pupils with special educational needs, and is additional to or different from the provision which is generally made in ordinary classes for pupils of the same age'.

Educational integration was defined as:

'the participation of pupils with disabilities in school activities with other pupils, to the maximum extent which is consistent with the broader overall interests of both the pupils with disabilities and the other pupils in the class/group'.

The Review Committee stressed that the primary consideration in devising special education provision is the need to take full account of the assessed needs of the individual pupil. While pupils may have a common impairment or disability, the special educational provision made for them must reflect the particular needs of each child and recognise the many differences between individual children.

In regard to the issue of integration, the Review Committee declared that it held no doctrinaire position regarding the integration into the ordinary school system of pupils with disabilities and/or special needs. They summed up their approach by saying that they were in favour of as much integration as is appropriate and feasible with as little segregation as is necessary. The Review Committee accepted that, as is the case in many other countries, the Irish system of special schooling is likely to contract over time as levels of provision grow in mainstream schools. They felt that, for the foreseeable future, the two systems – specialist and mainstream schooling – would continue to provide educational opportunities for disabled children and those with special needs.

The need for each child to have as complete a range of education options as possible was emphasised. Such options should range across a spectrum from full-time placement in an ordinary class to full-time placement in a special class or school to full-time placement in a seven-day residential special school, to part-time placement in a Child Education and Development Centre and part-time attendance at a Special School. Several other educational options were listed.

A particular development which was foreseen was the scenario where increasing numbers of pupils will receive part of their education in special schools and part in ordinary schools. It was envisaged that many special schools would enrol children with a variety of disabilities and special needs and over time become more in the nature of regional multi-category special schools. Many schools should, it was felt, develop outreach facilities for pupils in the ordinary school system. The Review Committee laid particular emphasis on the establishment and expansion of a school psychological service and the appointment of additional Special Needs Assistants to both mainstream and special schools.

It was recognised that, given the sparse population in parts of rural Ireland, it would not be possible or desirable to try to cater adequately for every pupil with a disability and/or special education needs, in every isolated school in the country. It was felt that in some cases a better option was to have certain schools designated to provide a complete and centralised special service. It was seen that in some circumstances it is better to bring the pupil to the service rather than bring the service to the pupil. It was argued that, where pupils with more serious learning difficulties are grouped together, they will be able to receive substantial periods of support teaching each day, while at the same time being given the opportunity of integrating into the ordinary class for appropriate periods of time. However, for those students with learning difficulties who attend isolated schools, it was recommended that a visiting resource teacher should be available.

National Rehabilitation Board submission

The National Rehabilitation Board of Ireland (NRB) in its submission to the Commission on the Status of People with Disabilities entitled *Equal*

Status – a Blueprint for Action (National Rehabilitation Board, Ireland, 1994) made over 40 specific recommendations on ways of reducing or eliminating altogether the barriers experienced by students with disabilities/special educational needs in gaining appropriate education at all levels of school and third-level colleges. In its submission NRB highlighted the importance of the then forthcoming Education Act, which was expected to set out the statutory responsibility for removing barriers to appropriate education and to specify the statutory right of persons with disabilities in education to receive appropriate support based on their personal needs and requirements.

The NRB recommended that there should be greater representation of pupils with disabilities/special educational needs in mainstream primary and post-primary schools, promoted by appropriate monitoring incentives and sanctions.

Many of the recommendations made by NRB were subsequently incorporated into the Report of the Commission on the Status of People with Disabilities.

Charting our Education Future

The White Paper *Charting our Education Future* (*op cit*) espouses the principle of equality of access and participation in the education system for all students according to their ability and potential. It recognises that equal access will need positive intervention to make this happen. This policy document commits itself to the objective of developing a continuum of provision to allow flexible access to students, in accordance with their needs.

Report of the Commission on the status of people with disabilities

The Commission Report, *A Strategy for Equality* (Department of Equality and Law Reform, Ireland, 1996), stresses that education must be equally available to everyone. To achieve this objective sufficient planning and resources must be applied. The emphasis in this report is on equality and maximisation of participation, enabling independence and choice. The Commission sets out key educational principles and proposals that should be enshrined in legislation, in regard to the education of every citizen with a disability.

In summary, these principles include the following:

• Appropriate education for children with disabilities to be provided in mainstream schools, except in special circumstances;

- The need to provide for the unique needs of each individual student;
- The primacy of parents in the decision-making process;
- The responsibility of schools to serve children in the least restrictive environment;
- The need for the State to provide the necessary resources so that education appropriate to the needs of all children can be provided in the best possible environment.

Getting into mainstream schools

Parents of children with disabilities and/or special needs require good information about available education options to enable them to make well-informed educational decisions. The non-availability or lack of information about schools, support services and available facilities, in some areas, has been widely commented upon (*eg* Working Group, 1996) and causes great anxiety and difficulties for parents. Those parents who have links with Non-Governmental Organisations (NGOs) dedicated to providing services for people with learning difficulties, for instance, seem to fare better in terms of obtaining appropriate information and support services (Colgan, 1998).

Significant information and support is also provided for parents through the eight Regional Health Boards. However, not all parents have developed satisfactory contacts with relevant agencies and not all parts of the country have an agency capable of providing the necessary supports. However many parents opting for mainstream national schooling for their child need or require very little additional assistance. They are in a position to make decisions based on their own evaluation of their child's needs together with inputs from professional assessment. Their decision to opt for mainstream schooling may be based primarily on their wish to keep their child in their own local community. Sadly for some parents, a choice of school for their child is not available because there is only one local school.

A structured method of providing information and advice for all parents on schooling options and facilities must be provided. Although, one must acknowledge that, at present, there is quite an extensive range of expertise and considerable resources within the health and educational systems.

The larger Non-Governmental Organisations (NGOs) for instance will, at the request of parents, provide medical, psychological, educational reports and other informal and formal reports to parents who are seeking placements for their children in mainstream pre-schools or primary schools. Many NGOs will provide information to parents on schools in the area and help them to make suitable choices. A lesser number of NGOs provide a multi-disciplinary service to mainstream schools, to support disabled children and those with special needs and continue to provide a full range of therapeutic inputs.

On a case-by-case basis, the health boards provide a certain amount of support for parents with educational decision-making and placement. The current development of Early Intervention Teams (EITs) by health boards may allow for an expansion of support services.

A report published in 1990 (Review Group on Mental Hardship Services) advocated the establishment of these multi-disciplinary Early Intervention Teams and recommended that one member of each team be assigned the role of 'Key Worker' to coordinate all necessary support services. In most instances, the Key Worker is the local community nurse or counsellor. The operation of the EITs and Key Worker system is currently being evaluated. The extent of their present or any likely future contribution to supporting parents to select appropriate schools for their children and provide other advice and support for both parents and children remains to be determined.

It should also be acknowledged that parent support groups and the Visiting Teacher Service play an invaluable role in providing readily accessible support and advice to parents. The idea of the 'Named Person', which is in operation in Great Britain on a voluntary basis, is another option currently being considered in Ireland.

Ongoing personal and social supports

Most children with special educational needs require access to supports such as personal assistants, transport, technical and mechanical aids and appliances, to enable them to participate fully in mainstream school.

At the present time, special needs assistants are available on an *ad hoc* basis only. Parents or school principals generally arrange for their employment through Government Community Employment Schemes. Arrangements have now been put in place (see below) for the widespread employment of personal assistants on a formal basis.

The issue of the extent of therapeutic supports and who should provide these is currently being debated. It is hoped to put in place the necessary structures and systems so that the current and evolving therapeutic needs of the vast majority of children with disabilities and special needs can be catered for in mainstream schools. It is expected that full use will be made of the skills and capabilities of personnel in the various specialist voluntary agencies.

School transport

The inadequacy of school transport provision to enable disabled/special needs children to attend the school of their choice, is of major concern. One of the earliest reports which drew attention to the lack of adequate facilities was drawn up by the Irish Wheelchair Association in 1977 (Faughnan, 1977). This report indicated that 53% of the members of the association (all ages) who wished to participate in some form of education could not do so because of lack of transport facilities.

The recently issued *Report of the School Transport Review Committee* (1998) examined in great depth the situation of students with special education needs in relation to school transport. It found that since the publication in 1993 of the Report of the Special Education Review Committee (*op. cit.*) there had been significant improvement in transport provisions. This report focussed on pupils with special educational needs who require transport to special schools and special classes. There was no particular focus on those children needing special transport to enable them to attend their local school. A controversial recommendation relates to the need for parents to increase their financial contribution. No additional funding for transport, currently costing the Exchequer around IR£36m per annum, was recommended. To those parents and others who were encouraged by the strong recommendations for improvement of school transport facilities contained in the Report of the Commission on the Status of People with Disabilities (p203) (*op cit*), the gaps and weaknesses in the Report of the School Transport Review Committee are likely to prove very disappointing.

Present supports for teaching and learning in mainstream schools

At present the main form of extra support for children with special educational needs in the mainstream classroom is provided through Resource and Visiting Teachers. There are currently (1998) 78 Resource Teachers and 48 Visiting Teachers in the system. In addition, there are 1,242 Remedial Teachers and over 500 Special Class Teachers.

An issue of contention in relation to the provision of Resource and Visiting Teacher posts for pupils assessed as needing special educational inputs has been the manner in which they have been provided in the past. Where teaching posts are 'surplus to existing needs' as a result of a drop in pupil numbers, they are re-distributed once a year to the area of education and of the county where they are most needed. As there is greater demand than supply of 'surplus' teachers, many areas are not adequately staffed. Many observers fear that the so-called 'demographic dividend', which facilitates this allocation of teachers, will shrink with recent increasing birth rates.

Another issue which gives cause for concern at present is the administrative arrangement through which children secure the services of Resource Teachers. Up to 1999 children with special educational needs entering mainstream schools did not have an automatic entitlement to the service of a Resource Teacher. In order to secure this service, between six and eight children (depending on the nature and degree of disability/special need) had to be in need of the service in a particular school or area. At present the amount of time which can be allocated by Resource Teachers to children with special needs, being educated in the mainstream, is between two and three hours per week on average.

According to ministerial press releases in the late 1998 and early 1999, it was hoped that recent arrangements regarding funding and the appointment of extra teachers by the Minister for Education and Science would result in improvements to services on offer.

The Report of the Special Education Review Committee (*op cit*) outlined the roles of Resource and Visiting Teachers and gave priority to their role in the direct teaching of individual children and groups, with some advisory and support work. The practice of withdrawing children with special needs from the classroom as the main means of supporting them and their teachers has been questioned (Hegarty, 1993).

Internationally, there has been a move away from the practice of withdrawing pupils from their class in order to offer special help, in favour of the Support Teacher working in the class with both pupil and teacher. In future, we must concentrate much more on interdisciplinary teamwork between the personnel involved – the class teacher, the support teacher, parents, special needs assistants, speech therapists and psychologists – if we are to avoid role conflict and provide the best possible educational opportunities for the children concerned.

The Education Act (1998)

This Act obliges the Minister for Education to ensure 'that there is made available to each person resident in the State, including a person with a disability or who has other educational needs, special services and a level and quality of education appropriate to meeting the needs and abilities of that person'.

This is an enabling Act which sets out the broad thrust of policy, while specifying the precise responsibilities of the Schools Inspectorate, Boards of Management and the proposed National Council for Curriculum Development.

Some of the sections of this Act which are relevant to people with disabilities are as follows:

Section 9 (a)

'Ensure that the educational needs of all students, including those with a disability or other special needs, are identified and provided for'.

Section 13: Sub-Section 3 (a)

This refers to the functions of the Schools Inspector who must 'assess the implementation and effectiveness of any programmes of education which have been delivered in respect of individual students who have a disability or other special education needs'. and

Section 13: Sub-Section 4 (b)

'Advise recognised schools on policies and strategies for the education of children with special educational needs'.

Section 33: Sub-Section (i)

The Minister may make regulations relating to, *inter alia*:-

'Access to schools and centres for education by students with disabilities or who have other educational needs, including matters relating to reasonable accommodation and technical aids and equipment for such students'.

Section 41: Sub-Section 2 (f)

This states that the Council must 'advise the Minister on the requirements, as regards curriculum and syllabuses, of students with disability or other educational need.'

Recent developments in the provision of special education services

In November 1998, the Minister for Education announced the following measures:

- The introduction of a formalised system of special teaching support for all children attending schools on a fully-integrated basis who have been assessed as having special educational needs;

- The introduction of a formalised system of child care support for all children with special needs, including those in special schools, who have been assessed as requiring such support;

- The strengthening of the National Council for Curriculum and Assessment by the appointment of extra staff to assist schools to meet special educational needs in mainstream schools. A Steering Committee with representatives of parents, teachers and school managements has been appointed;

- The establishment of a National Educational Psychological Service which will be staffed by approximately 200 psychologists;

- The commencement of an audit of needs nationally.

These measures are aimed at ensuring that all children with a special educational need, irrespective of their location or disability, will receive the support they require to participate fully in the education system. They extend across the entire spectrum of special needs and are intended to deliver extra teaching and child care services to all special needs children, whether in groups or in isolated settings. These measures ensure that each child has an automatic entitlement to the level of teaching and child care support which they need. When a group of children with special needs attends an ordinary school or adjacent schools, the support will take the form of full-time resource teachers or child care posts or both. The pupil/teacher ratio is reduced to 6:1. However, the level of response in each case will have regard to the severity of the disabilities involved. The Minister for Education and Science stressed that flexibility of response, based on individual assessed need, was essential. For example, children with severe or profound mental handicap now have an entitlement to two childcare assistants per class of six children.

For the first time, children with disabilities and special needs have a guarantee of special teaching support and, if necessary, childcare support. In the past, such support measures were unevenly available throughout the

State and there was no automatic entitlement to these services. Children who attended special schools or classes did, however, enjoy a special reduced pupil/teacher ratio. However, those who chose the integrated option had no guarantee of special teaching support. This was particularly the case in sparsely-populated rural locations, where small groups of pupils or isolated individuals were concerned.

Sufficient funding for the necessary extra teaching and childcare posts has been assured. An audit of the precise number of children with special needs and the exact nature of these needs is underway at present, so that the requirements of every special needs child are responded to.

As we look to the future, we must build a more inclusive education system for all, encompassing the strengths of both the special and mainstream systems. We must create a continuum of provision to cater for, and respond to, a range of learning needs. From an educational perspective, one of the great strengths of the continuum concept is that it embodies and is built upon the principle of catering to individual needs and strengths, a basic educational principle.

The system of separate provision for special education has developed in Ireland over many decades. Clearly the educational system in Ireland is in transition. We must work to develop greater links between the special and mainstream systems. The task of building an inclusive educational system, based on the concept of a continuum of educational provision, will require information provision, revised approaches to assessment services, systematic support systems for parents, a radical restructuring of the teaching support systems, an administrative infrastructure within the Department of Education and Science – all this facilitated and enabled by the newly laid down legislative framework.

References

Colgan, A (1998), *Access to Mainstream Classrooms: A Research Paper* (mimeo)

Department of Education and Science, Ireland (1998), *Report of the School Transport Committee*, Dublin

Department of Equality and Law Reform, Ireland (1996), *A Strategy for Equality: Report of the Commission on the Status of People with Disabilities*, Dublin

Faughnan, P (1977), *Dimensions of Need*, Irish Wheelchair Association, Dublin

Government Publications Office (1990), *Needs and Abilities – A Policy for the*

Intellectually Disabled: Report of the Review Group on Mental Handicap Services, Dublin

Hegarty, S (1993), *Meeting Special Educational Needs in the Ordinary School*, Cassell

Irish Department of Education (1993), *Report of the Special Education Review Committee*, Dublin

Irish Department of Education (1995), *Charting Our Education Future: White Paper on Education*, Dublin

National Rehabilitation Board, Ireland (1994), *Equal Status – A Blueprint for Action: Submission to the Commission on the Status of People with Disabilities*, Dublin

Working Group on Education for the Commission on the Status of People with Disabilities (1996), Dublin

Chapter 4

The rhetoric of political correctness: European Union perspectives on inclusion

Christine O'Hanlon

Introduction

There is one thing that characterises special needs education in Europe and that is its diversity and wide-ranging practices. Much of what has been written about Europe starts with the defining of what is meant by the term 'special educational needs' (SEN), which is socially determined within each country. Although the focus of recent European legislation has been to provide a common framework for the 'inclusion' of students and persons with 'special educational needs' throughout the EU, there is still a widely divergent variety of practice.

Since the 1960s, Europe has been pursuing the principles of integration and normalisation developed in Scandinavian countries (Nirje 1992, Wolfensberger 1972), to counteract the institutionalisation of children with disabilities in western society. Although the terms 'integration' and 'inclusion' have been raised in recent educational debates, consistently, in all the information sources in Europe on 'inclusion' in education, or the provision for students with special educational needs in mainstream schools, the term 'integration' is widely used in official education policy documents. This may be because the term is familiar in Europe, since the general political emphasis is on the 'integration' of all national political systems, *ie* in relation to policy development in the EU countries. It is a word often used in relation to unification and the dynamics of common economic, political and social actions which have shaped European developments over the past century.

Although the term 'Europe' brings different interpretations and responses from its citizens, in this chapter the term will be used to refer to the 15 countries which are at present members of the European Union, which is the present collective title of the member states.

Since the signing of the Treaty of Rome in 1957, the European Union has grown from being known as the EEC (European Economic Community), to the EC (European Community), and to the present title of EU (European Union). The EU has moved spasmodically in a social context with its own recognisable values of social solidarity, equality and the active participation in a new social-democratic or social-capitalist society (Wallace 1990). It is a society where people learn from each other. The economic integration of Europe has created a mixture of cultures, attitudes and expectations. European values and attitudes are in a state of constant flux. They are moulded by experience and social learning, by shared interactions over time, by the representation and influence of intellectual and political leaders, and by changes in the social environment.

The social integration of Western Europe has altered customary and popular assumptions about national identities and about the space and the culture which they share. It could be claimed that the notion of a distinctive European culture, in the context of the education of pupils with SEN, is promoted through the explication and sharing of education policy, tradition and practice, with their accompanying set of implicit values, which have political significance. Any promotion of ideas in a bounded area defines and draws the participants closer through their identification with shared experiences and traditions.

Since the inception of the EU, many working networks have been established, and much has been achieved through political bargaining over rules and conflicting interests, during multilateral and intergovernmental co-operation.

Europe is also a multicultural society with a myriad of languages set to defy even the best organised system towards integration. However, participation in the development of economic, social and cultural affairs has been experienced by EU citizens since its inception. Education and schooling are included in the overall aim for a European society which pertains to break down the barriers presently blocking any form of social inclusion. Inclusive education is integral to a democratic society. The study of inclusive practices in Europe has been slowly gaining pace as part of the democratisation of its society. Its roots go back to the response to fascism before and during the Second World War, in human rights movements, and in the drive towards 'normalisation', in which disabled people have rights to the same treatment as non-disabled people (Evans 1999).

Inclusive practice is the active process of progressing towards 'full participation' in society. The notion of full participation came about through the *UN Standard Rules*, which are based on a human rights perspective. The rules wished to remove obstacles from people with disabilities which prevented them from exercising their rights and freedoms to participate fully in the activities of their societies. The *UN Standard Rules* clearly state that it is 'the responsibility of States to take appropriate action to remove such obstacles' (para 15, introduction).

Full participation is the major aim for EU society which circumscribes its Laws and policies to support it, particularly in employment, training and education.

However, trying to make transparent the practice of other countries through written accounts requires a critical stance and an overview of the whole. Whether such a view is possible in Europe is debatable. However, the understanding of different educational, political and cultural systems allows its citizens to appreciate diversity in what is increasingly regarded as a cultural entity.

Movement of ideas and practices between countries throughout the world and in Europe has created multicultural societies (Bray *et al*, 1986), or it has been claimed the hybridisation of culture (McCarthy *et al*, 1997). World-wide, the integration of pupils with disabilities and special needs is gaining credibility and acceptance in mainstream society.

The European system

In order to fully understand the operation and funding of systems of education for pupils with SEN, it is important to realise how initiatives get funded and how the general mechanism of disseminating responsibility beyond Brussels operates in Europe. The principal institutions of the EU include the European Parliament, Council of Ministers, European Commission, and the Economic and Social Committee.

The Council of Ministers legislates for the Union, sets its political objectives, co-ordinates national policies and resolves differences between itself and other institutions. The Council of Ministers is the most powerful decision making body in the EU and it uses the Commission to carry out and take the lead in proposing legislation, action plans, policies and programmes. The Commission has 23 Directorates-General (DGs). The DGs carry out the decisions of the Commission. The DG of Social Affairs is DG V, which has two units, one of which is responsible for people with learning difficulties *ie* HELIOS. The Economic and Social Committee, on the other hand, gives 'opinions' on EC measures, policies and proposals. The Committee comprises nine sections, one of which is 'social, family, educational and cultural affairs'.

The EU sponsors the programmes run by the DGs, which are subcontracted to management groups, consultancies, networks and institutions, such as universities and schools. These are given programme titles and acronyms. Some are funding programmes, others are information networks, some have a policy and advisory role, many are a combination of all three. They provide opportunities for contact and influence for many organisations, especially in the voluntary sector and for educational professionals.

Involvement in the programmes provides a strong liaison among educational institutions and other groups, through which they can influence the institutions of the Communities and the Commission by making recommendations from the specialised programmes. Although some of the specialised programmes are termed networks, they should not be confused with the networks of non-governmental voluntary organisations (NGOs) in the EU like 'Handicap International'.

The European Regional Fund began in 1991 by funding up to 60 networks involving voluntary organisations, businesses, universities, schools and local authorities. There have been a number of specialised programmes which have been designed to promote cross-European training and educational experiences. They vary in scale. Some programmes are based on individual applications while others depend upon NGOs, schools, universities and other organisations, for example: ERASMUS, COMETT, TEMPUS, PETRA, ARION, LINGUA and SOCRATES. HELIOS was the first action programme in favour of people with disabilities and was launched in 1983.

However, in the field of policy making and programme funding in the EU, individual countries prefer to decide for themselves how the funds are to be spent. It is the principle of *subsidiarity* which allows different countries to keep Brussels at a distance when dealing with social and educational issues, believing that they should be left to themselves to organise their own priorities. Local governments apply to Brussels, receive the funds and then manage the programmes locally. This principle means that the EU is entitled to lay down minimum social standards – but leaves it to the member states to work out how they should be reached. The concept of subsidiarity is both a legal and a political principle. The principle was envisaged to respond to the discrepancy between 'political' and 'economic', by trying to define the political content of European integration, which includes social and education policies. Subsidiarity is capable of either supporting or undermining the legitimacy of EU policy. In practice it means a division of policy making responsibilities to achieve efficiency. It is used as a guiding principle in education to ensure that the exercise of power does not become an abuse of power. In keeping with the principle, the EU Treaty stipulates that it

'encourages co-operation between member states and supports and supplements their action, while fully respecting the responsibility of the member states for the content of teaching and the organisation of education systems and their cultural and linguistic diversity'.

(Maastricht Treaty 1992)

However, the concept itself is seen to be in need of some development to meet the needs of potentially disadvantaged groups and to prevent their further marginalisation. Daniels (1995) states that it is doubtful whether some students categorised as having SEN ever achieve formal representation in negotiations about educational support and placement. In the process of devolved decision making, only the most powerful local voices appear to be heard in local community decision-making processes (*ibid.*). Perhaps the devolution of policies and power from Brussels needs to be more specifically focused on mainstream educational support in schools in order that pupils with SEN can fully realise their rightful claim to mainstream education in all EU countries.

The development towards integration in Europe

The integration of Europe as a political system has been characterised by intense patterns of social interaction, following the dynamics of markets, technology, communication networks and social exchange, and the gradual growth of systems of interaction. Although the original Treaty of Rome did not mention education, collaboration between countries led to a first European Community conference organised by the Commission in Rome in 1978.

Queries about the benefits of special education began in the 1970s when the EC made its first moves to improve the services and opportunities for people with disabilities (Daunt 1991). It was not until the 1980s, after the UN declared 1981 to be the International Year of Disabled People, that the EC used the year as a springboard for a new level of Community action.

The first action was planned to last for four years, but went well beyond that time. This led directly to the first Community Action Programme (1983-87), which was concerned with the social and economic integration of adults with disabilities, but not yet directly concerned with the educational integration of children and young people with disabilities. After this, a Working Group on Educational Integration was set up by the Commission, and its first report entitled *Progress with Regard to the Implementation of the Policy of Integrating Handicapped Children into Ordinary Schools* was published in 1986.

The second action programme was entitled HELIOS and began in 1988. It was mainly concentrated on employment opportunities for people with disabilities and on mobility and transport issues. It was the networks of local model activities (LMAs) which focused directly on education. There were 80 LMAs, of which 21 were devoted to the educational integration of pupils with SEN (for examples see O'Hanlon 1995). The 'education network' had the organisational advantage of a relatively small membership and the asset of concentrating their exchanges on issues known to be prominent for practitioners and policy makers.

The third action programme, HELIOS ll, was designed to carry on the work of HELIOS 1 and was established in 1992. Two more social action programmes designed to 'mainstream' people with disabilities were HORIZON 1992, (a programme to reduce unemployment of people with disabilities through training and job creation initiatives) and TIDE 1991, (an action on 'technology for the socio-economic integration of disabled people and the elderly').

Central and Eastern European countries (CEECs) are also presently co-operating in EU programmes for disability and special needs. In 1993 the European Council agreed that those CEECs which had concluded an association agreement with the EU (the associated country) could join the Union, as soon as they were in a position to meet the political and economic obligations that membership implied. The associated countries at present are: Poland, Hungary, the Czech Republic, Slovakia, Romania, Bulgaria, Estonia, Lithuania and Latvia. The European Council has opened up a number of community programmes to the associated countries, along the lines of the measures already implemented for the EFTA states. Therefore, in addition to the community programmes already established for central and eastern Europe, such as PHARE, TEMPUS, COPERNICUS, participation in programmes has also begun in other initiatives, for example LEONARDO and SOCRATES.

The HELIOS 11 programmes ended in 1996. In the meantime, the HES-TIA study has prepared the way for greater understanding of initiatives for integration of disabled people in the Czech Republic, Hungary, Poland and Slovakia in the field of vocational training and employment.

The EU, through its HELIOS programme, has stressed the importance of professionals in the development of inclusive practices by providing opportunities for them to meet, to share experiences and to carry out research. Other government agencies, such as the Swedish SIDA and the Danish DANIDA, support inclusive practices in Europe. Beyond Europe the international dimension includes the US Department of Education, the US Department of Health and Human Services, the UK Commonwealth Secretariat, USAID, the World Bank and the Inter-American Development Bank (Evans 1999). The international community of people working for an inclusive society also embraces non-governmental organisations which play an active role in promoting 'inclusive' education.

The language of inclusion

The shared European language used for the planning and development of mainstream education is important. The use of the word inclusion implies the full participation of pupils in all school activities, and thus the concept of participation is increased with its usage. Although the term 'integration' was common in the UK until the 90s, now the term 'inclusion' is predominantly used in everyday discourse to replace it. This is because often it is seen to be more politically correct in spite of the fact that it refers more often, in practice, to 'integration'. The New Labour government in the UK has used the rhetoric of social inclusion as a main focus of its political policies since the election in 1997. In Europe, the Amsterdam Treaty (1999) continues to seek measures to combat social exclusion throughout the Community.

Inclusion is seen to be more closely linked to assimilation than to membership of a particular group in society and assimilation is a major aim for European countries. The term 'integration' could be seen to be the antithesis of 'segregation', in the same way that 'exclusion' is the antithesis of 'inclusion'. Segregated schooling is separate schooling which pupils experience as 'special education' throughout Europe. It is education in a special school or unit, which is separately funded with few or no links to mainstream schooling. Alternatively, 'exclusion' from education means no attendance at any school within the mainstream system. Alternative educational support may be found if country legislation decrees it.

The imperative towards inclusive (rather than integrated) education was given a boost in 1994 by a UNESCO Conference in Salamanca, Spain, which led to the 'Salamanca Statement on Principles, Policy and Practice in Special Needs Education' with its additional Draft Framework for Action (UNESCO 1994). The Statement reiterates much of the content of the 'Universal Declaration of Human Rights' (UN 1948) and the 'United Nations Standard Rules on the Equalisation of Opportunities for Persons with Disabilities' (UN 1993). The Statement begins with a commitment to 'Education for All', urging that children with special educational needs 'must have access to regular (ordinary) schools'. It continues:

> 'Regular (ordinary) schools with this inclusive orientation are the most effective means of combating discriminatory attitudes, creating welcoming communities, building an inclusive society and achieving education for all: Moreover, they provide an effective education for the majority of children and improve the efficiency and ultimately the cost-effectiveness of the entire education system'.

The 'Framework for Action' develops the basic principles specifically through the establishment of 'inclusive schools'.

> 'Inclusion and participation are essential to human dignity and to the enjoyment and exercise of human rights, through education for a genuine equalisation of opportunity'.

The document argues that special needs education incorporates proven methods of teaching from which all children can benefit. It accepts that human differences are normal and that teaching and learning must be adapted to the needs of the child, rather than have the child fitted to the educational process. The fundamental principle of the 'inclusive school', it adds, is that all children should learn together where possible, and that ordinary schools must recognise and respond to the diverse needs of their students, while also having a continuum of support and services to match these needs. Inclusive schools are the 'most effective' at building solidarity between children with special needs and their peers. It goes on to recommend that countries with few or no special schools should establish inclusive, not special, schools (UNESCO 1994).

However, in spite of the UK's declared support of the Salamanca Statement (DfEE 1997), through its inclusion policy it has been seen to be a deeply ambiguous document, constituting a somewhat shaky platform on which to base policy (Dyson 1999).

The debate about terminology

Concepts such as 'disability', 'handicap', 'special needs' and 'education' are culturally and contextually bound. The term SEN was introduced in the UK through the Warnock Report (DES 1978), which argued for the eradication of the traditional categorisation of pupils by disability. Most European countries still use the term 'disability' and 'handicap' to categorise their children according to psycho-medical labels.

The World Health Organisation (1980) positions 'impairment', 'disability' and 'handicap' along a continuum and defines the terms as follows:

Impairment is the loss or abnormality of psychological, physiological or anatomical structure or functions;

Disability is any restriction or lack of ability (resulting from impairment) to perform an activity in the manner or within the range considered;

Handicap is the disadvantage which results from the difference between what society expects of the person and he or she is capable of doing considering his or her respective disability.

Although recognised and used throughout the world, it can be asserted that these definitions have not received universal acceptance, particularly among disabled people and their organisations, because they have been based on able-bodied assumptions of disability, and consequently they do not accord with the personal realities of disabled people (Oliver 1993, p 61).

SEN is a term which originated in the UK in the 1970s to avoid the use of categorisation and its consequences, particularly for the largest group of children categorised in this way, who were children with 'mild mental handicap', which later in the UK was translated into 'moderate learning difficulties'. Before this, children who were categorised were subjected to a life in special school with limited curriculum opportunities and the stigma of association with other pupils who were similarly categorised. SEN moved away from the notion of providing for placement and services for 'categories' of children to emphasise instead the need for individualised decisions and instructions for specific services to meet individual educational needs. As a result, the focus in the UK moved to provision in the ordinary school to meet individual needs, rather than having whole schools resourced because they were 'special', to educate children with a specific category of disability for example sensory or physical.

In a sense, much of the debate in the UK and in Europe arises because of difficult decisions to be made about children with 'learning and behavioural difficulties'. It was, and still is, easier to classify and assess children with motor and sensory disabilities, but less clear how to categorise and plan the education of children who are less academic and amenable to the traditional aims and methods of mainstream schools. This is a common tension in the practical assessment and placement of pupils throughout Europe.

However, more often than not, the terms 'inclusion' and 'integration' are used as synonyms (Meijer *et al,* 1994) and are commonly interchanged in conversations and debate about school placements of children with special educational needs. In the UK, the use of 'integration' was used to describe the process of assimilating children with special educational needs into mainstream schools. Now 'inclusive' discourse refers to all children who may be disadvantaged within educational organisations, to raise awareness about them and to avoid any deliberate or unintended exclusion of them from mainstream education. 'Inclusion' emphasises the rights of minority groups to be offered equal opportunities in schooling and to be given whatever resources and help may be necessary for them to realise their full educational potential. Therefore inclusion refers to a wider group of children, in fact all children including, for example, second language pupils and children of travellers.

In the USA, 'mainstreaming' is the predominant term used for the same process of increasing the inclusion of pupils with special educational needs into ordinary schools or regular schools.

However, there is a danger in this kind of debate which assumes that, while the language of educational policies on disability may appear positive for inclusion in European countries, it may only be an up-to-date renaming of the traditional and familiar deficit-disabling discourse of special education. Much is hidden in the rhetoric supporting political correctness. Special educational research has been dominated by the psychological deficit medical model of disability, which masks as much as it discloses about the inclusion debate (Slee 1995).

Moreover, in spite of the economic advancement of countries in the EU there are still children and young people with special educational needs who are yet excluded (Hegarty 1993, Nesbit 1985, O'Hanlon 1995, Pijl and Meijer 1991).

Children and young people with special needs are increasingly being accepted and educated in mainstream settings in each EU country, with varying degrees of commitment and educational success. Traditions and values in education vary from country to country, and established views and attitudes are slow to transform the practical experiences of the children concerned in the decisions about 'where', 'when' and 'how' they are to be educated.

Booth warns that:

> 'The view that a concern with inclusion is primarily about the location of students assigned to a special education category can lead to the presentation of misleading statistics that imply that educational difficulties are to do with the numbers and placement of disabled students or others seen to have difficulties in learning ... such statistics distract our attention from the ways in which attitudes, policies and institutions exclude or marginalise groups of children and young people'. (Booth & Ainscow 1998)

It is in this spirit that we move to a country-by-country perspective of the education of pupils with special educational needs. A summary of the official position taken by governments in the EU (adapted from EADSEN 99), is expressed in the following separate country reports:

Country by country

Austria

In 1993 integration into primary schools was established by law. The inclusion of pupils with special educational needs is possible under certain conditions and through the use of specific methods and forms of provision. Before 1993 special schools were obligatory for children with certified special needs, except for a small number who were involved in pilot integration schemes. Parents are given the choice of integrated or special education and this is defined by availability of places and where they live.

Special schools since 1993 have faced the challenge of integration, which has led them to enter a competitive market where once they had the monopoly. They now offer 'attractive alternatives' to encourage parents to place their children with them. Special schools also offer support and expertise to mainstream schools.

Belgium

All children in Belgium have the right to special education after an extensive examination of their educational needs, in line with the 1970 Act.

Special education is perceived as offering pupils the opportunity to integrate where possible into 'normal' life.

In practice the mainstream schools in Belgium are not seen to have the resources to cope with pupils with learning difficulties. Integration is considered on an individual basis because the special education system is well resourced, so there is a reluctance to consider alternatives to it. Pilot projects encouraging co-operation between mainstream and special schools have demonstrated that there are inherent attitudes, barriers and practices in mainstream that remain to be addressed, although at present some integrational projects are in operation, funded privately by parents.

Denmark

A fundamental principle of Danish education is that every child should have the same access to education and training, basically free of charge, from five years of age. All pupils are entitled to instruction appropriate to their situation, the possibilities and their individual needs. The 1994 'Folkeskole' Act is the third and final stage in an extensive reform of both the management and curriculum of the 'Folkeskole'. The new legislation supports a comprehensive policy where pupils remain in the same class group from the first to the ninth form, sharing the same experiences with peers and covering a wide range of abilities.

Finland

The first preference for educational provision is to integrate pupils in need of specialist support into mainstream school, usually into a small teaching group. Failing this, education is provided in a special group, class or school. Children with severe and multiple disabilities are educated in a special school. There is the opportunity for part of the child's education to take place in both a special and a mainstream school. Children receive a modified curriculum in special school, where the general educational objectives and essential content are the same as the mainstream school. Integration is recognised as the right for pupils with special needs to have the same educational opportunities as other pupils. However, pupils still have limited access to the mainstream education system.

France

The Guideline law no75-534 (1975) defines the right of 'social integration' for people with disabilities, whether minors or adults. The Memorandums of January 28, 1982 and January 29, 1983 defined the strategies for implementing this policy. The Law has been seen to open the way to a policy of educational integration for children and young people with disabilities. Subsequently, in the Guideline Law on Education in 1989, the principle of educational integration has been reasserted. The legal framework has made it possible to set up a coherent system favouring integration initiatives, but it is seen as a major social challenge in France, because it means rethinking the acceptance and education of all pupils, especially those with educational difficulties.

Germany

The special education system for pupils with SEN is extensive and well-supported in Germany. In 1988 terminology changed from 'the need for special education' to the 'child with special educational needs', which put the focus on the child's needs, rather than on the location. From 1980, there has been a steady decline in the number of pupils in special schools. In 1994 the German government recommended that the education of children with SEN be the co-operative task of all schools, and that special education be seen as a necessary resource for mainstream education. Almost all Länder have adapted their educational Laws towards more integrational practices.

Greece

Officially the Ministry of Education in Greece aims to integrate all children with special educational needs into mainstream schools and is developing this aim through a number of programmes. The first step has been the establishment of 700 special classes throughout Greece since 1984. In addition, there have been a small number of projects developed in liaison with Higher Education institutions to integrate pupils with visual or hearing impairments, and 'mentally disabled' pupils into mainstream schools in remote areas. The official aims of special education are to ensure pupils' all-round and effective development and utilisation of a child's ability and potential; integration into productive life and society; and acceptance of and by society.

Ireland

It is current government policy to encourage the maximum possible level of integration for pupils with special needs into mainstream schools by providing the necessary support to facilitate it. The support offered takes the form of remedial, resource and visiting teachers. The pace of the integration process is seen to be partly determined by the capacities of individual children and the availability of resources. The Report of the Special Education Review Committee (1993) confirmed its support for integration by declaring that it favoured as much integration as was appropriate, with as little segregation as was necessary, and proposed a system in which there would be a place for both mainstream and special schools. It was proposed to establish links between the mainstream and special schools, which would involve the sharing of teachers and facilities, the interchange of pupils and their involvement in shared projects.

Italy

Legislation in Italy in 1976 and 1977 has led to the common practice of educating pupils with special needs in mainstream schools. As a result society, parents, teachers and other professionals have accepted the policy and given it full support. A child is recognised as having a 'handicap' when his/her physical, psychological or sensory disability is steady or progressive: it causes difficulties in learning, relationships or integration into working life, and is serious enough to lead to social disadvantage or exclusion. Serious conditions have priority in public service provision. Children with special educational needs are guaranteed a place in mainstream schooling from three years to university entrance.

Luxembourg

In Luxembourg the first special schools were opened in the mid-60s, catering for children with disabilities of various types. In 1973 legislation organised the various specialist centres and institutions into a coherent system under the Ministry of Education. In 1989 the regional special needs centres were then transferred from local authority financing into the state budget. There has been some movement in recent years towards integrating children with disabilities into the mainstream system. The special educational sector which was, up till now, seen as a parallel system since 1991, has been encouraged to act as a special support for pupils in preparation for mainstream schooling, at least for those children who are seen to benefit from it. When integration is not possible, a system of 'cohabitation', where schools provide special education classes, has recently begun with a view to systematic mixed provision in the future.

Netherlands

In 1985, the Primary Education Act set out its main aim to offer all children appropriate instruction and to guarantee them an uninterrupted school career. In recent years several policy papers have focused on reducing the segregation of pupils with special needs. More specifically, in 1990 a government policy document *Together to School Again*, aimed at the integration of pupils with special needs. Until recent years there had been a steady rise in the numbers of such children entering special education. More recently however, the numbers in special schools have been falling. For children for whom the special needs provision available under **Going to School Together** is not sufficient, personal budgets are to be introduced. The intention is that parents will in future be able to choose between an ordinary or a special school for their child. The entitlement to special provision will travel with the child.

Portugal

The Laws of 1986, 1991 and recent legislation in 1997 recognise the right to equal opportunities for pupils with special educational needs, to education in a local mainstream school as well as integration into the wider society. The new legislation of 1997 reinforces the movement towards integration that was established in 1986. The education system is focused upon adequate provision for pupils with special needs in mainstream schools.

Pupils with special needs have the right to the adaptation of the educational environment, as well as to the educational process itself, in order to remove barriers to their learning.

The number of pupils attending special schools is decreasing and several integration projects are under way. This trend is happening throughout all regions in Portugal.

Spain

The principles of mainstreaming and educational integration were established in the General Arrangement of the Education System (organic) Act 1/1990. Pupils with special educational needs are provided for within the mainstream system, which is allocated the resources required for these pupils to attain the general curriculum aims for all learners.

This principle stresses that children with special educational needs should neither use, nor receive, exceptional services, except when they are strictly essential, and therefore they should as far as possible make use of the system of general community services. The law encourages the main-streaming of children, to allow them to lead a normal life, and to be entitled to rights and duties in the same way as other members of society. In Spain the 'integration' principle is more akin to 'inclusion' because it is seen as active participation in all areas of life: in the school, the family the community and the labour market *etc*. It is not considered simply as 'putting together, or being together'. It is a functional concept which has an impact on all areas of a pupil's experience, in or out of school.

Sweden

In Sweden the education system is based on the philosophy that all children with special needs have the right to the same personal development and educational experiences as their non-handicapped peers. There are, however, special schools for children with severe language disorders and hearing impairments. Since 1996 children with severe learning difficulties are educated in special classes run by the municipalities.

Since the 1950s increasing numbers of pupils have been integrated into mainstream education and, at present, most pupils in need of special support are taught in mainstream.

United Kingdom

Under the terms of the Education Act 1996, local education authorities (LEAs) have the duty to place children with special educational needs in mainstream schools with their peers whenever possible. Placements are dependent upon the LEA ensuring that the child receives the full special provision required to meet their special educational needs. Only 1% of the school age population is educated in special schools. All children are entitled to receive the National Curriculum (Education Reform Act 1988), and to have their special educational needs identified, assessed and provided for. The Code of Practice (DfEE 1994) states that pupils should be involved in decision making about their learning as much as possible, including target setting, monitoring of progress and review. However, there are large regional differences in the degree of integration within LEAs in the UK. Tensions surround issues related to location and to forms of 'integration' in the UK.

Conclusion

In the preceding general outlining of policy in the 15 EU countries we must ask ourselves what the official policy documents and trends can tell us. Is there, in every country, a genuine policy statement to effect fuller inclusion in mainstream schools? Is there a support mechanism in place with judicial strength to ensure its recognition; and following that, are there many different ways of ensuring increased inclusion, depending on the situational context, in which the policies are implemented? What can we learn from the different practices for inclusion throughout the EU?

The general aims for special education are more similar than dissimilar in EU countries. All affirm the right of all children to equal opportunities, and support inclusive education as an egalitarian ideology. In practice, the aims of education in each of the countries vary considerably in relation to their traditional policies and forms of economic support. A common concern in all countries is for the equal opportunities of all its children to be partly resolved through the increased development of inclusive educational practice.

Countries with a relatively advanced special school system find it most difficult to move away from it and to educate all pupils in the mainstream system. Implicit in each country report is the premise that the focus for the development of inclusive practice should lie in the mainstream schooling system. Yet special schools cannot be considered as an alternative or parallel system. It is the main national systems of education in each country that must be re-evaluated. Everywhere in Europe there is 'special education', yet there are still a number of children who do not attend any kind of school. Identifying the countries concerned points to the need for resources and trained personnel. These are undoubtedly important, as too is the fact that rich countries find it easier to build the physical infrastructure required and secure the training and employment of expert staff, which gives them a signal advantage (Hegarty 1998).

I have written previously of the difficulties in making sense of data about 'handicapping' conditions across Europe and about the impossibility of trying to compare statistics that are based on divergent categories and values, and the changing emphasis in terminology (O'Hanlon 1993). The view from Europe is multifaceted and national perspectives give only a flavour of the tensions and problems experienced in the practical process.

The percentage of pupils in special schools in the EU varies from 1-4%, although the percentage of pupils recognised with special educational needs ranges from 1-10%, (Meijer 1998). Yet, as stated previously, these figures need to be viewed with some caution, because the study attempts to unify the statistical data by dividing the number of pupils with SEN by the total number of pupils in the same age group, in spite of the fact that there are different compulsory school age ranges across Europe. The authors themselves point out that it is often an arbitrary distinction deciding whether education is 'segregated' or 'integrated', in spite of their efforts to obtain data by age, SEN category and type of provision.

Pupils are assessed differently in each country, and provided for according to the prevailing traditions and norms of the 'main' education system. Many systems are heavily reliant on academic outcomes (France, Belgium), so integration is difficult and slow in such countries. Other countries put more emphasis on the 'social' rights of the child, and their need for full participation in the educational, social and cultural life of the community, (Spain, Sweden, UK, Denmark).

Some of the 'newer' countries to join the EU are using the 'politically correct' commitment to the education of pupils with special needs through 'integration' procedures, but are still in the process of changing attitudes and beliefs through conservative educational policies and practices (*eg* Austria and Finland). Some are experimenting about the possibilities of fuller 'inclusion' through 'integration' projects (Ireland, Belgium, France, Greece, Portugal and the Netherlands). Whatever the perspective, Europe is seen from the South as a group of countries in the Northern hemisphere, which, because of the long history of institutionalisation and special schooling, finds inclusive education a difficult and strong challenge (Kisanji 1998).

But what the success of 'integration' throughout Europe hinges upon is the quality of the provision, and the organisation and management of the teaching to support pupils' special educational needs in mainstream schools. Issues arise about the reality of the practices throughout the EU. In spite of the rhetoric about the all-encompassing 'inclusion' policies, there are issues related to the quality of participation and educational support offered to pupils with SEN. Now would be an appropriate time to create a large scale European research project focused upon the educational quality of mainstream practice for all pupils with SEN. It is time to evaluate the practices and claims made in the rhetorical gestures of government policies. What is the reality of the experience of mainstream education for pupils with SEN throughout Europe?

Nevertheless a recent report, supported by the European Commission, to reassess the current situation in relation to integration, and to describe developments since an earlier report in 1992, enlightens the situation further (Meijer 1998). A thematic overview of the issues dealt with shows that :

• some countries clearly define their special education system as a resource for mainstream schools, and others are now following this approach;

• parental choice in education has been included in legislation in some countries; and

• countries with separate laws for special and mainstream education are now developing one legal framework for both systems.

A number of discernible trends in special education are noted which are identical to those implicit in the foregoing country reports:

• that special schools are being used increasingly as resource centres;

• a wide range of facilities is available in most countries and is being used to improve integration conditions in the mainstream;

• most countries use individual education programmes (IEPs) for pupils with SEN, in which recommendations for the curriculum, resources, the aim and the evaluation of the approach are included; and

• parents are developing positive attitudes towards integration.

In relation to obstacles to integration, the appropriate funding system is important. Separate funding systems for special and mainstream education cause problems for flexible resourcing, as too do locational, rather than pupil-based, funding.

Four challenges for the future are identified as:

1. Tension between the pressure of academic output and its effect on vulnerable pupils.

2. Monitoring and evaluation procedures to measure the quality of services for SEN, and the role of IEPs in this.

3. The development of integration in secondary schools through improved teacher training.

4. Reducing numbers of pupils in segregated provision because it is increasing in countries that use it most (*ibid*).

The national commitments to inclusive policies are not enough on their own. In each country there are endemic constraints which make progress difficult or impossible. In the spirit of subsidiarity, it is up to the people concerned within each country to define, analyse and remove these constraints, because they are specific to national contexts. Much can be learned within the EU by sharing these stories about the practice of inclusion in the kind of depth that exposes the problematic nature of the exercise. Yet, in a positive mode, the Europe-wide egalitarian ideology witnessed in the country reports can only lead, in time, to the creation of more favourable conditions for the growth of the fully 'inclusive' society.

References

Booth, T (1987), 'Introduction to the Series in Including Pupils with Disabilities' edited by Booth T & Swann W, Open University Press

Booth, T and Ainscow, M (Eds) (1998), *From Them To Us: an international study of inclusion in education,* Routledge

Bray, M, Clarke, P and Stephens, D (1986), *Education and Society in Africa,* Edward Arnold

Daniels, H (1995), 'A Case Study from Denmark and Germany', in *Equality and Diversity in education: National and international Contexts,* edited by P Potts, F Armstrong and M Masterton, Routledge

Daunt, P (1991), *Meeting Disability: a European Response,* Cassell

DES (1978), *Special Educational Needs,* (The Warnock Report), HMSO

Department of Health (1989), *The Children Act; guidance and regulations,* HMSO

DfEE (1988), *The Education Reform Act,* HMSO

DfEE (1997), *Excellence for All Children,* Department for Education and Employment

DfEE (1994), *Code of Practice on the Identification and Assessment of Children with Special Educational Needs,* HMSO

Dyson A (1999), Inclusion and inclusions: theories and discourses in inclusive education, in *Inclusive education: World Yearbook of Education,* edited by D Daniels and P Garner, Kogan Page

EADSEN (1999), 'National Overview of Countries', European Agency for Development in Special Needs Education

Evans, P (1999), 'Globalisation and Cultural Transmission: the role of International agencies in developing inclusive practice', in *Inclusive education: World Yearbook of Education,* edited by H Daniels and P Garner, Kogan Page

Hegarty, S (1993), 'Review of Literature on Integration', *European Journal of Special Needs Education,* 8, 3, (pp 194-200)

Hegarty, S (1998), 'International Perspectives on Education Reform', in *European Journal of Special Needs Education,* vol. 13 no 1 (p 112 -133)

Ireland (1993), *Report of the Special Education Review Committee,* Stationery Office

Kisanji, J (1998), The March Towards Inclusive Education in Non-western Countries: retracing the steps, *International Journal of Inclusive Education,* Vol. 2 no 1

Maastricht Treaty (1992), EU, Brussels

McCarthy, C, Dolby, N and Valdivia, A (1997), The Uses of Culture: canon formation, postcolonial literature and the multicultural project, in *International Journal of Inclusive Education,* 1, 1, (pp 89-100)

Meijer, C (Ed), (1998), *Integration in Europe. Provision for Pupils with Special Educational Needs: Trends in 14 European Countries,* the European Agency for Development in Special Needs Education

Meijer, C, Pijl, S and Hegarty, S, (Eds), (1994), *New Perspectives in Special Education,* Routledge

Nesbit, W (1985), 'Integration In Britain: impact of the Education Act of 1981', in *Canadian Journal of Special Education,* 1, 2, (pp 147-156)

Nirje, B (1985), 'The Basis and Logic of the Normalisation Principle', *Australia and New Zealand Journal of Developmental Disabilities,* 11 (pp 65-68)

O'Hanlon, C (Ed), (1995), *Inclusive Education In Europe,* David Fulton

O'Hanlon, C (1993), *Special Education: Integration in Europe,* David Fulton

Oliver, M (1993), 'Re-defining Disability: a challenge to research', in *Disabling Barriers – Enabling Environments,* edited by J Swain, V Finkelstein, S French, M Oliver, London, Sage Publications and the Open University

Pijl, S and Meijer, C (1991), 'Does Integration Count for Much? An analysis of the practices in eight countries', *European Journal of Special Needs Education,* 6, 2 (pp 100-111)

Slee, R (1995), 'Inclusive Education: from policy to school implementation', in C Clark, A Dyson and A Millard (Eds) *Towards Inclusive Schools?* David Fulton

Thomas, G, Walker, D, Webb, J (1998), *The Making of the Inclusive School,* Routledge

UN (1948), *The Universal Declaration of Human Rights,* UN

UN (1993), *United Nation Standard Rules on Equalisation of Opportunities for Persons with Disabilities,* UN

UNESCO (1994), *The Salamanca Statement and Framework on Special Needs Education,* UNESCO

Wallace, W (1990), *The Transformation of Western Europe,* The Royal Institute of International Affairs London

Wolfensberger, W (1972), *The Principle of Normalisation in Human Services,* Toronto National Institute for Mental Retardation

Chapter 5

The integration into mainstream schools of pupils with Special Educational Needs in Southern Europe

Pilar Arnaiz

Introduction

With the exception of Italy, which started in the 1970s, the rest of the European countries implemented programmes of school-integration in the 1980s. The political, social and economic situation in each country undoubtedly contributed to this uneven emergence of integration programmes in Southern European countries.

The objective of this chapter, then, is to analyse the integration into mainstream schools in Southern Europe of pupils with special educational needs, with reference to Spain, Italy and Portugal. It places in context and suggests an interpretation of the legal framework which supports integration into mainstream schools and subsequent educational reforms which have facilitated processes of integration in each one of these countries. It will be noted in this respect that the Spanish case will be more widely examined, and those of Italy and Portugal by way of reference.

The case of Spain

Before going further into the current educational provision for diversity in Spain on the threshold of the year 2000, it would be appropriate to comment briefly on the background; that is, what occurred in the field of special needs education during the 1970s and 1980s. This will give us the key towards understanding the present situation.

The delay in planning a modern special education provision in Spain in comparison with other European countries can be seen as one of the most striking features of the Spanish educational system in the 1960s and 1970s. Thus we see that, whilst in Spain in the 1970s segregation of pupils with mental disabilities in special schools was just under way, in some other European countries (*eg* Denmark, Norway and Italy) the movement towards school integration was already well-established.

Effectively, given the legacy of the Spanish Civil War and the political circumstances created by dictatorship, up to the 1970s Special Needs Education was not seen as being within the remit of the Spanish educational system. The Education Law of 1970 prompted some decisions with regard to provision for pupils with mental disabilities in special schools and units. Until then only a few initiatives in the education of pupils with sensory impairments had been undertaken, along with some others – above all in the private sector – regarding the mentally-handicapped.

The Spanish transition to democracy produced the long overdue acknowledgment of human rights and concomitant respect for human differences, which provided fertile ground for the emergence of organisations which transformed these moral advances into reality, so that Spain was more in line with the rest of Europe. Among the committees created to implement specific actions were Royal Patronage of Provision, a Royal Decree for the provision of individuals with disabilities (Royal Decree 1023/1976 of 9th April 1976), and the drawing-up of the Magna Carta for Special Education in 1978, which was formulated in connection with the above-mentioned Patronage. This document acknowledged the rights of individuals with disabilities, and established the duty and responsibility of public bodies towards the fulfillment of these individuals' rights.

The arrival of democracy and the implementation of the Spanish Constitution (1978) established the need for a new legal framework in which the rights of individuals with disabilities were acknowledged. Subsequently, the Law of Social Integration for Disabled Persons was passed in 1982 in accordance with Article 49 of the Spanish Constitution. This stated the provision of various principles as enunciated in the National Plan for Special Education.

By bringing in this law, the Spanish government also adhered to the Declaration of Rights of the Mentally Handicapped (Art.2, United Nations, 1971) and to the Rights of the Physically Handicapped (United Nations, 1975). Although this was defined as a 'Social Integration Law', its scope for action was quite wide, tackling through its articles key issues relating to personal, health, educational and labour issues. It can be said that with this law the legal basis for school integration in Spain was established.

The Ministerial Order of 20th March 1985 on the Planning of Special Education and laying down of guidelines for school integration (BOE of March, 1985) initiated actions for school integration in Spain. This was set up as a pilot-experiment over three years (1985-1987). The order established the criteria to be followed by schools that wished to take part in this pilot-scheme on a voluntary basis.

Those schools taking part saw the reduction of the number of pupils to 25 per class, to include two pupils with special educational needs. This process of integration was to start from the nursery, from four-years' old and upwards, throughout the different levels of the education system. In order to support integration, support teacher teams were set up in schools, including teachers specialising in special educational methods applied to learning difficulties and sensory, speech and language impairments, as well as external support (a 'psycho-pedagogical team', comprising educators, psychologists and social workers).

The tenure and status of teachers were guaranteed in those schools taking part in the integration experiment, and participation in the project was rewarded with a 'system of teaching-merit points'. The scope and implications of these working conditions and the 'merit-system' do not come under discussion here, as these may not be directly related to the process of implementing integration.

With the start of school integration, numerous children had the chance to enter the mainstream school system instead of going to special educational schools. In this way, the pupil participated in school activities as far as possible as a member of a mainstream classroom, with any necessary extra assistance being lent him or her within that context. On those occasions when the integrated pupils required special support – difficult to provide in the mainstream classroom – they were given individualised support in carrying out an alternative didactic activity.

After the implementation and assessment of the Experimental Plan of Integration in the 1990s (MEC 1990; Garcia Pastor, 1991; Parrilla, 1992), we can affirm that, although the integration into mainstream classrooms has yielded positive results, it has also given rise to serious defects. These have come about on account of the difficulty of co-ordinating the Individual Development Programmes with the delivery of the mainstream curriculum.

It is clear that instead of facilitating the full inclusion of the special needs pupil into the mainstream, the special needs teacher, on the contrary, becomes an unwilling agent of segregation of his or her special needs pupils. Being the main, and at times the only, teacher of the special needs pupil in the mainstream class, serves as a kind of human barrier to such pupils, or an indicator of their differences from the others in the class. Classmates, who should have been the best facilitators of learning at integration-level, came to be seen as potential mini-helpers or social workers rather than as friends.

Often the integration of a pupil with difficulties in the mainstream classroom was linked to the features of segregated special education. Many of the pupils with special needs had their desks placed well away from the rest, in the majority of cases beside or next to the teacher's table or that of the classmate who was particularly responsible for assisting, faced a degree of isolation in order to minimise their potential for distraction. Such segregation within the mainstream class can be considered as a prelude to separation in the context of social integration, marking the life of these persons inside and outside the school environment.

Consequently the promise of integration had to be rethought and redefined, as it was reproducing the medical model centred on diagnosing disabilities and establishing specific teaching models taught by specialists. The planning carried out with respect to educational objectives, the nature of knowledge and the learning process, tend to cause one to fall back on a paradigm in which schooling is conceived as a process in which the teachers are the ones who know, and transmit their knowledge to those who need it *ie* the pupils. Formal mainstream schools, therefore, are converted into rational places of learning, organised to transmit knowledge (Skirtic, 1991).

Hence, those pupils who for mental, social or personal reasons do not take advantage of this knowledge in the doses required are considered disabled. They are isolated and treated individually according to their personal characteristics, so that their schooling process is hindered. All this involved the teaching/learning process of integrated children being carried out on an individual basis, geared to considering educational difficulties as arising from the characteristics of particular pupils, thus generating individual programmes of development that needed for their application more time in the special education classroom than in the mainstream classroom.

To sum up (See Arnaiz, 1998), in the 1990-1995 period a series of aspects became apparent that denoted the difficulties with which the school integration project was presented in the beginning:

- Absence of a preliminary period of preparation and/or planning by the schools and teachers involved capable of providing the necessary ideological debate on the budgets and goals which would form the framework of integration in educational discourse.

- Emergence of different training-proposals that, if anything, are incoherent and sketchily-developed; proposals which, moreover, treat these educational changes as technical processes, leading to a constructed outcome – a product – rather than as enabling schools to rethink and redefine themselves.

- An educational system with a closed curricular framework, which makes it difficult to achieve the equilibrium between the special needs of integrated pupils and the requirements and demands in which this curricular framework involved them. In the past, demands and differences were a never-ending source of failure and segregation of many pupils.

- Furthermore, integration highlighted the need to develop a project in collaboration with different professionals participating in the integration process. The appearance on the scene of new professionals (support-teachers, speech-therapists *etc*) called forth the capacity of schools to form communication-channels in anticipation of the new educational reality.

- The beginning of integration meant the abandonment of deep-rooted practices, usages and educational terminology. It even meant rejecting the conceptualisation surrounding the education of pupils who showed some sort of difficulty. Reclamation demanded a terminological change, a change in the practices of classification and labelling that, for a long time, contributed to the classification of two types of pupil – 'normal' and 'not-normal' – and, therefore, two types of education: *ie* mainstream education and special education.

- The placing of pupils with special educational needs in a mainstream classroom meant that this had to be reorganised in order to provide responses to their special needs and, at the same time, serve the needs of the rest of the pupils. This new situation demands of the ordinary classroom teacher a new way of teaching and thinking about education.

One could say that the new school integration movement produced a fairly general response from the schools and teachers. This meant an institutional/ideological adoption of integration, especially from 1987, when integration ceased to be a voluntary option for designated schools and, instead, hardened into general compulsory implementation by the Spanish Ministry of Education.

All these circumstances contributed to emphasise the need to reform the educational system from a basis that promoted a system of education which was comprehensive, open to diversity, and advocated equal opportunities. The promulgation of the Reform Law of the Educational System (LOGSE) on 3rd October, 1990, and its previous processes, articulated in White Papers on the Reform of the Educational System (1987) and in the 'Basic Curricular Design' (1989), with this objective, establishes a new model of treatment for persons with disabilities, which is open, flexible, prescriptive and need-orientated. This law, therefore, has been promulgated with the desire to overcome the shortcomings that were present in the educational system, and to provide a suitable answer to the demands of education for all citizens.

From this proposal a conceptual framework is established with respect to the aspects which characterise the two basic terms of comprehensivity and diversity (Puigdellivol, 1998). Thus *comprehensivity* is defined in terms of elements such as:

- Treatment of all pupils in accordance with their personal characteristics, with no distinction of any kind (physical or mental limitation, economic and cultural levels, race, sex, religion);

- Unified and identical curriculum for every pupil up to the age of 16, followed by movement to educational and job specialisations;

- Guaranteeing the right to education of all members of society;

- The right to achieve a common cultural education necessary for everyday life.

At the same time *diversity* finds its definition in the following criteria;

- The right of pupils to be considered in accordance with their previous knowledge and experience, ways of learning, interests, motivations, expectations, specific capacities and work-rhythms;

- The development of individuals in the light of their varied personal features, to the enrichment of a widely-varied society;

- Open and flexible attention provided at different levels, both with respect to the centre itself and the individually-considered pupils;

- The extension of support to all types of pupils who, on a permanent or a temporary basis, require complementary attention apart from the general education considered for the majority of pupils.

Thus, diversity and comprehensivity are constituted according to complementary principles which involve a commitment to providing a response to an array of interests, problems and needs that are present in real educational environments, compensating for inequalities, and bringing into effect the principle of equal opportunities (Munoz and Alsinet, 1990).

The LOGSE, then, tries to articulate this change in creating schools which promote respect and tolerance. The development of the capacity for co-operation, moral responsibility, tolerance and solidarity demonstrates this. It is manifested in a non-discriminatory spirit which advocates diversity, and in the objectives of compulsory education.

This law has brought special educational needs under judicial order as an alternative to the concepts of mentally-handicapped, disabled or physically-handicapped. By the means of special needs education we try to enforce the idea that dealing with a disadvantaged pupil means deciding case-by-case the specific help that he or she needs in its actual context, so that the pupil is able to meet the requirements of the established curriculum. Thus, with the implementation of the Royal Decree 334/1985, the LOGSE establishes the same educational objectives for pupils with special educational needs as for the rest of the pupils, according to the establishment of principles for the suitability or adaptation of teaching to the characteristics of these (Art.3).

Hence the onus lies not on the pupils with difficulties to adapt or 'conform themselves' to what is generally planned or developed in terms of teaching, but rather on what teaching has to offer to cater to the educational needs of the majority of pupils. Thus, teaching must be adapted to the learning styles and pace of learning of each pupil in accordance with their strengths and needs, special or not (Arnaiz and De Haro, 1997). This is achieved by adjusting the curriculum and the teaching so that they answer the needs of the diversity of pupils in educational categories in schools of Primary Education, Compulsory Secondary Education, Vocational Training and Special Education.

This framework presents us with a vision of pupils as individuals considered in a certain context, whose progress can only be understood and assessed in accordance with certain circumstances, tasks and a set of relationships. A framework within which teachers should have a greater capacity for interpreting educational events and circumstances, taking advantage of the insights of others in their milieu, in which the education-teams of the various schools, seeing the difficulties that pupils have in class, take stock and try to improve learning conditions. From this perspective pupils' difficulties will be considered as the source of information that provides food for reflection, and suggests changes in work-conditions in the classroom. Undoubtedly this will be an advantage to all the students in the classroom.

To sum up, for Spain, we could say that schools are places where teachers, parents and pupils must think about the problems and circumstances that surround them and jointly seek solutions, organisations in which all the educational community should work in a spirit of co-operation. Promoting collective solutions to problems means being aware of schools as organisations in which relationships and personal interactions are analysed, since in the end it is people who will make and change schools.

The case of Italy

The treatment of diversity in Italy, from the viewpoint of integration, has a lengthy tradition which goes back to the 1970s. This initiative coincides with certain political, social and cultural transformations, which have their origins in the change from the state governed by law to a social state. The principle of a democratic school open to everyone implicitly means the acceptance of diversity among pupils and, consequently, the integration of such pupils into the mainstream of schools. It was decided to face the increasing problem of schooling pupils with disabilities in schools and special classrooms, a fact which started to cause great public concern, as it reinforced and contributed to segregation.

As a consequence, the first parliamentary proposals for the provision, care and rehabilitation of these persons with physical, mental and sensorial problems began as a series of laws and rights which, at least on paper, have tried formally to establish developmental aspects. We should never forget that, with respect to this, Italian legislation in the matter of integration is among the most advanced in Europe.

The first stages are found in the promulgation in 1971 of the Law for Disabled Citizens, No 118, which stipulates in its Article 28 that compulsory education must be given in the mainstream school. On the same lines, Law 517 (1997) abolishes grading and 'removes' in the secondary school, and envisages forms of integration for disabled pupils, with the help of special education teachers both in elementary and secondary schools. This law reorientates the problem of integration in the field of planned, integrated school activities, with the objective of delivering individualised activities in relation to the requirements of each student.

This approach to the problem of disability is very important because it introduces new activities which, if applied with dedication, could eliminate the old didactic and pedagogical methods linked to the medical approach, and profoundly change the organisation of school work. This law advocates the constitutional right of each individual to achieve social and cultural goals that the school is obliged to provide for everyone, in order to achieve the personal development for all the pupils.

In 1979, a ministerial paper (CM of 28.7.79) defined the role of the support teacher in the integrating process, a role which is often not well-defined and unfortunately is not understood even today in many countries. Under this definition, then, a support teacher is described as being under the control of the normal class teacher or as a teacher who performs his or her roles independently and away from the mainstream classroom, yet who works in collaboration with the rest of the teachers in a school, and is immersed in different educational processes that could improve the quality of teaching for all pupils.

During the 1980s, once the integrating process had got under way, the Ministry promulgated a series of decrees and ministerial documents with a view to extending the roles of educational diversity (CM - Ministerial Document - 258 of 22.9.83; DPR 12/9 No 104 of 1985; CM 250, 3.9.85; CM No 1, 4.1.88; CM 262, 22.9.88). These indicate and clarify such topics as areas of definition and competence between different institutions implicit in the integration process (school, sanitary and local authorities). Here such questions are addressed as how to prepare schools for the educational demands of all the children, in order that equality and diversity may be adequately served. These can constitute the basis of school integration: the need is underlined for co-operation of family, school and socio-sanitary bodies in the direction of monitoring and remedial-action, in line with the individual levels and attainment-objectives of individual pupils.

Special mentions occur with respect to the importance of assessing the potential of individual pupils and their educational needs, rather than diagnosis of their disabilities. Thus it is desired to shift attention from disabled status to educational possibilities, capacities and abilities, so that these can be fostered promptly and early, there being a strong link between early attention and performance in primary and secondary school.

It is only in the present decade of the 1990s that all these matters relating to the integration in schools of disabled persons have been arranged *ab initio* in the Law of Ordination of Elementary Schools (L 23.5.90, No 148). This law reaffirms, *de liovo*, the constitutional principles concerning these persons, and the assessment of individual, social and cultural diversities (Article 1), committing the Ministry to carrying out biennial examinations of the integration project in order to inform Parliament or, in accordance with the findings of these examinations, to prescribe more appropriate services.

The articles of this law point out that attention to diversity does not have to be considered as a specific problem that requires a series of specialised interventions, but as one more response emerging from the continuum of the educational system. Education is a right of all citizens, who may accordingly demand it. Successive governmental applications have emerged, among which we would like to highlight the above-mentioned initiative of co-ordination of local sanitary units (DPR, 24th February, 1994), and the dispositions of the Ministry of Public Instruction with regard to examinations (OM No 80, March, 1995) and their successive modifications and integration.

However, having set forth all these laws and rights, we are not to think that ministerial commitment has produced a total pedagogical transformation. On the contrary, between the practice and the theory there is still a wide gap, hence the need to work determinedly and lead the debate (Cuomo, 1994) from a viewpoint of continuous research and experimentation, so that mainstream schools really are for everyone.

We could say that this policy of renovation has allowed us to give new weight to the phenomenon of diversity, understood as an essential category of epistemological and operative reflection, above all in pedagogical terms (De Anna, 1998). In this way, the concept of diversity is beginning to be valued and to be accorded positive significance.

As a consequence of this, and from the educational viewpoint, schools are trying to build pedagogical projects with the capacity to integrate diversity and to improve educational policy. Subsequently, a change has taken place in such a way that students are evaluated in accordance with the contributions of educational psychology, such as multiple forms of intelligence, diversity of cognitive styles – and therefore of learning – variety of forms of expression and communication and interactions within contexts. To sum up, a pedagogy which is open to a multiplicity of languages, intelligences, logic, cultures and interpretative hypotheses is what is required, and what is being aimed at in Italy.

The case of Portugal

As in the above-mentioned countries, the Constitution of the Portuguese Republic recognises the right to education of handicapped people; this is in Article 75, whereby:

• Citizens with a physical or mental handicap possess the same rights and are subject to the duties stated in the Constitution resulting from the exercise of the same by and on behalf of those who are disabled.

• The state sets forth its obligation to carry out a national policy of care and treatment, rehabilitation and integration of handicapped persons, to develop a pedagogy which makes society sensitive to the duties of respect and solidarity with others, and to be responsible for the effective enforcement of their rights, without prejudicing the rights and duties of parents or tutors.

The first pilot project in integration took place in Portugal in the 1960s, when the main education system was that of special schools and mainstream schools. They were good initiatives, and related to the blind or those with partial vision, helped by teachers specialising in this type of disability. It was necessary to wait till the 1970s to find the first legal measure relating to the education of children with all types of disabilities (Decree for the Integration of Students with Disabilities, 1975). The same occurred within the framework of the important reform of the educational system which took place at that time.

The promulgation of this decree made it possible for students with special education needs who attended special education schools, or who were confined to their homes, to receive an education in the mainstream schools. It was a change that triggered-off important discussions about attitudes regarding diversity, the role of mainstream teachers, the aims of educational integration and the social and professional future of handicapped people.

The influence exercised by the Warnock Report (1978) in the 1980s must be noted. This opened up a new horizon on attention to diversity in Portugal, and brought with it important changes helped by the Law of Educational System Basis (1986) and by the Law of Provision and Rehabilitation Bases for Handicapped People.

In Bernard da Costa's opinion (1995) four outcomes can be observed from this:

• The inclusion of students with moderate and severe learning difficulties in reference groups supported by a 'Special Education Team'.

• The evolution of a policy concerning educational integration: from the support given to students with different types of handicaps (sensorial, physical or mental), to the support given to students with special needs.

• The development of the support system from three new perspectives: the substitution of the medical report in order to establish the provision needed for special education by educational and psychological reports; the attention given to the opinions of parents concerning assessment and delivery in special educational provision for their children; and the establishment of individual educational plans and guidelines for all school intervention.

• At the beginning of the 1990s the promulgation of Law 319/91 marks the continuation of the integral policy which began in the 1980s, tending to conclude with the assistance model. With this aim in view, it points out the responsibility of the schools in this process of transformation, and in its articles sets forth a series of measures designed to transform mainstream schools so that they really can cater for everybody. In the context of these aims, we must highlight the need to understand the educational response as a process in line with the individual situation of each student. To achieve this, schools must make administrative, curricular and organisational changes, such as individual support, an adapted or alternative curriculum, and the use of special teams and special means of communication.

In concluding this work, perhaps it should be re-emphasised that the presence of students with special educational needs in the mainstream educational system, especially the difficult ones, entails a fundamental rethinking of education so as to create a whole series of new teaching/learning strategies to be used in classrooms. As teachers we are involved in this, and must look for a way of achieving it. Current legislation can help us, but in no case will it be the creator of this change. We must remember that the true reformers must be the teachers, professors, students and families, acting in a mutually supportive and integrated way.

References

Alnscow, M (1995), *Necesidades especiales en el aula*, UNESCO/Narcea

Arnaiz, P (1996), Las escuelas son para todos, *Siglo Cero*, vol.27 (2), No.164, (pp 25-34)

Arnaiz, P (1998), *Bases pedagogicas de la Educación Especial*, Universidad de MurciaIDm

Arnaiz, P and De Haro, R (Eds) (1997), *Diez Anos de integración en Espafia: Analisis de la realidad y perspectivas de flituro*, Universidad de Murcia

Bernard da Costa, A M (1995), Inclusive Schools in Portugal, in C O'Hanlon (Ed), *Inclusive Education in Europe*, David Fulton Publishers

Cuomo, N (1994), *La Integración escolar. ~ ¿Dificultades de ensenanza O dificultades de aprendizaje?* Visor

De Anna, L (1998), *Analisis histórico sobre la integración escolar de los niflos en Italia*, Modulo Europeo, Programa Socrates

Fulcher, G (1989), Integrate and Mainstream? Comparative Issues in the Politics of these Policies, in L Barton (Ed.), *Integration, Myth or Reality?* The Falmer Press

Garcia Pastor, C (1991), *Evaluación del Programa de Integración en Andalucia, VIII*, Jornadas de Universidades y Educación, Tenerife

MEC (1987), *Libro Blanco para la reforma del sistema educativo*, Ministerio de Educación y Ciencia

MEC (1989), *Diseno Curricular Base*, Servicio de Publicaciones del Mini steno de Educación y Ciencia

MEC (1990), Evaluación plan integracion, *Siglo Cero*, 135, (pp 54-62)

Mufioz, E and Alsinet, J (1990), Comprensividad y diversidad. *Cuadernos de Pedagogia*, 183. (pp 54-57)

Parrilla, A (1992), *La integración escolar como experiencia institucional*, Universidad de Sevilla

Puigdillival, I (1998), *La educación especial en la escuela integrada. Una perspectiva desde la diversidad*, Grao

Skrtic, T M (1991), *Behind Special Education: A Critical Analysis of Professional Culture and School Organisation*, Love

Valero, L and Arranz, P (1993), *El tratamiento de la Educación Especial en la LOGSE: 60 una realidad 0 un deseo? En: La necesidad de una educación para la diversidad*, Universitat Rovira i Virgili

Warnock, H M (1978), *Special Education Needs. Report of the Committee of Enquiry into the Education of Handicapped Children and Young People*, HMSO London

York, J *et al.* (1991), Integration-Support Personnel in the Inclusive Classroom, in Stainback, S and Stainback, W (Eds), *Curriculum Considerations in Inclusive Classrooms*, Paul Brookes

Chapter 6

Special Education in Bulgaria

Diana Tzokova and Philip Garner

Introduction: the historical underpinnings

As in other countries, historical developments in special education have contributed significantly to the philosophical foundations of present-day approaches in special education in Bulgaria. At a practical level, they help explain its current function, organisational pattern and practices at a time of dramatic and ongoing change in Eastern Europe.

The history of special education in Bulgaria begins as late as the end of the 19th and the beginning of the 20th century. Data concerning the education and care of handicapped children prior to this time is very limited and predominantly focused on attempts to 'heal the handicapped persons', exemplifying a medicalised paradigm of learning difficulty. In this early period, those involved in special education were ambitious people with medical or pedagogical backgrounds who had been educated abroad, mainly in Russia, Switzerland or other west European countries. These were 'pioneers' who brought the initial ideas for the education of disabled children into Bulgaria and who contributed greatly to practical initiatives in the field. Among them, the names of F Ulbrich, V Shumanov, D Katzarov, S Belinov, I Shishmanov, K Cholakov, B Tomov are especially distinguished (Dobrev, 1992).

The first official source to mention the education of children with disabilities was the General Education Law (1891) which was also the first piece of educational legislation following Bulgaria's independence from the Turkish Empire (1878). The Law stated that schools should be established to cater for the 'underdeveloped, disabled and feebleminded'. However, there is no evidence to suggest that such practical measures were ever implemented. In subsequent years, increasing numbers of medical doctors, educationalists and other professionals began to advocate support, care and education of handicapped children. Their efforts remained fruitless, mainly due to the shortage of funds and support from the community.

The substantive starting point for the education of children with disabilities was 1898, when a private special school for deaf children was opened. Subsequently, in 1906, the school was transformed into a 'State Institute for the Deaf'. For the next 30 years or so community unions for the protection of the deaf and a number of organisations involving deaf people themselves appeared.

Alongside these developments in the field of deafness there was an increased interest directed towards speech disorders (notably stuttering) in children, together with a developing awareness that services for children with speech disorders should be established. This resulted in the inauguration of the first separate special school in 1924. The initiative was, unfortunately, short-lived and in the following two decades speech and language disorders were treated mainly on a private basis.

The first special school within the general education system was established in 1905 as a result of the personal initiative of the Minister of Education at that time. It was called an 'Educational Institution for the Blind' and the curriculum placed particular emphasis on musical education. Special classes attached to mainstream schools were organised for children with intellectual disability from 1921. In the same year, leading medical doctors and educationalists established a 'Medical Pedagogical Society'. Its purpose was to enhance the quality of care for children with intellectual disability and to promote their education. Special classes for these children in mainstream schools subsequently appeared throughout the country as a result of the activities of the Society. As with other early initiatives in Special Education, the majority of classes did not survive long because of a variety of difficulties, amongst which the lack of teachers with specialised training in the field was a critical factor.

In 1936 the Medical Pedagogical Society was renamed the 'Society for Care and Protection of Children with Delayed Development'. The 'new' association was largely instrumental in the establishment of the first special school for children with intellectual disability in 1937. Again a similar pattern developed, with the school, like its predecessors, struggling to survive because of lack of funds, inappropriate pedagogy and the absence of trained teachers.

The period following the Second World War (1939-1945) brought a new era of development in special education in Bulgaria. In 1944 Bulgaria began its socialist and communist history. Almost axiomatically this was also the start of a systematic, centralised approach to the education of children with disabilities. With the Education Law (1948) all special schools were, for the first time, included in the general education system of the country. Initially, most activity in special education was directed towards the identification and registration of all children in need of special educational support. Responsibility for this work was gradually assumed by 'medical pedagogical commissions' and a hierarchy of agencies responsible for the screening, identification and assessment of different impairments in children.

These activities were largely based on the belief that special education ('defectology') is an interdisciplinary field, requiring the involvement of a range of professionals and others. They were immensely influenced by the Soviet's post-revolutionary and post-war special education tradition, in which children with disabilities were the subject of intense medical and psychological study aimed at determining their 'defective' characteristics and the peculiarities in their development (Georgieva, 1995).

The theory and practice of special education in Bulgaria began to evolve alongside, and in the context of, this orientation based on the threefold priorities of curriculum development, special education methodology (pedagogy) and teacher training. It would be fair to say that the influence of the Russian psychological and educational tradition has remained, tempered only by the onset of a dramatic and widespread exposure to 'western' approaches in special education since 1989.

Theorising the current approach

The concept of special needs in Bulgaria at the present time is based entirely on the so-called 'psycho-medical' paradigm, identified and described by Clark et al (1995). Special educational need or 'learning difficulty' is understood in terms of characteristics of the 'disabled' individual. As Dyson and Millward (1997) indicate, these characteristics are seen 'to account for the inability of certain children to flourish within the provision made in mainstream education' (p 53).

Probably the most influential figure in the development of Bulgarian special education is Vygotsky, and his theory of child development together with the fifth volume of his collected work, which focussed on 'Defectology'. Although the former is relatively well known (in translation) in Western Europe, North America and elsewhere, the latter is less familiar – to the extent that the use of the term itself is taken as a negative, even pejorative, descriptor for the child with learning difficulty.

Central within Vygotsky's work is the concept of 'abnormal development' which was viewed as being rooted in biological-social origins. Karagiosov (1996) looks back at Vygotsky's theory of Defectology in an attempt to analyse its core concept of 'abnormal development'. Vygotsky (1983) stated that children with biological 'defects' are not automatically abnormal from the originating point of the organic 'damage', but progressively deviate from a normal human onto-genesis. This deviation demonstrates itself in terms of a mismatch between that child's biological-social functions and the norms of an individual functioning within society (the societal norm), wherein the child is increasingly unable to meet the social demands and expectations placed upon him/her. In reality, Vygotsky comes to the conclusion that, by its very nature, abnormality is a social construct. Vygotsky also observed that physical impairments, blindness, deafness or inborn 'feeblemindedness' alter not only the way in which a human being relates to the world, but they also, importantly, influence his/her relationships with people.

Abnormal development is described by Vygotsky as comprising primary defect and secondary deviations. The primary defect has biological and functional dimensions. Among the latter are: disordered basic brain functions, connective malfunction of the central nervous system and impaired links between the first and second signal systems. Problems in any of these spheres account for secondary deviations, which are most usually expressed on a psychological level. They are usually manifest by under-development of the higher cognitive and reflective processes, personal characteristics, experience, emotions, language and communication and relationships. Typically, they affect the whole social formation of the individual. Vygotsky emphasised that 'the psychological' appears first socially (between people) and only afterwards as an internalised category (within the child).

Each of the theoretical positions and their underpinning principles provides the foundation of Defectology, which was the predecessor of special education in the former Soviet Union and, to a great extent, in Bulgaria. In the former USSR, for example, Diachkov (1964) defined Defectology as an '(interdisciplinary) science' that looks at the psycho-physiological peculiarities of children with physical and psychological insufficiency (abnormal children), and their education'. Dobrev (1992), in Bulgaria, defines it as a complex science concerning the development of children with handicaps, their educational and vocational preparation. He also states that 'defectology' has to be seen as a pedagogical field and its main focus should be on education, whereas its developmental psychological aspects are more of a logical prerequisite for the effectiveness of educational activities.

This latter argument played a considerable role in the establishment of Defectology as a young branch within education and the incremental shift towards more educationally-related terminology in the following years – notably the use of such terms as special education, learning difficulties and so on.

Despite these shifts in terminology, the 'medical model' of disability (Radoulov, 1996) is still largely dominant in the Bulgarian approach to special education at the present time. Disability is viewed as a characteristic of the child, with little recognition of environmental interaction (Tzokova, 1997; Dobrev, 1998). There is also a belief that there are categorical differences in children's development and education. Therefore, children can be categorised and labelled according to the type of primary 'leading' impairment: for example deaf, blind or mentally deficient. This has tended to deflect attention away from pedagogical matters, leaving widespread concentration on attending to the clinical issues of the disability.

Educational provision for children and young people who are categorised in this manner is currently characterised by (i) the pre-eminence of special schools (ii) the utilisation of special, adapted or modified curricula and (iii) teachers with special training, expertise and qualifications for work in segregated settings. Each of these characteristics varies according to the category of disability, and its severity (Tzokova, 1997). This results in the present arrangement within special education in Bulgaria, which covers several specialist strands (Radulov, 1996):

- education of visually impaired children – includes totally blind, children with light perception, partially-sighted (visual sharpness 0.01-0.04/0.05) and partially-sighted (visual sharpness 0.05-0.2) children. In addition this strand accounts for those children with multiple impairments when the leading impairment is visual;

- hearing and speech rehabilitation – includes children with socially adequate hearing (0-30db), hard-of-hearing (30-50db), practically deaf (60-80db) and deaf children (over 80db);

- education of children with intellectual deficiency – children with mild, moderate, severe and profound intellectual disability. (Until recently, only children with mild and moderate intellectual disability were covered by this strand);

- education of children with neurosomatic diseases. This includes children with diseases of the muscle and bone structure, together with children with diseases of the inner organs or the nervous system;

- speech therapy (logopedy) – children with wide variety of speech, language and communication disorders.

In considering these groupings it is worthwhile noting that children with emotional and behavioural difficulties (EBD) are not regarded as an object of special education and their educational problems are not addressed separately. The rationale behind this strategy is that such children do not fit into the accepted description of 'abnormal development' and that their difficulties are rarely persistent and relatively permanent (Dobrev, 1992; 1995; 1998). This position illustrates a point of tension in educational policy and provision for EBD children which is a familiar element, almost endemically so, of educational systems worldwide (Cooper, 1999).

Moreover, this position is indicative of how the predominant consideration in the establishment of a set of categories of disability is biological-psychological. And, whilst the severity and relative permanence of disability are also important considerations, social factors are continuously ignored. The Bulgarian interpretation of Vygotsky's theory, therefore, has worked to undermine one of its most powerful suggestions. Psychological components form the core focus of disability, whilst environmental influences in child development are continually underestimated.

Children whose EBD has resulted in antisocial behaviour associated with delinquency and criminality are considered without the education system; although the relevant strand, called 'ethopedy', has a relatively low status when compared to those which might be regarded as the 'traditional' strands, outlined earlier. The children and young people covered by the ethopedic strand have recently been referred to as children with specific educational needs.

There are obviously two contradicting trends apparent in the Bulgarian manifestation of the 'medical model' of disability which form the bases of special educational provision at present. On one hand there is a drive towards a more expansive interpretation of the special educational strands (differentiation), whilst on the other there is high degree of conservatism resulting in a rigid, narrow interpretation of what constitutes children's special educational needs. The recent shift in terminology, which comes closer to the language of education (rather than the clinical sciences), is not reflected in a parallel shift in philosophy and understanding.

Current legislation in SEN: provision and prospects

Earlier, we commented on certain aspects of the new legislation in relation to general education in Bulgaria. In this, special schools are not subject to the statutory educational requirements placed upon mainstream schools (General Education Law, 1991). Special school matters are, however, addressed in detail in the Regulations for the Implementation of the General Education Law (1992), Chapter Five. Thus, there seems to be an ideological notion of separateness, at national level, given the striking absence of special education considerations in such a fundamental document as the General Education Law. A number of reasons might lie behind this neglect:

* special schools (or, at least, some of them) are marginalised within society as a whole;

* special schools provide only a portion of the total provision for the child with special needs, who is seen as educable in terms of the mainstream education system;

* special education establishments for those who fall exclusively within special (educational) settings are the shared responsibility of the health, education and social care authorities.

The Regulations for the Implementation of the General Education Law (1992) state that 'Special schools are established to provide for pupils who need special care, help and protection on a behalf of the state and society. Special Schools are for children with chronic illnesses, permanent disorders and specific educational needs. The middle group includes children with intellectual deficiency, speech disorders, hearing impairment, visual impairment and allied damage'.

Special schools organise educational and rehabilitation activities for these groups of children that are directed towards correction and compensation of their impairments and the stimulation of the child's further development. Enrolment of children to these schools is based on the discussions and final decision of the Medical-Pedagogical Commission, whose members and working procedures are determined by the Ministry of Education and Science and the Ministry of Health.

The final responsibility for identification, and subsequent special school enrolment, is the responsibility of the regional inspectorates of the Education Ministry. There are some difficulties and disparities in this arrangement. For example, the current Instruction N 06/1977 of the

Education Ministry states that it strives to achieve a considered multi-professional assessment. In reality, however, there is a high degree of misinterpretation, on account of the lack of appropriate professional experience amongst members of the Commission. This results in the use of assessment tools, procedures and instruments which are inadequate and inaccurate; in consequence some children are still wrongly directed to certain inappropriate types of special schools.

Pupils with disabilities, corrected and compensated to a sufficient degree, could in principle be educated in mainstream schools, where they would follow a suitably amended programme. Correction and compensation of developmental disorders in pupils are also prioritised as main targets in speech therapy units and centres for the rehabilitation of speech and hearing. The latter serve both special and mainstream schools. Classes for children with permanent disorders in mainstream or vocational schools can be organised with special permission from the Ministry of Education.

In schools for children with intellectual deficiency, education lasts up to the eighth grade (elementary education), whilst children with hearing and visual impairments can graduate in middle, general or professional grades of education in accordance with the general State requirement.

It is apparent that schools for children with intellectual deficiency are, in the main, marginalised from the mainstream of educational culture. These schools, and the children they cater for, provide one of the reasons why State educational standards are not considered to be valid for special schools within the existing General Education Law.

Children who graduate from schools for pupils with intellectual deficiency receive a graduation certificate which is not part of the national accreditation scheme and, moreover, it gives the holder no rights of access to professional-apprenticeship schools (thus enabling them to acquire a professional qualification).

The number of professions for which pupils with intellectual deficiency can qualify (via vocational qualifications) is determined by the Minister of Health. Apart from the vocational training provided within special schools, these pupils are entitled to vocational training in 'social educational-vocational establishments', but do not have the right to continue their education in a higher grade.

Pupils with intellectual disability are being discriminated against under existing law. The centralised State view supports the idea that there is a 'ceiling' in their development and it seems only natural that measures might be taken, at some point in the future, to formally pre-determine this by statutory means. It is also worth reinforcing that special schools for children with intellectual deficiency accept only children with a mild degree of intellectual deficiency (according to the currently operative Instruction No 6/1977, referred to earlier).

Graduates from schools for pupils with visual or hearing impairment who successfully pass 'maturity exams' (the final, formal external examination) enjoy all the rights of graduates of middle education in the mainstream. Schools for the rest of the pupils with special needs are of a mainstream type and therefore a subject of the general state requirements.

Some aspects of current ways of working

Early intervention and pre-school education

The early diagnosis and identification institutions perform activities which often appear to be formalised and there is little evidence of satisfactory co-operation between individual institutions. The dominant role in early diagnosis and intervention is taken by the medical profession. Timchev (1997) points out that, due to the lack of commitment of paediatricians to the problem of psychological development and a commensurate lack of attention by psychiatrists, there is a considerable delay in identification and early intervention, particularly of intellectual disability.

Pre-school education centres often create their own assessment approaches and the mechanisms which might support them. As a general rule the main areas of assessment are language, perception and orientation, behaviour, attention, communication skills, gross and fine motor skills. There are pre-school centres, kindergartens and homes for pre-school children, differentiated on the basis of category and severity of disability.

Children who are placed in pre-school homes are not seen as a responsibility of the educational system but of the social care system, thus making difficult the task of quantifying the size of the various groups with disabilities. The age of children in most of these pre-school establishments is between 3-6 or 3-7 and the group sizes are 5-8. This pre-school data is made even more problematic in that pre-school groups attached to special schools are not included.

There is also some data overlap in the provision for children with severe, profound and multiple intellectual disability (SPMID): part of the same data is classified both under the pre-school section and the provision for children with SPMID. Nevertheless, Dobrev (1995) stresses that the number of pre-school education centres is insufficient, which leads to a delay in early intervention. Some of the pre-school centres are organised by the Ministry of Education and funded partly by it. Pre-school residential homes, as mentioned earlier, are the responsibility of the Ministry of Labour and Social Care.

Educational activities in pre-school institutions vary according to the specific characteristics of the particular disability type. They range from a more or less unified national pre-school curriculum to all sorts of therapies depending on children's needs:

• medico-genetic diagnostic and consultation services;

• maternity hospitals;

• child consultation medical services;

• 'Mother and Child' homes for abandoned children;

• kindergartens;

• schools;

• psycho-neurological services;

• summer diagnostic camps;

• regional medical-pedagogical teams.

Category	ID*	SLD*	DHH*	PD*
Total no. of centres	13	3	2	1

ID - intellectual disability; SLD - speech and language disorders; DHH - deaf and hardhearing; PD - physical disability

Table 1. Pre-school centres and homes for children with special educational needs (SEN).

Sub-category	SID*	MID & MoID	MoID & Autsim	MID
No. of centres	4	6	2	1

SID - severe intellectual disability; PID - profound intellectual disability; MoID - moderate intellectual disability; MID - mild intellectual disability

Table 1a. Pre-school centres and homes for children with ID.

Special schools

Most special schools are elementary schools and educate children and adolescents between the ages of 7 and 16. Types and numbers of special schools in Bulgaria are presented in Table 2.

Type	MID		LCD*		VI*		DHH		CP*	
No in	SS	P	SS	P	SS	P	SS	P	SS	P
1995	83		6		2		4		1	
1996	78	9157	4	273	2	308	5	689	1	no data

LCD - language and communication disorders; VI - visual impairment; CP - cerebral palsy

Table 2. Special schools (SS) and pupils' (P) numbers.

Depending on the type of school, the curriculum delivered might be either the NC (national curriculum), or a nationally unified, adapted and reduced version of it. In addition to the NC subjects there is a range of relevant developmental and therapeutic activities for children. The emphasis is on academic skills at the expense of social skills. Radoulov (1996) differentiates between general educational, adapted and specialised curricula for children with disabilities.

Some of the special schools follow the general national curriculum, with minor alterations providing for pupils with visual impairment and those with neuro-somatic illnesses. The 'adapted curriculum' is a version of the general education curriculum but reduced or modified in content to match the ability or aptitude level of pupils with different categories of disability. For example, the curriculum for pupils with intellectual disability is entirely adapted and modified, whilst only parts of the curricula in schools for pupils with hearing and visual impairments are adapted. Specialised curricula include social skills programmes and are relevant to the category of disability therapies. These form part of the whole curriculum in all special schools. Textbooks and workbooks are produced to cover all subject-content, usually developed by expert teams in open competition ('tendering'), organised by the Ministry of Education.

Vocational education and training

People with all types of disabilities aged 14 to 35 are offered vocational education, qualification and pre-qualification. Young people prepare for transition and gain initial vocational qualifications at school. Vocational training of people with visual and hearing impairment is often assisted by their Unions (charitable organisations, acting as interest/advocacy groups). The Unions of the Deaf and the Blind also provide protected employment in co-operative enterprises.

Vocational education of young people with intellectual disability is carried out in Social-Educational-Vocational Institutions (SEVI). Their number in Bulgaria is ten and they are regulated by the Ministry of Labour and Social Care. Administratively and financially they are subordinate to the municipalities in which they are located. Special education programmes in SEVIs include language, mathematics and additional academic skills which are regarded as crucial for the profession in which young people are to be trained. The professions offered to young people are mainly from the areas of agriculture, industry or services.

Children excluded from the special education system

The needs of children with severe and profound ID who have no access to the education system and are placed in social homes remain to a considerable extent unmet (see Table 3, below).

Category ⟋ age group	Persons with MoID, SID or PID — Number of Homes	Persons with SID and PID — Number of Homes
3 - 18	17	-
10 - 18	3	-
3 - 10	-	12

Table 3. Social Homes for Children with moderate, severe or profound ID.

The Ministry of National Health and Social Care experimented in developing a curriculum for the education of these children in 1982. This curriculum has been approved and recommended (1993) and is still followed by 90% of the institutions. Educational guidance is also available, together with instructions concerning the homes' status, differentiation, curriculum content and the formal organisation of the educational process.

At present the Ministry of Education is responsible for the guidance and the control over the educational process, whilst the Ministry of Labour and Social Care deals with organisational matters. Unfortunately the co-ordination between the two Ministries is sometimes problematic.

In 1996, an expert group was asked to evaluate the regulations concerning the Homes of Social Care, and present a set of recommendations for change. A project proposal has been produced. It strives to provide common educational criteria through a curriculum produced and co-ordinated by the Education Ministry. A developmental curriculum is proposed, with an emphasis on personal and social skills, communication, basic literacy and numeracy. The additional curriculum includes relevant therapies.

Another large group of children which has been excluded from the education system is that which includes children with autism, some children with physical disability and multiple (sensory and/or cognitive) difficulties. There are only two groups of autistic children in pre-school education; these are attached to a centre for pre-school education of intellectually disabled children. Methods of work and curriculum organisation are somewhat indeterminate: moreover, many of those working with young autistic children are often protective about the work they do, making even a broad interpretation of curriculum and pedagogy quite difficult.

Most children who experience severe autism are placed in children's homes at psychiatric hospitals. There is no research evidence of what happens to autistic children of school age. Identification and diagnosis is at an appalling stage and no specialised or otherwise provision is in place for these children.

Physically disabled children would normally enter mainstream schools without any specialised support or an ergonomically adapted environment. Apart from one indicated school for children with cerebral palsy, there is no other specialised educational service.

Finally, it should be noted that there must be either a very low prevalence of multiple sensory impairment in Bulgaria, or that the communicating systems are very unsatisfactory. For there were no children identified as being in need for a proposed one-to-one education programme funded internationally.

Children with multiple sensory and cognitive impairments often fall within the category of severe and profound intellectual disability and, in consequence, are a further group of children who are excluded from the education system.

An initiative for the future: 'Action on Reflective Practice'

With Central and Eastern Europe undergoing a period of rapid change, there have been opportunities in recent years to examine ways in which new approaches might be introduced to existing Bulgarian frameworks. 'Action on Reflective Practice' (ARP) was funded under the European Community TEMPUS programme from 1994 to 1997; a further one-year extension of the project enabled the participation of colleagues from

Macedonia. The project had the expressed aim of re-orientating and modernising Bulgarian teacher training in SEN, given that newly trained teachers would subsequently be likely to become 'change agents' in the new democracy. Its philosophy was based upon a synthesis of the differing traditions in teacher training for SEN and drew upon the experiences of teacher trainers in the Republic of Ireland and Greece, as well as involving other English and Bulgarian participants. It has been one of only a handful of EC TEMPUS projects to be directly involved in teacher training and SEN.

To achieve the project's principal aim, four targets were agreed upon. First, and bearing in mind the context-sensitivity required in East-West cooperation, a review of existing (*ie* pre-1994) teacher training practices was completed, based upon exchange visits by the participants. Next, a series of workshops and seminars was organised which considered the theoretical implications of 'reflective practice' for Bulgarian teacher trainers. Thirdly, work on revisions to existing curricula were undertaken in the training of teachers for work in SEN. Fourthly, a Bulgarian network of special educators, including teachers and others working in schools and other institutions was established.

These targets were achieved by three key strategies. First, the provision for teacher-mobility (a total of 63 exchanges of staff between the participating universities and schools were completed) within the project. This mobility was heavily directed towards East to West movement (80% of total movements), in order to avoid mistakes of several earlier TEMPUS projects, which did little other than foster 'academic tourism' by West European university teachers. Placements in schools and attendance at lectures and seminars in the host universities (in England and Ireland) were essential features of this mobility. Secondly, substantial funds (approximately 35% of the total three-year budget of Ecu 271,550) were contractually earmarked to upgrade SEN library facilities (books, journals, periodicals, CD ROM equipment) in two Bulgarian universities. Finally, the establishment of the first *Bulgarian Journal of Special Education*, distributed free of charge to all schools in the country, created an arena in which SEN matters could be debated more critically.

In the three annual reports of Project ARP there have been indications that, because of exposure to West European versions of SEN practice, the Bulgarian participants have increasingly recognised some important initial changes in their teaching approach in SEN. Many West European pedagogic practices, suitably modified, have been implemented, and the notion of 'theory into practice' by virtue of critical reflection has been enhanced. Many of these changes have been individual interpretations and 'borrowings' from West European teacher training and SEN provision. The current belief is that, by a process of osmosis from this small-scale programme, more widespread changes in pedagogic practice in teacher training will continue to result.

Special Educational Needs has, over time, become an increasingly important element in educational planning and resultant provision in most countries. It is also more susceptible to changes in the social and economic infrastructure of nations. As Europe adjusts to the radical changes in its organisation as a result of the political upheavals of 1989, SEN may be viewed as being at a crossroads in its development. In order to achieve further development in the field, participants in the struggle will have to convince national governments and other agencies of the efficacy of providing increased financial and human resources which are essential to guarantee the rights and status of those who have disabilities.

In spite of the difficulties facing teachers in SEN in East European countries, this is one group which can do more than most to ensure development in this area. In the face of other competing priorities, not least the economic regeneration of Eastern Europe and the climb out of recession for some of the West European states, the argument for rethinking along these lines will not be easily won. Ultimately the success or failure of the task may depend, as the case-study in this chapter suggests, upon the personal, rather than professional, beliefs, commitment and personality of teachers and teacher-educators themselves working in small-scale collaborative programmes. Moreover, local innovations which are culturally-sensitive, cost-effective and ethically-grounded may provide the best hope for educational development in the new democracies of Central and Eastern Europe.

Conclusion

The Bulgarian education system as a whole faces a wide range of difficulties at present due to the political, economic and social instability of the country. The changes of the political system affected the whole life of the society and people with learning difficulties are at the periphery of attention and therefore suffering most severely. The high degree of centralisation of the education system brings with itself disadvantages and inherent problems. Most importantly these are connected with rigidity and inhibition of creativity and innovation, as well as a lack of proper co-ordination between central government bodies responsible for special needs.

References

Diachkov, I (1964), 'Defectology', in *Pedagogic Encyclopaedia*, 1, Moscow

Dobrev, Z (1992), *Foundations of Defectology*, University 'St Kliment Ohridski'

Dobrev, Z (1995), *Mentally Delayed Children*, Sofia University

Dobrev, Z (1998), *Developmental Characteristics of Children with Mental Retardation: Social and Educational Aspects*, Agency Data Ltd

Dyson, A and Millward, A (1997), 'The Reform of Special Education or the transformation of mainstream schools', in S Pijl, C Meijer, S Hegarty (Eds), *Inclusive Education. A Global Agenda*, Routledge

Flemish-Bulgarian Forum (1996), *Guide to the Social Establishments for Disabled Individuals*, Centrum OBRA

Georgieva, A (1995), 'Speech Therapy in Bulgaria – The State of the Art in the mid-90s', *Bulgarian Journal of Special Education*, 1, 1, (p 8)

General Education Law (1991), *Republic of Bulgaria State Newspaper*, 86, Friday 18 October

Ministry of Education (1977), Instruction No 06, 'Instruction for the enrolment of children and pupils with physical or psychological insufficiency in special school and special educational establishments', Ministry of Education

Karagiosov, I (1996), 'Abnormal Development: the main issue in special education', *Bulgarian Journal of Special Education*, 2, 1, (pp 3-9)

Radoulov, V (1996) *Children with Special Educational Needs in school and society*, DARS

Tzokova, D (1995), *Education Opportunities for Children with Considerable Learning Difficulties,* Agency Data Ltd

Timchev, L (1997), 'The Normalisation Concept and the opportunities for social integration of individuals with mental difficulties in time of transition in Bulgaria', *Bulgarian Journal of Special Education* , 1, 1, (pp 21-27)

Vygotsky, L (1983), *Defectology. Collected Works,* Vol.5. Moscow

Vygotsky, L (1983), *Defectology. Collected Works,* Vol.4. Moscow

Chapter 7

Original power of expression: the Netherlands experience

Max Timmerman

Original power of expression demonstrates that people with intellectual limitations do not necessarily have to be handicapped in the field of expressive skills. They can create works of art which equal, and sometimes even outstrip, the expressive works of non-handicapped people, particularly in terms of originality, expressiveness and symbolism. After all, non-developed capabilities and intellectual limitations seem to play virtually no role in the expressive process.

To put it more strongly, handicapped people are not prevented by the desire itself to make something beautiful. First and foremost, they draw what they experience, not what they see. Intuition, use of primary colours and emotional tension take the leading roles. This makes the art of mentally handicapped people particularly valuable. The realisation is growing that they can make a significant contribution to our culture. Exhibitions always attract a great deal of interest.

This article makes the work of mentally handicapped people accessible to all interested parties. It explains how composition processes take place, making clear how composition is nurtured by pre-logical and expressive thought and sometimes, as it were, wells up from deeper layers of consciousness: the unconscious, intuition and affection.

The interest which was aroused, particularly during the 1980s, for the works of art of mentally handicapped people already has a long cultural background. Over the past two centuries, constant wonderment has been expressed for the expressive works of madmen, the mentally handicapped and primitive expressions of art.

During the Romantic Movement, around 1800, the conviction grew that the inner being of the artist is decisive in creating a work of art. During this period, the term 'divine inspiration', invented by Plato, was restored to its rightful place. The feeling was that genius was linked to being possessed. Not the artist himself, but other, preferably higher, eternal powers were using that person to express themselves. These powers could be divine, but they could just as easily be demonic, satanic inspirations. Madness and genius were linked together. Both concepts cover an area which exceeds the boundaries of what is normal and where terms such as possession, hallucination, melancholy, daydreaming and derealisation are used (Cimmermans, 1990).

Artists from this period found their inspiration in the world of feelings; a poetic state of mind tending towards sentimentality, but which also had its roots in a close association between man and nature. The work of art is then no longer an objective reflection of reality, but an illustration of the inner rationale of the artist himself (Didier & Boogd, 1992). The more tense the mind, the more expressive the painting (Goya, Munch, Van Gogh). The artist's perception is to play a leading role in the work.

The mentally ill

As a result of the growing popularity of and interest in the visual work of the mentally ill, madmen and schizophrenics, plus interest in non-Western art, in children's drawings and in so-called 'primitive' art, at the beginning of the 20th century, a cultural climate emerged in which the focus was on the inner message of the work of art. Being 'different', 'mad', deviating from the 'norm' became the potential vocations of the artist. The art produced by these people is characterised by an original, primitive, unspoiled, direct and uncultivated visual language.

Understanding of the true value of these works of art made a breakthrough in Europe with exhibitions in Paris and Germany of primitive sculptures and the art of 'outsiders'. In German expressionist journals such as *Aktion* and *Der Sturm*, the drawings and paintings of madmen, the mentally ill and children were given a prominent place. They were regarded as examples of an authentic, original and innocent art, free from upbringing or social influence and were emphatically displayed.

Surrealists, in particular, displayed much interest in the expressions of madmen, schizophrenics and children. They explored the fallow fields of the mind. After all, the impulses of passions and of the irrational were just as important as those of reason. The mysterious abilities of the unconscious had to be released in the service of artistic expression. Using dreams and hallucination, artists would be able to reveal a higher reality; a *surréalité*. Some artists went so far as to visit psychiatric institutions and to work with patients.

In 1992, Heidelberg psychiatrist Hans Prinzhorn published a book entitled *Bildnerei der Geisteskranken. Ein Beitrag zur Psychologie und Psychopathologie der Gestaltung.* In this much-discussed book, Prinzhorn demonstrates, using many fine examples, the fundamental and original creative power present in these works of art. Moreover, he provides an insight into the remarkable characteristic features which give the works such a special aura.

This extraordinary collection of works of art by psychiatric patients has been compiled over several years by Prinzhorn with the aim of publicising testimonies from the 'other side of reality'. The book and Prinzhorn's plan to include the collection in a museum for pathological art met with much resistance and lack of understanding from society. The Dadaists, however, led by André Breton, who in turn were searching for a situation of child-like creativity, explained this art, together with Indian art, as 'reservation art', as a way of expressing their appreciation.

Art Brut

From 1945 onwards, the painter Jean Dubuffet began to collect the best works of 'extra-cultural art' in Switzerland. Two years later, this collection was exhibited in Paris. Dubuffet called this art 'Art Brut' or raw art, thus laying the foundations of this artistic movement. However, not until 1976, after 30 years of collecting, was this vast, important collection given a permanent home in the Château de Beaulieu in Lausanne (Thévoz, 1990). The first museum for this type of art thus became a reality [see Illustration 1]. L'Art Brut and outsiders' art therefore became a concept and a permanent fixture of art theory in Europe.

Professional expressive artists such as Appel, Constant, Corneille, Miro, Kandinski, Picasso, Klee and De Kooning became more interested and were inspired by folk art, the art of primitives, the mentally ill and particularly the expressive work produced by children and people with mental handicaps. As early as 1912, referring to 'der Blaue Reiter', Paul Klee wrote about the value of children's drawings and the work of the insane. His work is very close to the unaffected method of expression used by children and to works from early phases of culture. At that time, however, no clear distinction was yet drawn between madmen and the mentally handicapped. Similarly, the Cobra painters drew their inspiration from the lack of cultivation, and the spontaneity and directness reproduced in primary shapes and colours in the expressive work of children, the handicapped and African art. "We had also captured an unrestricted freedom.

123

Illustration 1. The Chateau 'Beaulieu' at Lausanne, the first museum for Art Brut. From: Michel Thévoz, *'Art Brut: Kunst jensiets der Kunst*, AT Verlag, Aurau, 1990.

Illustration 2. From De Ontmoeting (the Meeting) by Karel Appel (reproduced in contour lines.

Children, primitives and psychopaths had our sympathy," explained Rooskens in 1984 about Cobra (Rooskens, 1994) [see Illustration 2].

Developmental psychologists at the beginning of this century also drew our attention to the importance of the expressive work of children, which visualises how they feel about reality. Children portray reality in a way which is very different from observable reality. Young children draw what they know and have experienced, not what they see (Breeusma, 1991).

Children have a natural ability to express themselves in visual concepts. They attribute emotional properties to objects and symbols. Their work can be characterised by pre-logical/intuitive thinking, by the use of primary colours and by an emotional tension. It therefore goes without saying that, through the method of depiction, the work of children, the handicapped and the mentally ill is associated with the cave drawings of our 'artistic' ancestors, also known as primitive art.

Primitive art

Our art history begins with what is known as 'primitive' or prehistoric art. This has become the basis of communicative transfer through artistic expression. Illustrations of animals drawn during the Ice Age, approximately 60-10,000 years BC, were discovered at the end of the last century on the walls of caves in France and Spain.

Not until the beginning of this century did archaeologists realise the particular importance of these artistic manifestations by our ancestors. These are pictures which reveal a high prehistoric civilisation and which turn on its head everything which research had until then revealed about the development of art. At that time it was thought that all artistic expression had developed – as in children's drawings - from a clumsy beginning with abstract representations into the more natural shapes of people, animals and objects.

The illustrations of animals from the Palaeolithic age, however, gave the discoverers a major surprise because they represented a fully developed naturalistic form of painting, based on accurate observation, without the preliminary stages. In the following period of cave painting came a phase during which the illustration of people became important, composition became simplified, more abstract and more symbolic (Valltortakloof, Spain, 7500 BC).

Two elements can be identified in the art of primitive peoples: an exclusively formal side, where the shape is the bearer of beauty, happiness and the perception of pleasure, and the other side, where the shape is the carrier of the intention and the meaning. This formal and symbolic representation appears in the art of all the races of the world in never-ending variations and techniques. Many experts have pondered on its correct interpretation (Boas, 1955).

Another important discovery with respect to the artistic expressions of the mentally handicapped in the formation of a theory concerning the development of art was the fact that many later artists sometimes achieved entirely abstract composition based on a naturalist representation. We can see this, for instance, in the works of Paul Klee (1879-1940), Picasso (1881-1973), Mondriaan (1872-1944) and Matisse (1869-1954).

The development of cave art, of non-professionally trained artists, thus seems to be at odds with development in the art of trained, highly skilled artists. This is a discovery which indicates that artistic powers of expression can be revealed, manifested and developed in different ways in pre-logically thinking people and in cognitively developed people.

The Stone Age wall paintings in the caves at Altamira, Trois-Frères and Lascaux consist primarily of the shapes of animals and semi-human beings, whose movements and positions in nature have been observed and reproduced with great artistic skill.

In addition to their naturalist reproduction, these pictures have great symbolic significance, for example hunting rites and holy sacrificial sites [see Illustration 3]. Many representations exist of animals, of people disguised as animals, masks and such like (Kühn, 1952). By portraying a hunting scene or someone wearing an animal or demonic mask, man is controlling his emotions and giving himself the spiritual strength of the animal, which he uses to attempt to conquer the alleged demons and other supernatural phenomena. The figure of the animal is usually symbolic of the primitive and instinctive nature of man (C G Jung).

Humans, with their tendencies towards symbol formation, subconsciously change the objects or shapes into symbols and thus attaches a significance which is psychologically very important. They express these symbols both in religion and in visual art (Jaffé, 1982). Well before the concept of art entered our thinking, people communicated with each other through pictures. The basis for this is formed by the urge present in everyone to make themselves visible, to express their preoccupations and in so doing to make contact with others. Visual manifestations, particularly in

Illustration 3. Prehistoric wall paintings reproduced in contour lines; left, a hind discovered in Siberia; right, a hunter from Rhodesia.

Illustration 4. Detail from 'Orpheus en de dieren' (Orpheus and the animals) (1952) by Lucebert (reproduced in contour lines).

our early cultures, are therefore not only determined by the portrayal of reality, but also by symbolic representation.

Interest in unusual stylistic thought and action in ancient civilisations, both within Europe and further afield, is therefore increasing. This wide appreciation brings with it an extension of the concept of art as well as increased enjoyment. Artistic status is now attributed to the visual manifestations of every group imaginable, such as children, farmers, indigenous peoples and the mentally ill and the handicapped. Art itself cannot be distinguished, the only distinction is in quality. Art thus acquires many faces and multiple forms.

Spontaneous expressions

The relationship between all these artistic expressions, for example by children, the handicapped, exotic artists and archaic folk arts, lies in the unconcealed manifestation in expressive thought which is visible among all these groups. Artistic manifestations are not yet subjected to the levelling influence of the abstract, verbal thought which so decisively controls all vital expressions in our present culture [see Illustration 4].

Initially, scientists made no distinction between psychiatric and mentally handicapped people. Scientific and, therefore, artistic interest focused primarily on psychiatric patients. The visual expressions of these people are largely generated within the context of therapeutic healing treatment. To begin with, an artistic approach to the power of expression is still entirely absent.

It was the French psychiatrist Réjà who carried out research among both psychiatric and mentally handicapped patients. In *L'art chez les fous* (1907), he wrote that the expressive works of mentally handicapped people gave a particular impression of the inner creative and artistic processes. Réjà discovered that a specific individual feature of the conceptualisation process became visible in the works of mentally handicapped people.

These visual works were overwhelmingly characterised by a fixed, concise expression of an early thought level. At this level, known compositional principles can be recognised which also occur in children's drawings, in those of untrained adults, among so-called primitives and among the mentally handicapped. At a very early stage, Réjà also pointed out that the creative developments which also apply to non-mentally handicapped people, as well as the original artistic views, are also particularly clearly expressed in the art of these people.

Professor Max Kläger, in particular, updated all these assumptions by carrying out research into 'original' expressive thought (*urtümliches Gestaltdenken*) in mentally handicapped people. In so doing, he made a major contribution to the equality of mentally handicapped people within the artistic manifestations in expressive art.

The cultural climate changed dramatically, during the 1960s, towards increased understanding of individuality. The 'principle of normalisation' made its appearance in health care. Centres of creativity mushroomed. Once society paid more heed to the equal rights of people with a mental handicap, the living environment in the health care establishments or institutions changed and more account was taken of the applicable standards and values in society. As normal an existence as possible for our handicapped fellows and their integration into society then became political aims. Consequently, smaller institutions were created, together with surrogate family homes, day centres for the elderly and various centres for day activities. A new phenomenon emerged in the daily activities of mentally handicapped people, namely artistic or creative activities.

Expressive thought

In order to gain a greater understanding of the role which thought and imagination play in the creative process, research has been performed by American psychologists Torranco and Guilford, among others, into the relationship between verbal and non-verbal expression. Initially, following the findings of Freud, Jung, Prinzhorn, Réjà and others, they attached great value to the meaning of the non-verbal forms of expression of so-called patients. By analysing the creative process, they gained an insight into the function assumed by thought in this process and the role which intelligence – developing or not – plays in the process.

Referring to the experiences of Torranco and Guilford, Van Praag (1971) writes, in his article on creativity: 'The movement from representation to abstraction is characteristic of thought'. This is also known as the abstraction process, or the dissociation of reality.

Thought therefore moves from concrete reality towards the higher levels of obscurity. Imagination, by contrast, begins with emptiness, from where it is given shape and form. Imagination is characterised by visualisation, the expression of an idea. If thought and imagination are used in an inventive way, we can talk of intelligence and creativity.

It is striking that intelligence is based precisely on the abstract, while creativity finds its origins in solid matter, in other words physical and material reality. This is because both functional abilities – creativity and intelligence – are based on the intention of thought and imagination. Creativity should be distinguished from expression and intelligence, but cannot be fully separated from either.

Discovery, or intuition, plays a major role in the process of composition. By intuition, we mean the flash of inspiration which comes from outside and is decisive for decisions which are taken during the creative process. It is an irrational, incalculable aspect of the creative process [see Fig. 1].

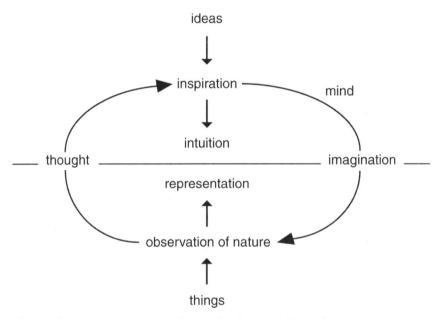

Figure 1. A Represenation of Imagination and Thought.

This irrational aspect, which is the basis for choices, can be found in many of the expressive processes of mentally handicapped people. It is the logical step forward in the representational thought of the artist, which has to do with the role played by expression – the artistic manifestation of the feelings of the inner life.

The Austrian psychiatrist Viktor Frankl pointed out that verbal expression often leads to aggression and fanaticism, while creativity – the power of expression – usually leads to solidarity and tolerance. This is linked to the fact that verbal expression is always subjective and all forms of resistance are in the first instance perceived as frustrations, while resistance in creativity implies a challenge to mastery. The danger that spoken words are adapted to acceptance of the environment is as large as life and is based on the ability to think in terms of cause and effect. By contrast, the danger that images which are recorded on paper in pictures or symbols are adapted to the acceptance of the environment is smaller because rational thought is often positioned between them.

For this reason, the non-verbal form of expression is more direct and of essential significance in achieving a correct and complete picture of the artist. It is more original in terms of significance, more concrete in terms of its primary observation. This principle applies to all people and it goes without saying that the mentally handicapped do not form an exception to this rule.

It is my firm conviction that conscious thought requires a high level of understanding and insight into natural and spiritual reality. Above all, it is the integration of these two aspects which makes us into fully-fledged beings. Since mentally handicapped people are handicapped in terms of mental, and perhaps also physical, abilities as a result of physical, organic or hereditary causes, depending on the extent of disintegration, they will never be able to comply with this ideal image. Moreover, their level is often expressed as what is known as an intelligence quotient (IQ). Depending on this IQ, terms such as idiot, imbecile and subnormal are used. Often, through the incorrect use of these terms, they have acquired negative connotations. Moreover, the fact of mental handicap cannot be remedied.

This point of departure provides us with the possibility of accepting mentally handicapped people and of meeting them in their own manifestation, which is immensely exciting in all its diversity. This manifestation is made clear to us in its personality expression (*Gestaltwerdung*), which in turn is possible through the vital creative power and the fundamental ability for imaginative thought and action, the unconscious imaginative thought aspect.

The rationale behind expressive thought is formed by linking the concept of primitive with primitive thought processes, also known as early thought processes, Arnheim (1978) claims that the brain controls the hand, a psychomotor action through which the person is shaped. That means that, using artistic-expressive, it is possible to recreate the regressive, chaotic, subconscious processes as a unit. Through an executive action using the hands, a representational concept is created. In this way, form is born out of rudderless chaos.

The mentally handicapped person is hardly disadvantaged, if at all, in the creative power of expression, despite an intellectual shortcoming or mental limitation. Precisely in the presence of sufficient artistic space and freedom of expression, this force fulfils a decisive and irreplaceable role in the acquisition of self-understanding and self-appreciation. It also generates an entirely individual figuration, which cannot be distinguished in origin from the products of the non-mentally handicapped. Compared to children's drawings, a temporal phase shift is detected as well as stronger psychomotor diversity.

Going one step further, it can be alleged that everyone who is intellectually and verbally handicapped actually has an advantage in the expressive and creative field because he or she is much closer to the origin of the artistic and symbolic meaning than the non-mentally handicapped person, who has been one-sidedly cognitively standardised through education and socialisation. In the mentally handicapped person, thought is not yet dominated by a practical, rational faculty. Intuition and instinctive faculties play an important role in making oneself known and understood. It is precisely in the artistic field where the mentally handicapped person is equal, in fact can sometimes even create more significant pictures which are more full of meaning than those of their fellows, who often feel they are superior.

As far as these problems are concerned, I would again like to stress that communication difficulties are often caused by the fact that the non-handicapped person tends to impose rational criteria on those who do not think rationally. When one is aware of the fact that feelings can be expressed in different ways, that not everyone thinks according to the same patterns and can express themselves at a rational level, it can also be acknowledged that intelligence is not the only criterion for being a fully-fledged individual. This gives us the opportunity to restore the balance of verbal and non-verbal expression, which has become skewed over the years.

Devoting attention to, and creating possibilities for, non-verbal expression, through artistic forms of expression specifically for people who do not have adequate verbal faculties, gives them a range of new possibilities and opens up to us an unknown world of perception. It is also possible to assess accurately the skills of mentally handicapped people.

The starting point often – and entirely incorrectly – selected is that of what it is impossible for handicapped people to do, which can be explained by their mental handicap. In this way, the handicapped person is taught to be helpless, is treated as incapable, in brief, is hospitalised. It is all too quickly assumed that 'they certainly cannot do that'. This is merely an excuse for not devoting any energy to them.

In recent years, happily, the reverse has been revealed in expressive, performing and musical arts launched by pioneers. People working in specially equipped studios prove that anyone can assume the talents present in us and in particular the artistic abilities described in this article. Mentally handicapped people reveal an original expressive thought which has its origins in the early thought level. At this level, thought takes place in the field of accumulated experiences, paradigms, which the person initially reproduces in pictures. Our distant ancestors did this in their cave drawings. This visual communication, however, has been replaced during human evolution by spoken language or by a combination of both means of communication.

Memory

A great deal of information is stored in our memories, which we have obtained since our early childhood. Using memory blocks, this information is processed and stored by our brains. The total of cohesive information about a certain subject is called a paradigm. A great deal of information in our memories is latent or unconsciously present. Information which does not fit into the paradigm is not only not processed, in other words placed in a cohesive context and structure, but often it is simply not included. In the creative thought process this is included and, using non-paradigmatic information, a new, improved memory block is formed. More or less unconsciously reproduced information in images helps the person to select its processing in the brain, to treat it and to apply cohesion in consciousness.

In general, information is only included and correctly processed when it forms part of a mutually cohesive whole. The highly structured process of selection, processing, treatment and storage of information is a memory lock-forming process (Van Dort, 1981). This process enables the person to bring about integration between the experienced outer and inner world, in brief, to function correctly.

The expressive work of the mentally handicapped, which is produced from the early thought and expression level, displays a high degree of unity in image and perception. Rational thought has not intervened. For this reason, the work is a direct expression of the perceptions of the artist. It is more specific in terms of the primary observation and more original in terms of meaning. Their work is a complete personal reproduction of everything around and within them. It has a raw form which is closer to the origins of artistic-symbolic meaning than much of the work of socially and cognitively trained people. This primary orientation is of essential importance for understanding the perceptions of mentally handicapped people.

Development

Over the years, many theories have been formulated about the development of drawing, specifically by children, by, for instance, Kerschensteiner, Goodenough and Piaget. These obsolete theories still use cognitive development as their basis. Observing, arranging and thinking are the intellectual activities which serve as a basis for the progressive development of drawing in children (Snoeren, 1993). Psychologists and theoreticians such as Kellog, Golomb, Arnheim and Matthews start with the development of drawing, alleging that the child gains understanding into the cohesion between things through drawing. The psychologist Golomb based her ideas on Arnheim's concept of differentiation.

The law of differentiation is based on the preconceived idea that observing and understanding progress from the general to the particular. Observing is responsible for the development of drawing: *'Jede Form bleibt so undifferenziert, wie die Auffassung des Zeichners von seinem Zielobjekt erlaubt'* [Every form remains as undifferentiated as the artist's conception of his target object allows] (Klager, 1987a).

Differentiation or diversity refers to the addition and restructuring of details in a drawing or painting. In other words, it is about the development from the simple to the complex. Through a difference in differentiation, drawings display a difference in size, proportion and orientation. The law of diversity does not accurately indicate which ages correspond to certain results, nor is it directed at the role of intelligence. Its emphasis is on inner, essential aspects of growth rather than outer, external aspects, such as imitation for example. The concept and the experience of development is due more to the evolution of natural capacities than to their training.

Research indicates that the development of drawing in mentally handicapped people probably takes place slowly and is perhaps not completed in the same way as in non-mentally handicapped people; nonetheless it is not faulty, not deviant and it follows the normal course of differentiation. The findings support the idea of a universal graphic use of language in the early and elementary phases. We can indeed talk of drawing development in the mentally handicapped, and IQ should not form an obstacle. Cognitive knowledge and an ability to learn are not necessarily responsible for the development of drawing or for artistic performance.

According to Arnheim's theory, representation is based on observation (visual thinking). This claim is based on the expressive observation from *Gestalttheorie*. Furthermore, in Arnheim's theory, observation and the production of drawings are associated with the natural observation of the real world (Arnhem, *op cit*).

Both natural observation and image observation are primarily concerned with structure and form and, secondarily, with the differentiation of details. The expressive work of the mentally handicapped is characterised by directness, simplicity and the primary and elementary form and use of colour. The drawn representation is hardly ever reality reproduced in a realistic way, but a reproduction of an experienced reality, abstract in form, extremely imaginative and highly personal, with great power of expression. The primary thought-process is expressed in the visual work, where the unconscious is dominant. The creative process is controlled by non-verbal thought-processes and takes place outside rational control.

Visual works from this level of consciousness often contain archetypal images and strong symbolism. I will look in more detail at this aspect in the section on image and meaning. This composition is also characterised by visually symbolic thought and action. The dimension of time is introduced into the secondary thought process; here and now, yesterday and tomorrow. We can talk of the reality principle. In this phase, concepts such as colour, composition and dimension play an entirely different role in representation because they are placed within the prevailing social structure, for example, beautiful – ugly, far – near.

Forming from the unconscious

To the mentally handicapped person, visual expressions are an illustration of their clearly visual, predominantly non-linguistic thought and action. They represent an entirely mental performance which consists of observing, perceiving, thinking and feeling. A purposeful hand movement makes this into an image. All the senses are involved, in particular visual observation, as well as the sense of touch and the bodily rhythm of the artist [see Illustration 5].

In the work produced, representations of existence and the world of the handicapped person in terms of content are visualised. Problems such as 'In what way should I portray something?' and 'Using which shapes and colours?' must be resolved through expressive thought. In this case, the artist cannot fall back on mental, reasoning faculties and finds solutions in instinct and associative ability.

As I described earlier, discovery plays an important role in composition. To a large extent, intuitions determine the choice of shape, image, symbol and colour, which create the overall picture as a representation in an unreasoned, irrational way. The way in which this intuition comes about has to do with the 'logical' step in the visual thought and action of the creator. It is the inner urge, the vital creative power from which expression emerges which reveals the inner life.

Expression – in signals which can be recognised and perceived by others – can lead to communication. Associations which arise during the expression process also determine visual thought and depiction. Associations, feelings and emotional aspects are linked from previous paradigms and they give the representation its emotional and symbolic tone. The composition thus created is fitted into certain, fixed, psychological structures – the paradigms – as a result of which they are processed and can be integrated into the person. In expressing oneself, the problem arises of using tools to transform spatial perception, the third dimension, into the second dimension. A well-known example of this is rails which disappear into the distance. This is incidentally a problem which affects everyone. The difference is that, in most people, this visual thought declines in intensity throughout the school years. Understanding, verbal thought takes over the role of visual thought.

In mentally handicapped people it does not work like this because verbal domination is much less prevalent. The basic structure of visual thought is often especially clear in the visual work of mentally handicapped peo-

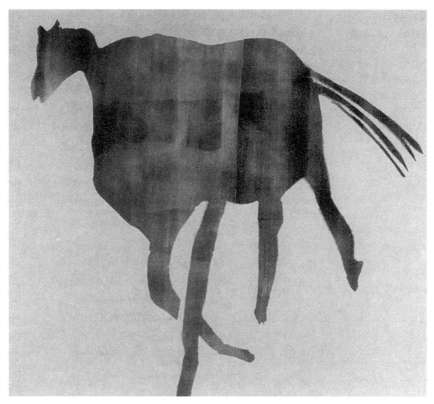

Illustration 5. Piet Koopman: 'Running Horse' (1980).

ple. Mentally handicapped people therefore participate, through their creation, in an original and archaic universal language, a primitive cultural language which is global and timeless (Klager, 1987a). As far back as 1907, Réjà wrote that the artworks of the mentally handicapped were particularly demonstrative of inner artistic processes. Their work portrays a specific individual character of the representational process. It is overwhelmingly characterised by a fixed, concise expression of an early creative and thought level.

If we assume that the fundamental primitive structures which determine the representational thought and action of men are carried over into adulthood, it should also be possible to apply these latent thought processes to mentally handicapped people and giving them the opportunity of achieving their own individual form of expression. This method can also lead to differentiation of these structures and to refinement of creative thought. This interpretation of expressive thought has a general human origin. Various views of this type of thought are possible. In addition to the view already described, we can also speak of visually graphic and presentational thought.

The brain

It has been discovered that the left-hand side of the brain favours speech and linguistic ability and verbal analytic thought. This left-hand side, which functions in 'internal' time, is concerned with logic, analytical faculties and practical, routine tasks such as organising one's surroundings. It also acts as a translator for the operation of the right-hand side of the brain. It codes, explains and communicates and, under certain circumstances, suppresses the functions of the right-hand side of the brain.

Over on the other side, the right-hand side of the brain specialises in spatial understanding and non-verbal thought. It controls the primitive, non-differentiated consciousness faculties. This right-hand side of the brain, which governs creativity, spatial observation, abstract thought and musical and visual observation, operates in 'external' time, a state of timelessness, hence its link with the supernatural (Hope, 1990). According to Fischer, creativity in the artistic process is based, at least partially, on a function exchange between the mutual halves of the brain and on integration by the brain stem, which forms the link between the two brain halves (Fischer, 1970). When the creativity process takes place, the body and the brain are subjected to great stresses. In other words, a high level of interaction takes place with the old cerebral cortex structures, the mid-brain. At the same time, a change in the information process takes place, from the left-hand side, the 'intellectual' brain, to the right-hand side, the 'intuitive' brain.

According to Kläger, the insights described here should be used to decipher the creative process in mentally handicapped people. If, for one reason or another, the left-hand side of the brain is unable to fulfil its functions adequately, for example as a result of the use of drugs or alcohol or because of a chromosome deficiency, the right-hand side of the brain will function more autonomously. The increased physical subordination will activate the limbic system, in other words it will appeal to the brain activity around the central stem, which chiefly influences the emotional, motor behavioural pattern of the individual. At the same time, the reserve stock of general symbol formation and abstracting ability increases (Martindale, 1975).

Pictures produced from this stage are particularly difficult to decipher. Ultimately, the pictures will be completely inaccessible if the artist does not provide any spoken or written explanation. We may assume that the translation has taken place inadequately, if at all, or that the right-hand side of the brain has its own primitive processing.

Our intelligence and our understanding are directly dependent on our brain functions, which are very probably determined by hereditary factors. 'Wild' or 'raw' thought reveals itself in language and in conceptual art.

Handicap

The cause of mental deficiency lies in a defect in the cerebral cortex, caused by a defect in construction or by damage to the nerve tissue. In all cases, damage to this tissue leads to disruptions from a slight to a very severe nature in mental and often physical abilities too.

The assumption is now that the translating function of the left-hand side of the brain is limited in mentally handicapped people, in particular those with Down's syndrome. As a result of their limited abilities, these people are not able to establish a connection with the right-hand side of the brain which is in turn not activated. This specific handicap suppresses the usual tendency to want to explain and to codify. Moreover, the left-hand side of the brain fails in its task of producing understandable evaluations in a verbal way.

As a result of the lack of interaction between the two halves of the brain, or distorted interaction, visual thought and expression is influenced in a particular way. In this way, the 'raw' or 'wild' thought process will manifest itself in drawings and paintings and other forms of expression. The right-hand side of the brain is then put in a position to use the emotional forces supplied by the mid-brain. This old region of the brain, the brain stem, reacts typically and characteristically, as if everything were meaningful, as if nothing in the world were meaningless. It links everything to the I of the person, just as in dreams. All this results in a continually strengthening, albeit erratic, figurative distance between formal structure and the literal reference in the works of art produced. The works of art of mentally handicapped people often present us with problems when we attempt to understand and appreciate them.

The insights of researchers in the field of neuropsychology have been used by Kläger as a basis for assumptions which provide possibilities for explaining the creative ability. The findings of researchers such as Fischer and Gazzaniga provide indications for resolving the problem of deciphering visual language (Fischer, *op cit*; Gazzaniga, 1986).

If we suppose that mentally handicapped people lag behind in mental development, then we can and must conclude, fortunately, that an adult handicapped person with the mental age of a child is capable of symbolic and abstract thought.

Piaget assumes that symbolic thought – thinking without any deeper or actual significance – begins even before the third year of life. He believes that the development of thought progresses in phases, the order of which is fixed but the age at which that phase is achieved is not fixed; this depends on a variety of factors affecting the individual and their environment (Saunders-Woudstra, 1990; Piaget and Inhelder, 1972). He first of all identifies sensory-motor thought, a phase primarily involving the coordination of locomotion and observation and which last from birth to the age of two.

Pre-logical thought is a phase in which thought is not yet linked to reality, everything is still open and free and everything can be linked together, thought is fairly I-oriented: time, place and relationships do not yet play an interfering role. In this phase, human features are attributed to animals and objects (animism) and everything has a purpose, things live and living is associated with movement (anthropomorphism). In this type of thought, until approximately the seventh year, magic and reality are still intertwined, events are linked together and still have no isolated meaning (syncretism). An important phase in pre-logical thought is intuitive thinking, from approximately four to seven years. Objects are arranged on the basis of obvious details on the basis of the individual's observation [see llustration 6].

Concrete-logical thought, from seven to twelve years, is the phase during which an understanding of reality emerges. It is now possible to see and to make logical associations. Content, dimensions, gravity and similar concepts acquire a realistic meaning (principle of observation). Relationships between two or more objects can be made and order, quality and quantity can be tackled rationally.

Finally, Piaget identifies abstract thought – from twelve to fifteen years of age. This involves expectant thought, subtlety and problem-solving, almost scientific thinking – from the general to the particular. The abstraction ability is used to separate information from reality in order to compose new realities.

In Piaget's view, we must bear in mind that, although it provides a great deal of insight into the development of thought, it cannot adequately be applied to mentally handicapped people because phases of development are intertwined at various levels, such as mental, emotional, social and

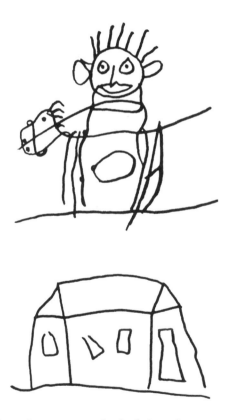

Illustration 6. The primary or pre-logical thought process: above, a horse and rider drawn by a four-year-old child; below, a house drawn by a six-year-old child; this house is a fine example of simultaneous perspective (taken from *Mamma ist ein Elephant,* Otto, F G Melin, 1979).

physical. The level of development between these areas can vary greatly from one to another. A mentally handicapped person who, in our eyes, operates socially at the level of the child, does have adult physical development and the associated experiences. This, in addition to the roles played by the unconscious and the hereditary, will strongly influence creation in the emotional and symbolic sense.

Arieti also talks of different types of cognition. He calls one of these amorphous cognition. Amorphous means without form; we could therefore talk of formless thought, not yet concrete and differentiated. This is a type of cognition which operates even in the first years of life and which exists separately from images, words, thoughts or actions. He places endocept - unconscious image and experience - alongside concept, conscious image. The endocept includes experiences which are not conscious and which exert indirect influence on the person. One way in which this formless thought can be expressed is via non-verbal media; artistic means are ideally suited. In this way, endocepts can be translated into meaningful symbols which can be observed by everyone and can lead to communication (Cimmermans, *op cit*).

Primitive structure

In the works of art of mentally handicapped people, continual interaction takes place between the meaning and emotional value of the picture. The enforcement of inner logic in visual thought is also characteristic, what we, in any event, observe is the surprising capacity of the handicapped person to transform shapes and meanings into genuine works of art.

Visual expression is characterised by a particular representational logic. This logic is a primitive structure of the visual thought capacity which has been associated with the development of early human nature and which is influenced by the processing method of the right-hand side of the brain. It can also be found in the artwork of children, the 'primitive art' of so-called outsiders and of consciously primitive artists.

A major problem in producing an artistic work is the conversion of the depiction of a three-dimensional experience or perception into a graphic presentation in a two-dimensional way. Observations, memories, experiences, feelings, dreams and the associated symbolic values must be converted into credible images. This is a high-level mental performance, requiring and employing all the psychological and motor forces (Kläger, 1984).

Illustration 7. Representation of an animal from Africa; a good example of the vital power of expression present in all people.

In order to understand and evaluate the artistic products and processes of the mentally handicapped, it is necessary to expose visual thought. The special artistic imagination has its origins in a type of thought based on an unusual way of observing. This thought has, as previously indicated, a general human origin, specifically the need present in man to express himself, the vital expressive power [see Illustration 7].

Imagination

In addition to expressive thought (Arnheim 1976), we can also talk of visually graphic and presentational thought (Langer 1965). According to more recent neuropsychological understanding, this thought is apparently based on the individual's own observational and the processing style of the right-hand side of the brain, which maintains a close association with the primitive structure and original function of the brain. Artistic imagination and expression are characterised here by a strong instinctiveness and definitely by less of a distinction from consciousness (Watzlawick, 1977).

One other important aspect of visual thought is the phenomenon of isomorphism or uniformity; in other words, evaluating the things of the world according to the similarity of properties of the shape. The artist creates a structural similarity between the symbol and the portrayal. This produces tendencies to merge meanings. These are expressed within a constant action and comparison. Comparisons come about through the application of relatively raw additions, comparisons in a hierarchic way within the merger of form and feeling, of shape and inner value.

Observation and the processing of observations are highly instinctive. This is also evident from the preference for expressing the faces and bodies of people in everyday situations. While we are busy being expressive, we do not reproduce what we see or believe we are seeing, but what we perceive while we are seeing!

Arnheim calls this portrayal of observation reproduction diagrams or observation models. These models are not learned, but are rather fixed spontaneously and through heredity. They are genuinely existent, global, simplified and fused together and are therefore not so easily labelled as understanding.

In the *Gestalt* theory, it is also assumed that visually absorbed information is organised into groupings or formations by the fundamental laws of perceptual, intellectual observation. Observation consists of the organisation of physiological, natural reactions into shapes. This organisation is innate and based on natural mechanisms and forces in the human brain. The most basic meaning of these shapes is the structure which they take. This structure is based on various laws of the organisation of observation and perception, such as unity, balance and association, for example. The onlooker is enabled, through these laws, to understand the meaningful structures or patterns. Arnheim calls these structures 'visual concepts of objects' and they have three qualities: they are three-dimensional, have a constant form and are not confined to projecting, such as plane or line aspects. Concept and perception, idea and perception are closely linked (Snoeren, *op cit*).

Creative observation forms the basis for idea formation and concept formation; they are the thought carriers. People think in images linked to experiences which they have stored in their memories over the years. This is the phenomenon of paradigms which was described earlier.

The depiction of the inner world is always associated with observation of the actual world. In most people, both natural observation and illustrative observation take place at the level of primary shape and structural perception and with differentiation and detail observation. As observation progresses from the general to the particular, in portrayal or expression, particularly where cognition is undeveloped or inadequately developed, man will in the first instance portray his world in global shapes and structures: a so-called 'simple' translation of reality which, however, this in no way represents. The global shapes and structures, universal images or as Jung said, archetypes, the unconscious primitive memories, have only partial detailing or differentiation, if any. However, since the pictures are reproduced in a highly simplified way and they are the carriers of the emotional perceptions and thoughts of the artist, they are often highly charged and full of symbolism. This effect is often further reinforced by the use of primary colours and shapes [see Illustration 8].

This method of observation and portrayal is correctly associated, by Arnheim and Kläger, with unconscious archaic clear thought, in other words with the way in which our prehistoric ancestors in ancient civilisation expressed themselves. As far as mentally handicapped people are concerned, we could say that unconscious archaic thought is not suppressed by the intellectual definition of development. This is the case in non-handicapped people, because reason occupies an important place in their conscious thought.

For this reason, an obvious similar development takes place in children and adult mentally handicapped people. In both groups, the fatal separation of global unity from form-symbol and feeling has not yet started. In children, we can see that a clear logic is visible in their drawing and painting up to primary school age. This logic displays a close similarity to that of mentally handicapped people in the intellectual and symbolic illustration of their world. This symbolic and emotional illustration is also central to some artistic eras, such as prehistoric art, what is known as primitivism, in some forms of naive painting and indigenous art, in some Cobra artists and individual artists, for example Miro, Klee and Picasso.

Concrete, exploratory visual thought makes it possible for children, the mentally handicapped and artists to change a three-dimensional reality of the world into shapes on a two-dimensional plane of a certain size, using

Illustration 8. 'Konijnepoep' (Rabbit droppings) by Ria Mul (40x50 cm).

expressive means. In this context, perspective drawing – with its caricatures which are culture-bound and which have to be learned – is entirely inapplicable. Kläger illustrates this using a quotation by Picasso, "If I want to paint a cup, then obviously I draw it round. But it may well be that the general degree of movement and the structure of the shape forces me to depict this roundness as square."

This quotation by Picasso shows that artists maintain just as special an access to archaic thought or that they can rediscover it. However, at the same time, they form part of a particular artistic tradition and thus can be distinguished from children and most mentally handicapped people. They expose themselves to the cultural spirit of the age and work with certain time-related techniques for the outside world.

Mentally handicapped creators, by contrast, seem to work undisturbed, not hampered by cultural standards, based on an original power of expression which is driven by intuition, not learned. If this ability is structurally stimulated by creating ideal conditions in space, resources, calm and acceptance, they too can achieve their own unmistakable style and artistic level and can be regarded as artists (Kläger, 1978).

Rationale

Nowadays, the rationale of the artworks of mentally handicapped people is derived, wrongly, from this relationship with the aforementioned artistic expressions. However, this relationship indicates only that the path along which expressive creative ability progresses in various times, cultures and people does not exclude identical processes. In all the artistic trends mentioned, in children's drawings and in the expressive work of mentally handicapped artists, the creative process develops from pre-logical, unconscious, archaic, clear thought. Kläger calls this *"urtümliches Gestaltdenken"*, which I have explained and described as "original power of expression" with respect to the works of art of mentally handicapped people.

Many experienced and trained artists of our time have consciously revived in the influence of the rational, cognitive, intellectual process in order to work and to paint on the basis of this original, archaic, unconscious world, which they refer to as primitive. The indication of parallels in the expressive world of these art forms is important for providing us with an insight into the way in which the power of expression is generated. Despite the similarities in the power of depiction of mentally handicapped artists, their work may not simply be referred to as Cobra, naive or primitive art.

The similarities I have described give an idea of relationship and expressive skill taking place at a recognisable level, as in the expressive work of the aforementioned artistic trends or cultural expressions. However, it would be over-simplifying to say that mentally handicapped artists only express themselves primitively or naively or that we want to determine the value of the expressive work by equating it with the work of, for example, the Cobra painters. This distracts from the importance of the impressive creative process of the mentally handicapped artist, as I described it as far back as 1984. The importance cannot only be determined by comparison or the link with so-called famous artists, but precisely through the individual value of the autonomous work of art itself, in the communicative and artistic sense.

It is also a misconception if we refer to the work as 'outsider art'. This is a terminology which is used for the works of art of artists who produce highly praiseworthy work but who often, for widely varying reasons, consciously remain aloof from social cultural life in society. It seems obvious to draw this parallel because the mentally handicapped person has long stayed aloof – quite against his or her will incidentally – from this social, cultural life.

Precisely through expressive work, the mentally handicapped person escapes from his withdrawn, secluded position and participates in life to the full. Integration into social life is therefore an aim much referred to in the various facilities. The expressive art of mentally handicapped people therefore has nothing to do with outsider art in terms of qualification. Being an outsider is merely a temporary phenomenon in the emancipatory process of the mentally handicapped artist. Appreciation of the works of art of the mentally handicapped person lies in the evaluation of the specific and unique artistic capacities which he or she displays. In other words, the yardstick for being an artist lies in the intentional method in creative expression and in the continuing expressive qualities of the work of the person – handicapped or not (van der Berg & Wouters, 1993).

Summary

The disadvantage of cognitive, intellectual people is that they constantly want to know and understand. For instance, I too have been preoccupied for years with the question of how people with a mental handicap can achieve such exceptionally artistic processes, how they possess this 'original' power of expression.

The essence of expressive thought lies to a large extent in the way in which our ancestors in prehistoric times were able to convert their perceptions and actions into images so that they obtained the possibility of communication. Creative willpower, present in rudimentary form in everyone, irrespective of any handicaps, is the source of primitive thought processes. The ability of everyone to represent the world in graphic, clear, composite forms is the underlying idea for expressive thought. Here, early thought is linked to the concept of 'primitive' which again means primary or 'original'.

Creative willpower ensures that personal expression takes place through a psychomotor activity controlled by the brain. That means that the creative impulses incite the brain to convert the regressive, chaotic, subconscious processes into a unity of observational concepts and pictorial forms and, through an executive action involving the hands and an artistic medium, to transform them into a picture.

In children and young adults, the cognitive and intellectual powers develop still further, as a result of which the verbal, formative illustration makes an increasingly explanatory meaning possible. This can be at the expense of the primitive early sentimental values, which do not have to be entirely lost, as long as they can be maintained. Put differently, if we assume that the fundamental primitive structures which make expressive thought and action possible are carried through from childhood to adulthood and that they are not completely dominated by the developing cognition and intelligence, then it is always possible to use these archaic structures again for individual expressive processes.

In mentally handicapped people whose cognitive and intellectual development is incomplete as a result of limited mental functions, either innate or acquired in early childhood, or as a result of their stunted development, this domination is barely present, if at all (van Germart et al, 1995). The vital formative power and expressive thought are thus much closer to the surface and are directly available.

Despite or precisely because of this cognitive, intellectual shortcoming, this artistic, creative power of expression manifests itself particularly clearly. 'As a result of the absence of the intellectual superstructure which controls the daily life of the average normal person, it seems to have released the realms of creativity' (Arnheim).

To take this even further, in the expressive field, this intellectually and - within the conventional meaning – communicatively handicapped person is closer to the origin of the artistic-symbolic meaning than the non-mentally handicapped person who has been unilaterally cognitively standardised by socialisation and education. This makes it possible for the mentally handicapped person, in all their directness and enthusiasm, to create an expressive world which is characterised by an original power of expression. This can create a form of communication which makes a considerable contribution to their participation in society and which brings the artist out into the open. For the mentally handicapped person it is a form of emancipation, to stand in the midst of life through art.

References

Arnheim, R (1976), *Visuelles Denken*

Arnheim, R (1978), 'Kunst und Sehen Eine Psychologie des Schopferischen Auges'

Boas, F (1955), *Primitive Art*, Dover Publications

Breeusman, G (1991), 'Een portret van het jonge kind als kunstenaar', in *De psycholoog*, 26, 3, March

Cimmermans, G (1990), 'Opvattingen over kreativiteit en de betekenis voor kreative therapie', in *Tijdschrift voor Kreative Therapie*, 1

Didier, M and Boogd, T (1992), 'Rare Kwasten', in *De groene Amsterdammer*, 11 March

Fischer, F (1970), Uber das Rhythmisch-ornamentale im Halluzinatorisch-schopferischen, *Conferentie Psychologie*, 13

Gazzaninga, M (1986), *Facts and fiction in brain asymmetry*, Symposium on symmetry in science and art Technische Hochschule Darmstadt, June

Hope, M (1990), *De psychologie van heit ritueel Verschijningsvormen, historie en betekenis van een wereldwijd fenomeen*, Bres

Jaffé, A (1982), 'De symboliek in de visuele kunsten', contribution to C G Jung, *De mens en zijn symbolen*, Lemniscaat

Kläger, M (1984), 'Beeldende uitdrukkingen, een fenomeen van de duidelijke logica, special imprint from *Geestelijke belemmeringen*, 4, (translation by Max Timmerman)

Kläger, M (1987), 'Gestalten aus dem Unbewussten', article in *Wir haben euch etwas zu sagen Bildnerisches Gestalten mit geistig Behinderten,* Bundesvereinigung Lebenshilfe für giestig Behinderte, EV Marburg und das Bayerische Nationalmuseum in München

Kläger, M (1987b), *Non Verbal thinking and the problems of decoding Exemplified by artworks of mentally retarded persons,* paper at the INSEA conference

Kühn, H (1952), Kühn's research into prehistoric art, in *Die Felsenbilder Europas*

Langer, S K (1965), *Philosophie auf neuem Wege*

Martindale, C (1975), *Romantic Progression,* The Psychology of literary history, Hemisphere

Piaget, J and Inhelder, B (1972), *De psychologie van het kind, Lemniscaat*

Prinzhorn, H (1922), *Bildnerei der Geisteskranken Ein Beitrag zur Psychologie und Psychopathologie der Geltaltung,* 'Die Prinzhorn-Sammlung'

Rooskens, A (1994), 'Het Jungle avontuur', quotation from Rooskens, A (1994), *De A van Cobra,* Leo Duppen

Sanders-Woudstra, J A R (1990), 'Zwakzinningheid', Chapter 5 of *Leerboek kinder – en jeugdpsychiatrie* Van Gorcum

Snoeren, H (1993), *Van tekenen en van schilderen – het beeldend werk van verstandelijk gehandicapten,* Doctoral thesis General Arts, University of Utrecht

Springer, S and Deutsch, G (1981), *Left Brain, Right Brain*

Thévoz, M (1990), 'Art Brut', *Kunst jenseits der Kunst,* AT Verlag

van Dort, M M (1981), 'Psychologische aspecten van creativiteit', in *Intermediair*, 17, 23, June

van den Berg, E and Wouters, M (1993), *Impressies van het symposium 'Kunst of gunst',* Report of the forum discussion, Chapter 4, NGBZ & Stichting, Agora

van Gemert, G H *et al* (1985), *Leerboek zwakzinnigenzorg*

van Praag, H (1971), 'Kreativiteit, een inleidende beschouwing', in: *Intermediair*

Watzlawick, P (1977), *Die Moglichkeit des Andersseins,* Huber

Addendum

Interview with Max van de Bruinhorst

Studios: Sterrenberg, Huis ter Heide

What is interesting in Max's work is the clear development in his expressive ability. His first drawings depicted primitive, archetypal and organic shapes. Within the technical process, he experimented by printing the stencils on top of each other, thus producing a double effect. This was how the picture 'Organische vormen' (Organic shapes), dating from 1977, was produced. From a technical and content point of view, he works entirely independently, which is no mean feat when it comes to the technique of stencil printing.

Over a process lasting many years, geometric shapes gradually emerge, which form a functional unit, together with clear plant images. One example of this is the stencil print entitled 'Vaas met bloemen' (Vase with flowers) from 1979.

This are intermediate forms which ultimately lead to the wholly abstract, most asymmetrical and geometric illustrations, consisting entirely of circles, triangles, rectangles and squares.

During drawing, the preliminary studies for the stencil printing and while painting, Max has only an roughly preconceived idea of what he wants to depict. The design emerges as he works. Particularly when painting, he changes the design constantly.

His abstract paintings always contain figurative elements which, despite the level of abstraction, are clearly recognisable. A clear example of this can be seen in the large painting entitled 'Abstract/figuratief' (Abstract/figurative) from 1991. In it, he depicts a bird with a beak and a fish, surrounded by colours and flowers. We can also see a brown animal in the background. "Drawing well is simply something inside me," explains Max, "and inside my memory. Let me put it this way, I am an artist!" The huge quantity of stencil prints, drawings and paintings he has produced since 1976 confirm this statement. His process of expression surprises us every time because various developments succeed each other. For instance, he goes from figurative, realistic to abstraction, only to add figurative and realistic image elements once again. Max develops his power of expression in the studios in consistent continuity. He fully explores various subjects, such as the series of flowers, vases, vase with flowers, teapots, harlequins and geometric representations. This produces amazing series of works of art on one subject, with a clear progression of style and illustration.

'Organische vormen', - 1977, 29x37.5cm.

'Vaas met bleomen', 1979, 20x19.8cm.

Developments in the way in which he depicts the subjects can be particularly clearly observed. Large or small stencil prints and paintings are no problem for him; rather, they present a new challenge. For instance, in 1992, he produced a few enormous billboard paintings measuring two by four metres. The showing at the 'Project 12' exhibition in Utrecht was extremely colourful.

His work is permanently represented in the Sterrenberg art library and Very Special Arts Nederland. It has been seen at many exhibitions all over the world, including in Brazil, Belgium, the UK, Germany, Taiwan, America and the Netherlands.

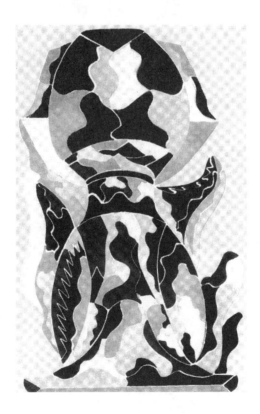

'Dubbele vase', 1990, 65x55cm, stencil print.

'Abstract', 1983, 41x28.5cm.   'Bleomen', 1978, 34x43cm.

'De klomp met bloemen', 1994, 57x40cm.

Chapter 8

Education for all young children

Dale Goldhaber and Jeanne Goldhaber

Introduction

The provision of educational services to young children from birth to age eight with special needs in the United States has undergone a significant transformation over the past 25 years. This transition has reflected changes in the social fabric of the nation, specific federal legislation relating to children with special needs and the continuing debate over best educational practices. To understand the current situation with respect to the education of young children with special needs requires an understanding of each of these three changes.

Before we begin a discussion of these three changes however, an important caveat is in order. Education in the United States is very much a local matter. Although there certainly are both federal and state level laws, mandates and guidelines designed to regulate the provision of educational services, the actual character and quality of these services reflect the particulars of each local school district and often even the particulars of each school within a school district. The character and quality of educational services within a district is in turn, to a large degree, a reflection of the financing of the school district.

School finance is based primarily on the property values of the homes and businesses in each community. Property-rich communities are able to provide more money for their schools than poor communities even though, ironically, the property tax rate may actually be lower in the rich community than the poor community. This funding inequity across school districts can be very striking. Suburban communities can often have twice the per-pupil expenditure than a neighbouring urban community (Kozol, 1991).

This funding inequity is now the focus of many legal challenges in state courts. A few state courts have already mandated that the property tax, as a means to finance education, is unconstitutional since it is inherently unfair. Legislatures in these states have been forced to draft 'Robin Hood' style equal funding legislation to resolve the issue. Such legislation has, in turn, led to court challenges from property-rich communities attempting to reverse the new legislation. This issue of funding is far from resolved in any of the 50 states and is likely to continue to be one of the major educational battlegrounds for the coming years. This issue of the inequity in educational funding, coupled with the regulation of education residing in the local community, makes clear why discussions of national trends must always be interpreted cautiously.

The changing social fabric of the United States

It is often hard to pinpoint when social changes begin to occur but the year 1954 does serve as a significant milestone since it marks the United States Supreme Court decision in the matter of Brown vs The Board of Education. The court, in its decision, ruled that the 'separate but equal' laws that had made racial segregation in the schools legal since the Civil War 100 years earlier were unconstitutional. The court agreed with the argument that to be separate made one inherently unequal and therefore was a violation of the equal rights provisions of the Constitution.

The ruling that racial segregation in education was unconstitutional had two additional consequence besides the legal requirement that schools be desegregated. The first consequence was that the court's decision made clear the more general precedent that actions on the part of the federal government concerning educational practice can take precedence over state law and custom. The second consequence was that the court's decision also established the legal precedent to consider the legality of both explicit and implicit 'separate but equal' practices involving groups defined in terms of characteristics other than race. The social, political and legal actions which have occurred in the United States since Brown vs The Board of Education have been to remove the legal barriers and social practices which have restricted individuals' access to equal opportunity.

By the 1960s the focus of efforts to establish equal opportunity broadened to include the issue of segregation due to economic disadvantage. This effort was reflected in the War on Poverty of the administration of President Lyndon Johnson and perhaps has its most visible continuing legacy in the form of Project Head Start. Mallory (1994) describes this broadening of social welfare policy as having a focus on reducing 'cultural disadvantage'.

'The guiding assumption seemed to be that children belonging to minority groups were inherently disadvantaged, or deprived, in comparison to children growing up in white, middle-class families. This generalization has obvious stigmatizing consequences. While efforts were made in later years to emphasize *economic* (italics in original) disadvantage rather than *cultural* (italics in original), in order to reduce the judgmental aspects of the latter, the notion of 'bootstrapping' minorities into the mainstream culture remains an implicit goal of social policy'. (p 45)

More recent efforts to provide equal opportunity for all have focused on matters of gender equity, equal opportunity and practice irrespective of sexual orientation and, of greater relevance to this discussion, on matters of equal educational opportunity for children with special educational needs. Although in all of these cases it is important to recognize that the United States is still far from its goal of equal opportunity for all of its citizens, it is nevertheless significantly closer in law, practice and attitude toward achieving this goal than it was in 1954.

Legislation relating to children with special educational needs

It is useful again to make use of a specific date to mark a transition. In this instance the date is the year 1975 and the transition is the passage of public law (PL) 94-142, which mandated the free, appropriate education for all children with special educational needs in the least restrictive environment. But, as was true in the case of Brown *vs* The Board of Education, law and practice are not always synonymous. In the first case, PL 94-142 did not require states to provide free, appropriate educational services to children below the age of six. This exclusion was corrected in 1986 with the passage of PL 99-457 which broadened the educational mandate to include all individuals between the ages of three and 21 who either have a diagnosed disability or who demonstrate a 'developmental delay' or are seen 'at risk for a developmental delay'. The law also provided funding for services to children under the age of three who have conditions likely to lead to developmental and educational disabilities (Bergen, 1997; Mallory, *op cit*).

Even though the passage of these two laws firmly established the concept of free, appropriate education for all children in the least restrictive environment, states (and in practice even local school districts) were left the responsibility to define what an 'appropriate' educational experience was for a child with special educational needs and what 'a least restrictive environment' actually is for such children. Bergen (*op cit*) provides a good description of how these terms were interpreted from 1975 to the early 1990s.

'As identification and placement decisions began to be made by schools, and in response to the way restricted funding sources were accessed, there was often a limited set of options available for child placement. Options may or may not have included receiving service within the regular classroom, but usually placement was in a separate classroom within existing school buildings. Even this 'inclusion' in the same building was initially considered a potentially traumatic change because, before that time, children with disabilities were rarely even seen by typical children. For the past 20 years, special education placements have been primarily in these self-containing settings staffed by teachers trained to work specifically with children who had been identified as having a particular type of disability (*e.g.* learning disabled, multi-handicapped). Although some of these children were 'mainstreamed' into regular art, music and other classes for part of the day, their basic instruction took place in separate or segregated settings'.

(p 159)

So, by the late 1980s, even though the necessary enabling legislation was in place to provide a free appropriate education to all children in the least restrictive environment, actual practices in most districts fell short of this goal. School districts often argued that full inclusion was not always in the best interest of children with special needs, that the nature of their special needs often required more specialized placements. Courts often upheld this interpretation of the law.

This continuing segregation was particularly evident in early childhood programmes. Since schools are not required to provide instruction for children under the age of five, locally-funded early education for typical children is very rare. Early education programmes which receive state or federal funds are always targeted for a particular population. Early childhood programmes catering to typical children are almost always funded solely by parents, through private fundraising and through subsidies in the case of employer-sponsored early childhood programmes. The two rarely overlap since private early childhood programmes have, in practice, not been held to the same accountability under these laws as have public school systems. As a result, there often are no 'least restrictive environments' available for most special needs children under the age of five because there are no publicly-funded classrooms for typical children. The consequence has been that children with special educational needs receive services in essentially segregated settings, sometimes with one or two 'peer models' added, through home and clinic-based services or, more rarely, by having these children placed in local, private early childhood programmes.

The decade of the 1990s has witnessed an increasing effort to make the free, appropriate education for all in the least restrictive environment concept a reality for all young children with special educational needs. This effort has been spearheaded by parents who have found themselves needing to become more politically and legally active to ensure that their children receive what they believe to be the full benefits of the special education laws, and by a growing number of educators who want nothing less than the elimination of special educational services and the inclusion of all children in regular education classrooms. These radicalizing educators (Fuch & Fuch, 1994; Stainback & Stainback, 1992) argue that a distinct special education system within the school system reflects the same 'separate but equal' logic found unconstitutional in 1954. They further argue that fully integrated classrooms would force regular classroom teachers to better appreciate the diversity inherent in all classrooms and therefore practice a more individualized approach to learning for all children. They also argue that such fully-integrated classrooms are of greater potential benefit to all children since all children would develop a greater appreciation for diversity.

Whereas the debate in the 1970s and 1980s focused on legislation mandating appropriate practice in the least restrictive environment, the debates in the 1990s have focused on the theoretical and practical issues involved in making such a goal reality. There are two aspects to this debate. The first concerns the identification of the best setting in which to educate children with special educational needs, *ie*, are there times when full inclusion is not in the best interests of the child? The second aspect of the debate concerns the nature of the instruction most appropriate to providing a suitable education to children with special educational needs. Are the instructional practices common to regular classrooms appropriate for children with special needs as well?

Best educational practices for all young children

The Question of Placement

Few educators today argue for the total segregation of children with special educational needs. The real issue is the degree of integration. More to the point, the real question is whether or not children with special educational needs can have all of their particular needs met within the routines of a regular education classroom (Bergen, *op cit*; Demchak & Drinkwater, 1992; Diamond, Hestenes, & O'Connor, 1994; Dugger-Wadsworth, 1997; Miller, 1992).

Proponents of partial inclusion recognize the importance of the peer socialization experiences that inclusion provides but also express concern that, given the reality of regular public education, children with special needs are less likely to have their particular needs met than they would by spending at least part of the day in a self-contained classroom. Their concerns focus on three issues. First, since most regular classroom teachers have limited preparation and experience in working with special needs children (Miller, *op cit*), there is the concern that these teachers are less able to meet children's special needs. And, because they are less able, perhaps they will be put off by children's special needs and therefore they will be less inclined to make the extra effort to meet those needs.

Second, the current educational and political climate in the United States is for higher standards and achievement. Competency-based testing and accountability have become the latest 'buzz words'. Teachers are feeling increasing pressure from all sides to make sure that their students are able to pass grade specific exams. In such a pressured climate, having the time to meet the needs of those who may be the least skilled or the most challenging in the class is seen as a significant problem.

Third, most teachers report that given the financial limitations that exist in many school districts, they feel overwhelmed meeting the educational needs of a typical functioning group, much less one also including children with special needs. Proponents for partial inclusion also argue that it is equally likely that children with special needs will not be readily accepted by their peers. Such rejection is seen as further damaging a potentially already shaky sense of self.

Proponents of full inclusion argue that if children are going to learn to function in the mainstream as adults, a clear social policy value, then education needs to begin as early as possible in a full inclusion programme.

They cite the potential value of inclusion in terms of positive peer relations and the development of appropriate social skills. They also argue that a well-designed inclusive classroom can be as effective in promoting academic achievement as a segregated classroom. Proponents also argue that full inclusion is an equally valuable experience for typically functioning children since it provides them a greater appreciation of diversity and opportunities for nurturance. In addition, full inclusion proponents argue that, since the evaluations used to place children in special education classes are far from perfect, a full inclusion policy removes the potential for misdiagnosis.

This issue of misdiagnosis is a significant political and social issue since a disproportionate number of children from racial and ethnic minorities in the United States find themselves placed in special education programmes. Full inclusion proponents argue that this disproportionate placement rate suggests that what are often interpreted as deficiencies on the child's part may in fact be failures on society's part to first, provide full opportunity for all of its citizens and second, to recognize and value cultural diversity. In effect, proponents for full inclusion are making the argument that all children, irrespective of their particular circumstances, are more like each other than they are different from each other and as such can all benefit equally well from a common educational experience.

Full inclusion proponents working with children under the age of six are also quick to note that the structure of the early childhood classroom is significantly different than that of the primary grade classroom, and therefore at least at the birth to age six range, the concerns of the partial inclusion advocates may have less weight. Early childhood classrooms are more likely to have a heterogeneous age grouping. Early childhood teachers, having been educated to develop a child-centered curriculum, are better able to design curricula to meet the individual needs of children. Moreover, the teacher-students ratios in early education classes are typically better. In other words, to the extent that the partial inclusion arguments have merit, they do so primarily at the primary grade level (grades 1 through 3). Consider how Bergen (*op cit*) frames the distinction:

'Implementing inclusion is often a different matter for teachers in early childhood classrooms at the kindergarten and primary grade levels, because the teacher's structural constraints, personal resources, and instructional methods differ. For example, teachers rarely have even one other adult in the classroom even though there may be 25-30 children in the class. Moreover, there has been increasing pressure on these teachers to focus on getting every child in the class to meet a certain level of performance, regardless of their special needs, learning modalities or developmental status. Thus, although individual teachers may wholeheartedly embrace a developmentally appropriate philosophy, they may still be subjected to external pressures from state-mandated proficiency tests beginning at the primary grade level and subsequent directives from administrators to meet standard test score criteria'. (p 157-8)

Given the nature of the arguments in the debate over inclusion, it is possible to consider the proponents of the partial inclusion as realists and the proponents of full inclusion as dreamers. It is equally possible however to consider the proponents of partial inclusion as pessimists and the proponents of full inclusion as optimists. Which perspective you take depends on your belief as to the likelihood that the regular education classroom can in fact meet all of the educational needs of special children. The answer to this question, in turn, depends upon your belief as to the types of instructional strategies that are more effective in working with children with special educational needs.

The question of practice

Perhaps because regular and special education have been practiced as distinct endeavours, their instructional strategies have also come to differ. It is actually this question of instructional strategies that is at the heart of the debate over full inclusion of children with special educational needs into the regular education classroom, since debates about inclusion are debates over whether instruction in the regular classroom can as equally meet the needs of special as typical children.

Best practices in special education

Instructional strategies within the separate special education classroom have two defining characteristics. First, the focus is on the child's disabilities (Dugger-Wadsworth, *op cit*; Mallory, 1992; Mallory, *op cit*; Novick, 1993). Second, the intervention strategies are more often than not very behavioural in nature (Atwater, Carta, Schwartz, & McConnell, 1994; Carta, Atwater, Schwartz, & McConnell, 1993; Carta, Schwartz, Atwater, & McConnell, 1991; Strain, McConnell, Carta, & Fowler, 1992). One does not necessarily preordain the other but, in practice, the two are closely intertwined.

Special education as a distinct educational effort exists to deal with particular problems, disabilities, and/or deficiencies in children. As such, special educators have typically seen their mandate as different from that of the regular educator. This distinctiveness is further heightened by legislative mandates defining the focus of special education intervention, the mandates of the funding supporting special education, and both the professional preparation and practice of those providing services to children with special educational needs. The sum of these defining characteristics is that special education practice has typically been categorical in structure and has focused on eliminating, or at least reducing, the gap between children with special needs and others with respect to one or more specific, definable characteristics. Such an orientation reflects the categorical, bureaucratic nature of the service delivery systems in the United States. Each disease, disability, deficiency, problem, *etc* has its own funding sources and often its own educational systems and practitioners. It is the 'medical model'. In such a system, it is not uncommon to find a child with multiple problems having several service providers, each focused on a particular aspect of the child's disability and each offering an intervention strategy specific to their area of interest and expertise.

Within the United States, the most common approach to meeting the mandate of special education has been the behavioural model as it has evolved through the early work of Watson (1930), Skinner (1938 and 1984), and Bijou and Baer (Baer 1973; Baer, Wolf, & Risley 1987; Bijou 1979; Bijou 1989; Bijou & Baer 1978). The defining element of a behavioural model is the contingent relationship that comes to exist between a response and its consequences. With respect to children with special educational needs, this concept forms the basis for the planning of specific, deliberate, usually adult defined and regulated, interventions in which specific desired behaviours on the part of the child are systematically shaped through the use of contingent reinforcement until some predefined level of proficiency is obtained. The process is individual and highly quantitative.

Competency is typically defined in terms of a child demonstrating a behaviour at the appropriate time and place and in a prescribed manner on a certain high percentage of the times the request for the behaviour is made. Because the focus of the interventions is always domain specific, attainment of any particular goal then leads to a new intervention within the same domain toward a still higher level of competence. In other words, once the child is able to reliably demonstrate one word responses at the adult-defined appropriate time, the goal then becomes the demonstration of two word responses, and so on. There is clearly a focus and sense of urgency in these efforts which reflect both the need to demonstrate the efficacy of their efforts and provide what behaviourists consider the best educational services possible. They are quick to point out that they do not enjoy what they see as the 'luxury' of the more relaxed approach typical of regular classroom teaching.

Instructional practices in regular classrooms depend to a large degree on grade level. Early childhood classrooms typically have a different approach to instruction than primary grade classrooms. Kindergartens usually fall somewhere in between the two extremes, depending largely on the educational approach of the district and each school within that district. Since the question of full inclusion is largely a question of whether or not the regular classroom curriculum can be effective in meeting the education needs of special children, there are potentially really two answers to the question of placement. Not only are there two answers but they are in fact very different. That the two answers are so different reflects the fact that early childhood education and primary level education have even less overlap in the United States than do regular and special education. We shall address each answer in turn.

Best practices in the regular primary grade classroom

Full inclusion of children with special educational needs into the regular primary grade classroom is at present not an easily accomplished goal in the United States (Krogh, 1997). Regular education in the United States most often involves a single teacher working with 20 to 30 approximately same-age children in a self-contained classroom. The curriculum is primarily defined in terms of academic subject matter (math, language arts, science *etc*) and increasingly, primary grade teachers are being asked to teach to a set of externally-defined academic standards and are increasingly being held fully accountable for their students' test scores on measures of these externally-defined standards. There is little room in the curriculum to meet the unique needs of individual children, to focus on issues of socialization and peer relations or to introduce teacher-defined subject matter. Increasingly teachers in the United States report that they feel that they have no choice but to 'teach to the test'.

In such an educational climate, a child with special needs is clearly an outsider, one not easily integrated into the mainstream of the classroom. When children with special needs are found in regular education classrooms, they are often there with part or full time aides (depending on the child's needs). These aides are poorly paid and rarely have any formal preparation in either special or regular education. Rather than serving as an aide to the teacher so that the teacher can more easily accommodate the needs of all of the children in the class, aides more typically function solely in relationship to one child. Their primary task is to help the child implement his or her special curriculum, a curriculum often neither similar to that of the other children nor created by that child's regular classroom teacher. In effect, the child is in the classroom but not part of the class.

Although there is clear pressure from many levels to more fully integrate children, especially as a way to control special education budgets, the reality is that the regular classroom teacher is given little, if any, additional support to make a true inclusion possible, much less successful. In fact, as noted above, those who argue for full inclusion at the primary level do so as much in the belief that such a move will force drastic changes in regular primary level instruction as they do out of a belief in the best interests of children with special educational needs. Unfortunately, given the current emphasis on standards-based achievement, such a radical shift is unlikely. However, if there is anything that characterizes educational practice in the United States, it is its fadishness. It is quite possible that the educational winds will blow in a very different direction in the coming years and that successful full inclusion at the primary level will become a realistic goal. It is also likely that this fully inclusive classroom of the future will look remarkably like most early childhood education classrooms of today.

Best practices in the early childhood classroom

The issue of inclusion at the early childhood level is a very different matter. In the first place, the structure of the early childhood classroom is usually very different than that of the primary level classroom. The early childhood classroom is more likely to be multi-age in composition, to have a better teacher-student ratio and to focus on social/emotional as well as academic topics. In addition, the curriculum tends to be presented in an integrated fashion and the teacher's preparation more likely involves both knowledge of families and work with children with special needs. All of these elements reflect an approach to early childhood education which is known as 'developmentally appropriate practice' (DAP) (Bredekamp, 1987; Bredekamp & Copple, 1997; Bredekamp & Rosegrant, 1992). DAP has come to be the focus of discussions on full inclusion in part because the approach does lend itself to working with a broad range of children and because the curriculum revisions recommended for the primary grades tend to look very much like DAP.

DAP is not a prescribed curriculum. Rather it is a set of educational guidelines which reflect the application of child development principles, most notably those consistent with the developmental theories of Jean Piaget (Piaget, 1952; Piaget, 1964; Piaget, 1970; Piaget, 1978/1985; Piaget & Inhelder, 1969) and Lev Vygotsky (Vygotsky, 1962; Vygotsky, 1978; Vygotsky, 1997; Vygotsky & Luria, 1993).

Vygotsky's theory, rooted within the sociocultural context and proceeding in a direction of increasingly effective use of sign and tool systems, and Piaget's theory, rooted in a dialectic process of successive knowledge constructions at increasingly more abstract and integrated levels, provide a framework for design, implementation and assessment of educational experiences.

Notwithstanding their theoretical differences, Piaget and Vygotsky do nevertheless offer very similar views as to the characteristics of mature adult development. In both cases, the emphasis is on the differentiation of form from content, the effective use of metacognitive skills to self-regulate action and thought, and the recognition of the probable as a special case of the possible. For both, the attainment of these mature adult thought characteristics is the fruition of a sequence of qualitatively distinct reconstructions of an individual's cognitive or meaning making mechanisms.

Further, for both, progress through this sequence is strongly influenced by the quality of one's social and non-social interactions. There may be important differences between the two perspectives as to the specifics of the mechanisms regulating development, but both are clear as to the interactive nature of the process.

Even the points of divergence between Piaget and Vygotsky can been seen as complementary elements in the foundation of a developmentally appropriate approach to education. Four are worthy of note. The first is the relative emphasis that each placed on the importance of reciprocal and complementary relationships (Goldhaber, 1986; Goldhaber, 2000) in fostering the course of development. Vygotsky's perspective places greater emphasis on complementary relationships; that is to say, those in which the rights, competence and responsibilities of one participant are different from those of the other(s). Complementary interactions define the exchanges that Vygotsky saw as occurring within the 'zone of proximal development'. Piaget placed greater emphasis on reciprocal relationships. Reciprocal relationships are between equals. Each participant shares the same rights, competence and responsibilities as the other.

The second difference reflects the belief each held about the degree of continuity across developmental domains. Piaget's model leads one to expect a high degree of continuity across developmental domains; Vygotsky's theory makes no such claim. Piaget argued that this interdomain continuity reflected the fact that children at any particular developmental level apply the same set of cognitive operations to all tasks. Any developmental differences that might exist between domains, circumstances that Piaget referred to as horizontal decalages, were not a function of the child's developmental level but rather a reflection of situational circumstances, including the specifics of a task (Goldhaber, 1981). Interdomain discontinuity is a more likely prediction within Vygotsky's theory since there is no necessary reason to expect that the contextual origins of sign and symbol systems would be uniform across subject matter domains.

Third, the theories differ in terms of the universality of developmental patterns. Piaget's theory, with its strong evolutionary base and its focus on 'species typical' patterns, argues for a view of development that transcends social place and historical time. Vygotsky's theory does not oppose this conceptualization but instead argues that the course and content of development is largely a reflection of the particular social structure in which that development occurs. This contextualist belief is perhaps most clearly reflected in Vygotsky's efforts, across the span of one generation, to introduce the symbol systems of formal literacy into a rural agrarian society in central Russia (Vygotsky, 1978).

Finally, Piaget and Vygotsky differ as to the process by which new knowledge is acquired and old knowledge restructured. For Piaget, the process is largely a constructive effort; for Vygotsky, it is portrayed as a process of co-construction. For Piaget, construction occurs internally as individuals continuously attempt to make meaning out of their everyday experiences through the processes of organization and equilibration (Piaget, 1978/1985). For Vygotsky, the co-construction of knowledge occurs as a social process, both in terms of the creation of new sign and symbol systems and the internalization of these co-constructed systems of meaning making (Rogoff, 1990).

Fundamental to DAP is the concept that effective educational practice must be based on an understanding of children's level of development as well as those characteristics typical of the child's cultural heritage and those idiosyncratic to each child. As Krogh (1997) describes it, 'The challenge for teachers is to create curricula that match each child's developing abilities while also providing the right level of challenge and interest'. (p 32).

To accomplish this challenge, teachers practicing DAP develop broad-based, integrated curricula incorporating many subject matter domains, allowing for multiple means of expressing uncertainty and competence and responding to all aspects of a child's developmental makeup (*ie*, physical/motor, cognitive, social and emotional). The development of these curricula is not arbitrary or adult predefined but rather is based on teachers' systematic observation of children's interests and investigations. These observations lead to the teacher's providing concrete, meaningful opportunities to explore ideas, materials and relationships which are designed to both further the child's development and meet the educational objectives of that setting. In some cases, these opportunities might involve direct interaction with an adult, in others, cooperative interactions with other children and, in still others, individual investigation of some material or setting. All three forms of engagement are seen as having equal educational value.

DAP and children with Special Educational Needs

The Concerns

Special educators who favor partial inclusion strategies tend to be sceptical about the ability of DAP to meet children's special needs (Atwater, *et al*, 1994; Carta, *et al*, 1993; Dugger-Wadsworth, *op cit*).

They typically mention four problems. First, special educators express concern about the ability of a DAP curriculum to allow the necessary frequent and exacting assessment that many special education mandates require. Second, they express concern that DAP is not designed to accelerate the rate of development, that is to reduce the gap between the developmental level of typical children and those with special educational needs. This issue of acceleration is also discussed in terms of the need to ensure that children with special needs are ready to function effectively in the public school setting. Atwater, Carta, Schwartz and McConnell (1994) express this concern about the appropriateness of acceleration:

'From the DAP perspective, this practice, especially as it applies to school environments, sometimes has been interpreted as an inappropriate downward shifting of academic standards from elementary grades to the preschool and kindergarten levels. From the ECSE perspective, however, preparation for the next environment directly serves the goal of facilitating a child's progress through a natural succession of inclusive educational environments. Because we, as interventionists, want children to flourish in those environments, we place importance on preparing the children and the environment in advance. Children with special needs often have problems with major educational transitions (*eg*, from home-based interventions to preschool, from preschool to kindergarten to first grade), because they have not had sufficient opportunity to learn and practice skills that will be expected in the future environment. (p 191)

DAP proponents counter with the argument that special educators often incorrectly equate DAP with maturationally based Programmes and as such many of the concerns that are expressed are inappropriate. Consider the comments of Johnson and Johnson (1992):

'The developmental approach, in contrast to the academic or maturational approach, is the third prevailing force in ECE and takes a contextualized, holistic view of the child and asks not what the child *can* learn but what *should* and *do* children learn. The teacher must be an astute observer of children's activities and behavior in all areas of the curriculum, understand the curricula area and development of the child in relation to the curricular area, and provide for learning opportunities accordingly. A balance is sought between teacher-led or convergent-thinking activities and child-initiated or divergent activities. The teacher does not accommodate to the child all the time in all ways, nor, on the other hand, expect of the child overly rigid adherence to the task or what might be called the teacher's agenda. (p 443)

Third, there is concern that what is seen as a play-based, self-directed approach to learning cannot guarantee the types of systematic, deliberate interventions that an adult-directed programme can provide. Special educators see this issue as particularly relevant for children who, at least initially, need a high rate of contingent reinforcement to initiate and maintain new behaviors and who need a highly structured and deliberate presentation of learning materials. Fourth, special educators express concern that DAP does not easily accommodate itself to the work of special service providers, such as physical therapists and speech and language teachers.

The solutions

In all likelihood, the commitment to providing a free, appropriate education to all children in the least restrictive environment will continue in the United States. The law is clear about this mandate and the costs of maintaining two separate educational enterprises, one for special children and one for typical children, is simply prohibitive. The question then becomes how can full inclusion be accomplished so that the developmental and educational needs of all children are most likely to be met. There does seem to be a shared consensus that DAP can serve as the foundation for inclusionary programmes at the early childhood level and that if inclusion is to be successful at the primary level, a 'DAP-like' curriculum will also need to be established at this level. For such an integration to be successful at both the early childhood and primary level, there will need to be a recognition on the part of both special and regular educators that the efforts of the other are equally legitimate to your own, and therefore both efforts need to be included for any inclusionary programmes to be successful. Accomplishing this integration will require that special educators recognize that a 'developmentally appropriate' classroom is equally appropriate for all children and that regular educators recognize that meeting the needs of children with special educational needs might require a higher degree of deliberateness.

This mutual recognition has six components. In the first place all educators need to recognize that children, like adults, function in an effective, rather than an objective, environment (Futterweit & Ruff, 1993; Krogh, op cit; Ludlow & Berkeley, 1994). That is, consistent with both Piaget and Vygotsky (Goldhaber & Goldhaber, 1996; Goldhaber, J, & Capone, 1998), we construct meaning out of our understanding of our experiences. These constructions resemble, but are never an exact copy of, either 'reality' or the constructions of others. Ideally, these experiences should be ones most consistent with our knowledge about child development. In particular, these environments need to be natural settings for children, not artificial or clinical in nature. For interventions to be maximally effective, they need to occur in a child's natural environment (Berkeley & Ludlow, 1992; Ludlow & Berkeley, 1994).

Second, the design of interventions within a natural environment cannot focus on one behavioural domain but must be holistic in structure (Berkeley & Ludlow, *op cit*). Our understanding of children's development tells us that focusing exclusively on a child's cognitive development or a child's social development may actually be counterproductive since activity in each developmental domain influences that in other domains.

Third, effective intervention must make full use not only of the direct efforts of the teacher but also of the role peers can play in motivating and facilitating children's activity (Guarlnick, 1993) and in the physical arrangement of the environment as a prompt or scaffold for children's investigations (Berk & Winsler, 1995).

Fourth, assessments must be authentic. That is, they must sample through deliberate observation and documentation naturally-occurring episodes of children's competence. Authentic assessment is a much more valid form of assessment since it measures the child's behaviour when the child is fully engaged in an activity (Bergen, *op cit*).

Fifth, special service providers, such as physical therapists and speech and language therapists, must function as consultants to the classroom teacher rather than as direct service providers to children physically removed from the classroom. Such a strategy will increase the likelihood that the child's special needs will be met in a natural setting and also increases the frequency of these special interventions since they can potentially occur throughout the school day (Bergen, *op cit*; Goldhaber, *et al*, 1998).

Finally, full inclusion for children must also mean full inclusion for prospective teachers. Separate teacher preparation programmes for regular and special educators must merge so that all teachers acquire the confidence and skills necessary to work with all children (Miller, *op cit*).

Bibliography

Atwater, J B, Carta, J J, Schwartz, I S, and McConnell, S R (1994), Blending developmentally appropriate practice and early childhood special education, in B Mallory & R S New (Eds), *Diversity and developmentally appropriate practices,* Teachers College Press (pp 185-201)

Baer, D M (1973), The control of developmental process: Why wait? in J R Nesselroade and H W Reese (Eds), *Life-span developmental psychology: Methodological issues,* Academic Press (pp 187-196)

Baer, D M, Wolf, M M, and Risley, T R (1987), Some still current dimensions of applied behavioural analysis, *Journal of Applied Behavioural Analysis*, Vol 20, (pp 313-327)

Bergen, D (1997), Perspectives on inclusion in early childhood education, in J Isenberg and M R Jalongo (Eds), *Major trends and issues in early childhood education*, Teachers College Press (pp 151-171)

Berk, L E, and Winsler, A (1995), *Scaffolding children's learning: Vygotsky and Early Childhood Education*, National Association for the Education of Young Children

Berkeley, T R, and Ludlow, B L (1992), Developmental domains: The mother of all interventions; or, The subterranean early development blues, *Topics in Early Childhood Special Education*, 11 (4), (pp 13-21)

Bijou, S W (1979), Some clarifications on the meaning of a behavioural analysis of child development, *The Psychological Record*, 29, (pp 3-13)

Bijou, S W (1989), Behavioural analysis, in R Vasta (Ed.), *Annals of child development*, JAI Press (pp 61-84)

Bijou, S W, and Baer, D M (1978), *Behavioural analysis of child development*, Prentice-Hall, Inc

Bredekamp, S (Ed.) (1987), *Developmentally appropriate practice in early childhood programs serving children from birth through age 8*, National Association for the Education of Young Children

Bredekamp, S, and Copple, C (Eds) (1997), *Developmentally appropriate practice in early childhood programs: Revised*, National Association for the Education of Young Children

Bredekamp, S, and Rosegrant, T (1992), Guidelines for appropriate curriculum content and assessment in programs serving children ages 3 though 8, in S Bredekamp and T Rosegrant (Eds), *Reaching potentials: Appropriate curriculum and assessment for young children*, National Association for the Education of Young Children (pp 9-27)

Carta, J J, Atwater, J B, Schwartz, I S, and McConnell, S R (1993), Developmentally appropriate practices and early child special education: A reaction to Johnson and McChesney Johnson, *Topics in Early Childhood Special Education*, 13(3), (pp 243-254)

Carta, J J, Schwartz, I S, Atwater, J B, and McConnell, S R (1991), Developmentally appropriate practice: Appraising its usefulness for young children with disabilities, *Topics in Early Childhood Special Education*, 11 (1), (pp 1-20)

Demchak, M, and Drinkwater, S (1992), Preschoolers with severe disabilities: The case against segregation, *Topics in Early Childhood Special Education*, 11 (4), (pp 70-83)

Diamond, K E, Hestenes, L L, & O'Connor, C (1994), *Integrating children with disabilities into preschool*, ERIC Clearinghouse on Elementary and Early Childhood Education (No EDO-PS-94-10)

Dugger-Wadsworth, D E (1997), The integrated curriculum and students with disabilities, in C H Hart, D C Burts, and R Charlesworth (Eds), *Integrated curriculum and developmentally appropriate practice: Birth to age eight*, State University Press of New York (pp 335-361)

Fuch, S, and Fuch, L S (1994), Inclusive schools movement and the radicalization of special education reform, *Exceptional Children*, 60 (4), (pp 294-309)

Futterweit, L R, and Ruff, H A (1993), Principles of development: Implications for early intervention, *Journal of Applied Developmental Psychology*, 14, (pp 153-173)

Goldhaber, D E, and Goldhaber, J (1996), Theory guided early childhood teacher education, paper presented at the *Piaget/Vygotsky Centenary Conference*, Brighton, UK

Goldhaber, D E, Goldhaber, J, and Capone, A (1998), Education for all, paper presented at the *National Conference for Special Educational Needs*, University of London, Surrey, UK

Goldhaber, D E (1981), On asking the right question: a review and critique of research evaluating the concept of stages within the Piagetian model, paper presented at the *Annual Meeting of the Jean Piaget Society*, Philadelphia, PA

Goldhaber, D E (1986), *Life-span human development*, Harcourt Brace Javonovich

Goldhaber, D E (2000), *Theories of human development: An integrative approach*, Mayfield Publishing Company

Guarlnick, M J (1993), Developmentally appropriate practice in the assessment and intervention of children's peer relations, *Topics in Early Childhood Special Education*, 13 (3), (pp 344-371)

Johnson, J E, and Johnson, K M (1992), Clarifying the developmental perspective in response to Carta, Schwartz, Atwater, and McConnell, *Topics in Early Childhood Special Education*, 12 (4), (pp 439-457)

Kozol, J (1991), *Savage Inequalities*, Crown Publishing

Krogh, S L (1997), How children develop and why it matters, in C H Hart, D C Burts, and R Charlesworth (Eds), *Integrated curriculum and developmentally appropriate practice: Birth to age eight,* State University Press of New York (pp 29-48)

Ludlow, B L, and Berkeley, T R (1994), Expanding the perceptions of developmentally appropriate practice, in B Mallory and R S New (Eds), *Diversity and developmentally appropriate practices,* Teachers College Press (pp 107-118)

Mallory, B (1992), Is it always appropriate to be developmental? Convergent models for early intervention practice, *Topics in Early Childhood Special Education,* 11 (4), (pp 1-12)

Mallory, B (1994), Inclusive policy, practice, and the theory for young children with developmental differences, in B Mallory and R S New (Eds), *Diversity and developmentally appropriate practices,* Teachers College Press (pp 44-61)

Miller, P S (1992), Segregated Programmes of teacher education in early childhood: Immoral and inefficient practice, *Topics in Early Childhood Special Education,* 11 (4), (pp 39-52)

Novick, R (1993), Activity based intervention and developmentally appropriate practice: Points of convergence, *Topics in Early Childhood Special Education,* 13 (4), (pp 403-417)

Piaget, J (1952), *The origins of intelligence in children,* International Universities Press, Inc

Piaget, J (1964), Development and learning, in R E Ripple and V N Rockcastle (Eds), *Piaget Rediscovered,* Cornell University Press

Piaget, J (1970), *Genetic epistemology,* Columbia University Press

Piaget, J (1978/1985), *The equilibration of cognitive structures,* The University of Chicago Press

Piaget, J, and Inhelder, B (1969), *The psychology of the child,* Basic Books, Inc

Rogoff, B (1990), *Apprenticeship in thinking: Cognitive development in social context,* Oxford University Press

Skinner, B F (1938), *The behavior of organisms: An experimental analysis,* Appleton-Century-Crofts, Inc

Skinner, B F (1984), The shame of American education, *American Psychologist,* 39, (pp 947-954)

Stainback, S, and Stainback, W (1992), Schools as inclusive communities, in W Stainback and S Stainback (Eds), *Controversial issues confronting special education*, Allyn and Bacon (pp 29-43)

Strain, P S, McConnell, S R, Carta, J J, and Fowler, S A (1992), Behaviorism in early intervention, *Topics in Early Childhood Special Education*, 12 (1), (pp 121-141)

Vygotsky, L S (1962), *Thought and language*, The MIT Press

Vygotsky, L S (1978), *Mind in Society*, Harvard University Press

Vygotsky, L S (1997), *Educational Psychology*, St Lucie Press

Vygotsky, L S, and Luria, A R (1993), *Studies on the history of behavior: ape, primitive and child*, Lawerence Erlbaum Associates

Watson, J B (1930), *Behaviorism*, The University of Chicago Press

Chapter 9

Illustrations of Special Needs Education service provision across Canada

Dan G Bachor and Markus R Baer

Introduction

Special needs education in Canada is influenced by a combination of geographical, historical-political, and cultural factors. One important geographical influence on the delivery of special needs education is the manner in which the population is distributed across the country. Based on the 1996 census data, Canada's population increased to approximately 29 million, which is about 0.5% of the world's population. Thus, Canada has, by world standards, a low population density spread across a large geographic area. However, this low population density needs to be qualified to some degree in that the vast majority of Canadians live in the southern portion of the country, approximately 85% of the Canadian population being clustered within 300 kilometers of the 49th parallel, the Canada-USA border. Thus, as we will argue below, special education emerged unevenly throughout Canadian history and, even today, special needs education service provision is more readily available in areas of greater population concentration. In addition, we will illustrate that historical-political and cultural developments within the Canadian context have had a significant impact on the development of special needs education service provision across the country. Two examples that are reviewed in this chapter are the political decision by the federal government to encourage multiculturalism, and the introduction of the Charter of Rights and Freedoms. Finally, it will be apparent that the cultural context both within and without Canada has had significant influence on the development of special needs education service provision. For example, the introduction of individual plans to guide instruction for persons with special educational needs followed from work in the USA.

In this chapter, we have attempted to provide an overview of special needs education in Canada. Given the diversity of policy and practice in the

Canadian context, we have assembled information from government policy documents, resource guides, website sources, and personal communications. The information presented in the following pages provides an illustrative, rather than a comprehensive, picture of the Canadian history and trends in policies and practice for special needs education. This chapter is organized into four main sections: 1) a brief description of the Canadian educational context; 2) a presentation of the history of special needs education in Canadian schools; 3) an examination of policy and practice in Canada; and 4) an overview of emerging trends in the area, along with some concluding remarks.

The Context of the Canadian Educational System

It will become apparent that, although we are discussing special needs education in Canada, we cannot provide a true Canadian picture as this country is one of the few countries in the world that does not have a national educational system. There is no Canadian central agency devoted to education; rather education falls under the exclusive jurisdiction of the 10 provinces and 3 territories[1] that constitute the country. There is one federal agency, the Council of Ministers of Education, Canada (CMEC); this office can be found on the Internet at http://www.cmec.ca/ in both English and French. The CMEC provides a mechanism through which the various provincial and territorial ministers can discuss educational issues of concern; however, the CMEC has no regulatory power. It does, however, issue periodic reports – see for instance, the Report on Education in Canada, issued in 1995 and, the most recent one published in 1998, both of which are available on the Internet. In these reports, CMEC captures the major challenges facing the Canadian educational system. For example, in the 1998 report, the CMEC observed:

'Twenty-five years ago, reform of education systems focused on encouraging girls and young women to continue their studies, preventing drug abuse, and building new facilities. Today, some of those issues remain. But we also face a new set of issues: improving student achievement in an increasingly complex and difficult social and economic climate, ensuring value for money, and closing half-empty institutions. Our education systems must also cope with child poverty and youth unemployment, and with conflict and even violence in the classroom. Increased youth unemployment, among other factors, is also making it more difficult for educators to motivate students – boys and young men in particular – to stay in school (CMEC, 1998, p 4).

It is noteworthy, while not directly relevant to special needs education, that young men have now replaced young women as a focal point. This trend has been emerging for the last ten years as, for example, registration in post-secondary institutions by young women has exceeded that of men (Statistics Canada, 1996). Far more germane to the topic under consideration, are the issues of youth unemployment, classroom conflict and violence, both for the immediate impact on society and for the possible long term inter-generational consequences that might emerge in the future. The latter concern, for example, has resulted in the Province of Ontario issuing a Violence-Free Schools Policy (Ontario, Ministry of Education and Training, 1994).

The CMEC has also developed the School Achievement Indicators Program, which is a national assessment program designed to provide Canadians with information on students' achievement in mathematics, reading and writing, and science. This is one of the few national educational initiatives undertaken in Canada and is part of an increasing focus on assessment practices across the country (Anderson & Bachor, 1998).

The lack of a Canadian office of education has resulted in considerable diversity in the governance and organization of education (*ibid*). Each province and territory has, the exception being Nunavit, a provincial or territorial act designed to regulate education. This legislation is wide ranging in scope and typically includes such things as the organization and structure of schools and their governing bodies, the definitions of responsibilities for personnel associated with educational delivery, and fiscal policies. As legislation is amended infrequently, each province or territory also sets a variety of policies and regulations that are revised on a fairly regular basis. For example, in British Columbia the 1978 BC School Act was rewritten in 1989 and the regulations were updated in 1996. These documents are available on the Internet at: (http://www.qp.gov.bc.ca/stat_reg/statutes/41200.htm).

Each jurisdiction has a Ministry of Education, although the name changes slightly from one area to another: for example, it is called the Department of Education in Prince Edward Island and Alberta, the Ministry of Education and Training in Ontario and Manitoba, and the Ministry of Education, Skills, and Training in British Columbia. These Ministries have responsibility for educational policy and regulation. As a rule, each Ministry of Education is sub-divided into a number of different branches, with responsibilities over such matters as special needs education service provision, curriculum, finance, and assessment. More precisely, each branch is charged with a specific obligation. For example, 'Curriculum' varies from prescribing learning outcomes in various subjects matters to checking to ensure that local educational authorities[2] follow provincial guidelines. In the case of special needs education, however, the overall responsibility may be sub-divided into more than one branch. Two examples of such subdivision are: 1) guidelines on the preparation of instructional plans for students with special educational needs may fall to a curriculum section; and 2) reporting on provincial resources allocated to local authorities might be the responsibility of an accountability or assessment section. In British Columbia, for example, special education needs is housed in the Ministry of Education, Skills, and Training under the jurisdiction of Special Programmes. As in the above example, some responsibility for special needs education falls under two other branches:

• Curriculum and Resources, which provides curriculum guidelines for all learners; and

• Evaluation and Accountability, which has responsibility for such matters as provincial learning assessments (subject specific assessment completed on a rotational basis, for example in Social Studies in 1996) and provincial examinations. Students with special education needs are expected to write these examinations. In sitting such tests, they may be allowed specific accommodations – such as permitting the use of a scribe to record their answers.

In addition, in some regions of the country, provinces and territories co-operate extensively with one another to plan policy and products. For example, Newfoundland and Labrador, Nova Scotia, New Brunswick, and Prince Edward Island have worked in concert to develop curricula and assessment materials for use in schools under an umbrella known as the Atlantic Provinces Education Foundation (APEF).

The geographically concentrated population of Canada, as noted in the introduction, has implications for special needs education in Canada. In one sense, the implications are positive. This population concentration in urban areas results in a reasonably efficient pool of services for the majority of Canadians. If, however, geography – notably distance – is used as a framework to examine the provision of special education, service delivery is both costly and inefficient for the minority of the population. For example, in several areas of the country schooling is provided to a scanty population, spread over several hundreds of square kilometers. In any given service area there may be only a few people who require special needs education support and they probably are located across the catchment area, rather than clustered in one location. In some cases, even in isolated settings, there are attempts to concentrate special needs education service provision; for example, in regional centres. These efforts to pool services, however, usually result in at least temporary dislocation and upheaval for families as they are required to travel to the service provider to begin to receive the assistance they want.

This geographical complexity is often complicated by two other factors: 1) a variety of language(s) are spoken in Canada; and 2) there is an increasing cultural diversity across the country. While Canada has two official languages (English and French), there is a growing number of individuals who speak another native language; for them English or French may be a second or third language. In part, this increase in languages is due to the Canadian policy of supporting multiculturalism. Thus, there are areas of the country where the majority cultural group is, for example, Chinese, Greek, Indo-Canadian or Inuit. This increase in cultural diversity is not limited to the sparsely populated regions of Canada; for example, according to a 1998 article in *The Globe and Mail*, English has now been reduced to a minority language status in Vancouver and Richmond, British Columbia ('English', 1998). The consequence of this admixture is that service providers must 1) be aware of the impact of diverse cultural values when conducting assessment or implementing interventions; 2) be sensitive to the possibility that different languages are spoken at home, at school, and in the community which may affect everything from communication to home support; and 3) provide the required services at a reasonable cost in an era of diminished fiscal resources (Bachor, forthcoming).

History of Special Needs in Education in Canada

The history of special education in Canada is too lengthy to describe fully in the context of this chapter. However, it is important to outline some of the key events that have helped to shape current service provision, and so the following events and trends have been selected as instrumental to the development of the provision of special needs education in the Canadian context.

Early efforts

As in other countries, special education has evolved through a number of stages, whereby the nature, scope, and location of service provision has been modified over the years (*eg*, for a US example, see MacMillan & Hendrick, 1993). Special education services were first initiated in Canada in the mid-nineteenth century whereby children were placed in institutional settings (Winzer, 1987). The provision of these services within the context of the 20th century might be seen as restrictive and confining, however, all historical services need to be reviewed from the perspective of the service provision mandate of the time period. Thus, for example, Bunch (1994) argues that service provision within institutions was a first step toward inclusion, in that people who had not received special needs education service provision were being helped for the first time.

Recent history

The beginning of the twentieth century resulted in the expansion of services being offered to individuals with special needs in two ways. First, schools were initiated for individuals with physical disabilities (deaf, blind), and second, the scope of services offered was expanded to encompass habilitative services to people with intellectual and behavioral handicapping conditions (Bunch, *op cit,* Winzer, 1987, 1989). Adopting a geographic perspective, however, services were still not available within many communities, especially those that were smaller or rural. By the beginning of the 1950s, segregated classroom-based service provision was becoming commonplace in urban centres; children were categorized based on a traditional delineation of special needs using a medical orientation. Thus, services were developed for discrete categories by various professional groups (Winzer, *op cit*).

This trend continued into the middle of the 1960s, whereby special education developed more rapidly in larger cities than in rural communities. However, there was considerable interprovincial/interterroritial variation in service provision (Hutchinson & Wong, 1987). As of 1969, there were offices of special education in half of the provincial Ministries or Departments of Education with approximately 3% of school-aged students receiving special education services (*ibid*). A marked change was clearly established in the 1960s and early 1970s, whereby advocacy groups – consisting of both parents and professionals, acting both separately and together in a variety of associations, such as the Association for Children with Learning Disabilities – were firmly established to lobby for additional funding and services provisions. Winzer (*op cit, 1989*) notes that during this time period, funding increased dramatically and professional and community interest in the problems associated with individuals with special needs multiplied. Thus, the demand for special needs education service provision was established and continues to influence program delivery today.

The next key trend that has influenced current service provision was the introduction of legislation or policy in which the moral obligation to provide special education, primarily in the form of segregated classes offered as an instructional cascade of services, was dominant (*eg* see Reynolds & Birch, (1977) for three variations of the cascade of service provision covering the period of 1962 to 1977). In some jurisdictions this also became a legal obligation. Partly as a result of the development of the instructional cascade, in the period from 1969 to 1972, seven provinces (British Columbia, Alberta, Saskatchewan, Manitoba, Ontario, Quebec, and Newfoundland) advanced new or revised legislation or policy and the remainder committed to change their special education legislation or policy (Hutchinson & Wong, *op cit*). At about this time, a committee of the Council for Exceptional Children in Canada prepared a report which advanced principles to govern legislation for children with special needs (Treherne, Dice, Grigg, & Sanche, 1974). Discussion and debate resulting from this report also had considerable influence over the legislation proposed in several different provinces/territories. This trend has continued, with the most recent change, the introduction of the Canadian Charter of Rights and Freedoms – which is discussed below – having a national impact on special needs education service provision.

Another major focal point for special needs education service provision, which emerged during the early to mid-1970s, was consideration of the standards regulating professionals. Hardy, McLeod, Minto, Perkins, & Quance (1971) produced an important document, *Standards for Educators of Exceptional Children*, that contains both a set of minimum standards and a model of training for teachers of exceptional children. This report was influential in the preparation of professionals across Canada; for example, a summer-based graduate program was developed at the University of Victoria and implemented during the 1980s, which incorporated some of the *Standards* recommendations. This concern about standards of professional training has continued into the 1990s. Recent policy documents developed by The Council for Exceptional Children (1991, 1997, 1999) have resulted in a set of recommended international standards of professional practice and the emergence of a code of ethics for special educators (The Council for Exceptional Children, 1991, 1997).

During the mid-1980s, it was estimated that 12% of the school population required some form of special education. However, the accuracy of this estimation was questionable since, as we noted earlier, there is still no national office of education in Canada and provinces reported, and continue to report, incidence data differently. By this time, every province had published legislation, regulations, policies, and/or guidelines for special education. The predominant models of service delivery were adapted from the USA and Europe, ranging from segregation to integration. In addition, individualized educational planning had become an important hallmark of special needs education service provision.

During the mid-to-late 1980s, the trends established during the middle of the decade continued. However, some notable Canadian developments occurred as well. One of the most significant influences on Canadian special education, the Canadian Charter of Rights and Freedoms, mentioned above, was introduced in 1982. The full impact of this Charter was not, however, felt by special educators until Section 15 was implemented in 1985 (MacKay, 1987). Section 15 contained the following key clause: 'Every individual is equal before and under the law and has the right to the equal protection and equal benefit of the law with discrimination and, in particular, without discrimination based on race, national or ethnic origin, colour, religion, sex, age or mental or physical disability'.

MacKay (*ibid*) noted that Section 15 could provide the legal grounds on which to request the provision of well-funded special education programs and to challenge the segregation of children, but such a provision has not resulted, partly due to the fiscal constraints and budget reduction priorities established by most provinces and territories. The latter challenge – in the form of integration and inclusion – certainly has emerged, but it is unclear to what extent this shift was the result of the introduction of the Charter, other international forces, or the combination of both of these influences. Interestingly, provinces/territories still can sidestep the implications of the Charter by invoking the 'notwithstanding' clause declaring that the education statute operates notwithstanding the Charter; however, no jurisdiction has elected to exercise this option to date.

There were also shifts in the nature of available instructional materials that were developed to prepare special educators to face classroom challenges. For the first time, Canadian special educators introduced professional texts that initially were adaptations of work published in the USA (for example, Hammill, Bartel, & Bunch, 1984), but subsequently were written specifically for Canadian audiences (for example, Bachor & Crealock, 1986). This trend has continued into the 1990s, with both adapted (for example, Friend, Bursuck, & Hutchinson, 1998) and unique texts (for example, Andrews & Lupart, forthcoming; Crealock & Bachor, 1995) continuing to materialize. The emergence of a distinctly Canadian literature to assist teachers, at minimum, has meant that the unique features of the geographical, political, historical, and cultural aspects of the country have been highlighted in discussions about special needs education service provision over approximately the last 15 years.

During this period policies and practices established in the USA and, to a lesser extent, Europe, continued to influence service delivery models adopted in Canada as well. One notable example was the regular education initiative (Reynolds, 1989; Reynolds, Wang, & Walberg, 1987), which led to the introduction of the full service school – that is a school in which the full range of services are provided to all students, regardless of special educational need, in the local community. Further, partly as a result of a British influence, many Canadian school systems have changed to school-based management, which has resulted in increased parental advocacy for all children and, in some provinces – Ontario, for example – the establishment of parent advisory councils. Deinstitutionalization gained momentum, with the closure of 1) provincial schools for the deaf and/or blind, with services being shifted to local school jurisdictions; and 2) provincial institutions for the 'retarded', with accommodation and services being provided in the local community through group homes and other facilities.

During the 1990s, the dominant theme in special education at the school-level has been a devolution of services. Oderkirk (1993), for example, points out that by 1991 only 26% of students requiring special needs education service provision received instruction in a special class or school. The introduction of inclusion, whereby most students remain in the regular classroom, has further decreased the number of students served outside this context.

There has been considerable debate, however, over the merits of inclusion as there are no clear criteria to evaluate this practice. Thus the discussion surrounding inclusion is often based on rhetoric rather than evidence. Proponents argue for the benefits of social interaction, some academic gains, and the tolerance and acceptance learned by other children/adolescents in the classroom (Hutchinson, 1996; Inclusion, 1996; Lupart, 1996; Lupart & Webber, 1996). Critics raise the problem of how to determine whether inclusion is appropriate for all students, that the costs of inclusion are not recognized, and that children that require special needs education service provision are being short-changed (Breakdown, 1997; Kauffman & Hallahan, 1995). Despite this debate, most current government policies across the country have been designed to support inclusion, although conditions for effectiveness are sometimes attached. For example, the policy of the Northwest Territories includes the following statement: 'Inclusive schooling is both a philosophy and a practice. However, including all students in regular classrooms with their age peers, and responding to individual needs and strengths, requires a number of conditions and practices ... [listing of territorial, regional, and school-based requirements for inclusion is given]' (Northwest Territories, Department of Education, Culture, and Employment, 1998). As a consequence, the regular classroom has become the home-base of most children and adolescents with special needs and curricula adaptations are made if required.

Three final comments round up our historical discussion and take us into the current era: estimating incidence rates, extended service within the community, and increased technology. As we indicated earlier, it is very difficult to estimate realistically the percentage of individuals with special educational needs being served in total across Canada. Obtaining this calculation is further complicated by the 'inclusion' trend, making it difficult to track accurately who is receiving services, as individuals are not necessarily designated, and by the inter-regional variation in service provision and reporting standards that has existed for some time. As a very crude approximation, however, about one to three percent of students are still being provided services within non-graded special education classrooms. Within communities in Canada, an important change that has been taking place over the last decade or so, from approximately 1989 to 1999, is that there are increased transportation options and greater environmental accessibility.

Notable examples are the emergence of a paratransit systems, such as minibuses, and, most recently, the introduction of city buses that are wheelchair accessible; modifications in sidewalk kerbs so that they are accessible to wheelchairs, and the introduction of sound-signal-cues at traffic lights for the visually challenged. Even more recently, barrier-free schools are being designed; for example, the Peel Board of Education in Ontario was, at the time this chapter was being prepared, constructing the *Rick Hansen Secondary School* – a name which will be familiar to many readers because of his world-wide wheelchair tours and advocacy efforts. This new school, when completed, will set a new standard of expectations for environmental accessibility ('Barrier-free', 1999). As with previous trends, however, these two options have begun in urban settings and only some of them are slowly devolving to smaller and more rural communities. Finally, increasingly sophisticated assistive technology, which is not limited by geography so much as by fiscal resources – such as high speed computers, with voice input or adapted keyboards, allowing individuals to attain full employment and specialized telephone systems to facilitate communication – has become available. The availability of this technology has resulted in increased accessibility for individuals with special needs. Each of these shifts at the school and community levels has been tempered by the emergence of conservative budget policies by provincial/territorial governments. This fiscal policy has meant that the major priority has been on balanced budgets and all service provision within the school system and the community has been judged against a budgetary standard. In the next section, we continue to discuss selected current trends in the delivery of special needs education service provision.

Current Policies and Practices

Again as a reminder, any discussion regarding the current policy and practice of special needs education in Canada, and its future development, is necessarily limited by the aforementioned diversity of the Canadian education system. The lack of federal directives relegates general policy and funding decisions to the provincial/territorial Ministries, while local educational authorities, and more often schools, set the particulars for practice. Although a clearly articulated description of special education is not possible, overlapping themes and overarching trends may be culled from the Ministry, local educational authorities, and school levels. We have identified four persistently occurring directives:

- the implementation of individual education plans for designated pupils;

- a focus on the integration and inclusion of special needs students into the 'regular' classroom;

- an emphasis on the use of technological aids;

- the need to account for transitional periods as individuals move between grade levels, schools and on to work settings.

As has been the case historically, some of these trends are consistent with those noted by counterparts in the USA (see for example, Ludlow & Lombardi, 1992), in Britain (see for example, Thomson, Ward, Riddell, & Dyer, 1993) and elsewhere (Wilton, 1988). Prior to discussing these four topics and citing examples of how they manifest themselves in various regions, some background information on the current status and definition of special education appears appropriate. In addition, a brief mention of several undercurrents that make their way into special needs education may help set the stage for the more notable directives.

Current conception of special needs education

What exactly is encompassed by the title special education just prior to the beginning of a new century, and what populations are included within its boundaries, still exhibits some regional variation, albeit not to the extent that practices do. The East Coast province of Prince Edward Island lists nine categories of exceptionality in its review of special education (Prince Edward Island, Department of Education, 1999). These categories, or some variation of them, are utilized by most provincial and territorial jurisdictions. They include the following nine classifications: gifted; intellectual disabilities; emotional/behavioural disorders; learning disabilities; sensory impairments; physical disabilities; communication disorders; health and neurological disorders and developmental delay. While some Ministries highlight specific diagnoses, such as autism in Ontario, and others use combined categories, such as multiple disability in British Columbia, the PEI example illustrates the range of populations that are included under the banner of special needs education service provision or, in more tradition terms, special education.

The manner that funding is arranged across the country for special needs education service provision also varies across Canada. In a recent evaluation of special education services in Manitoba, the authors of this report summarized the funding arrangements in Canada for special needs education service provision as follows:

> Canadian jurisdictions use a variety of funding models. The Maritime provinces tend to fund on a block per pupil basis. The Western provinces provide a basic instructional block (or core grant), supplemented with specific (categorical) funding for special education students. Saskatchewan is similar to Manitoba in that it provides base funding, plus a combination of an additional block and categorical. Base funding is determined on need and the local Board's ability to pay; that is, the greater the disparity between the need and the ability to pay, the greater the grant.

> In other Canadian jurisdictions there is a trend to provide categorical funding based on student needs rather than on labels. The intent is to determine student needs and then place students in categories depending on support requirements rather than labels. (Manitoba, Ministry of Education and Training, 1999, Chapter II, Section D, p 1).

This latter trend is taking on a higher priority within educational jurisdictions as provinces and territories grapple with ways of providing special needs education service provision while attempting to avoid stigmatizing individuals due to the manner in which people are classified.

Further, while designated funding categories have been the cornerstone of education policies, they actually account for only a small portion of the population receiving special needs services within local educational authorities. For example, a recent British Columbia survey conducted by the Ministry of Education concluded that only 26% of the current caseload of students obtaining learning assistance support[3] came from designated funding categories (British Columbia, 1997). The remaining 74% of students were composed of pupils with mild to moderate learning difficulties or learners who are otherwise deemed to have low ability in some general sense. These students received services either in pullout classes or within the classroom, as arranged by individual schools and districts through block funding allocated under the heading of learning assistance.

The category of students grouped under the rubric high incidence (specific designations might include mild/moderate Learning Disabilities, Attention Deficit Disorders, and emotional/behavioral disorders) compose the largest segment of students obtaining special assistance in Canada. Some of this group is the population that is generally not included in specific Ministry protocols, as they are often clustered under the block-funding category that is utilized by this province at the local educational authority and school level to employ special education assistants, purchase learning materials, hire other paraprofessionals and so forth. There is a paucity of information on this non-designated segment of learners, although the British Columbia Ministry of Education estimates place the number of students receiving services under some form of learning assistance at somewhere in the area of 10%, while those with more 'severe' disabilities account for approximately 1-2% of the student population (British Columbia Ministry of Education, Skills and Training, 1998a).

However, even these generalizations are tempered by regional differences. For example in the Northwest Territories, it has been estimated that 30-45% of students require one or more specific supports (Northwest Territories, Education, Culture and Employment, 1999a). Geographic and demographic variables, as we have already observed, cannot be underestimated in a country where, for example, some regions (such as the Yukon) have a ratio of 1 school per 16,700 square kilometers of land (and some of these schools have an enrolment as low as five pupils) (Yukon, Department of Education, 1999). It is with this ubiquitous diversity in mind, both in terms of the country and in relation to special needs categorization, that any discussion of common themes and trends must take place.

Nonetheless, there are several noteworthy themes or undercurrents that come to the fore in various education Ministries of Education across the country. A call to establishing standards is highlighted in several jurisdictions, such as in Prince Edward Island (1998). Whether those standards deal with professional expectations, reviewed earlier, and hiring criteria for special needs educators or curriculum and individual education program policies, discussed below, there is a move towards greater standardization in several regions. The province of New Brunswick, for example, established resource teacher and guidance counsellor hiring criteria in 1997/98 (New Brunswick, Department of Education, 1998).

Part of this move to establishing standards and accountability often takes the form of greater parent and community involvement. Creating community linkages has become a common directive in recent years. In provinces such as Alberta, the need for school boards to consult with parents prior to placing any child in a special education program has been written into the School Act (Alberta, Alberta Education, 1997) while other regions such as Ontario and Manitoba have increased the right of parents to participate in discussions and meetings concerning their children (Manitoba, 1999; Ontario, 1998a). The effort to foster ties between schools, parents and community agencies is being discussed at all levels.

Of particular concern for many parents and educators alike is the early identification and intervention for students who require special programs. Several regions have recently identified the need for increased special education initiatives in the early school years; the Manitoba EIEP (Early Identification and Education Program) is one such example (Manitoba, 1999). The shift to special needs identification and program implementation among younger students is something that will no doubt continue to be discussed by planning and policy makers. Although the issues of standardization, parent/community involvement and early identification/intervention are discussion topics, if not practice, in many provinces and territories, they take a variety of forms and shapes depending on the particular directive. While these themes do present common threads that run through special education in Canada, and in some jurisdictions they are paramount, they tend to reflect influential undercurrents rather than unilateral trends *per se*. Their direct and indirect impact on both policy and practice, however, should not be underestimated.

Individualized plans

Among the four more salient directives noted in Canadian special needs education, the use of individualized plans to detail personal learning goals has become pivotal. Although the names vary, from Personal Program Plans (PPP) in Saskatchewan and Individual Pathways for Learning (IPL) in Quebec, to Individual Program Plans (IPP) and Individual Education Plans (IEP) in Alberta and British Columbia respectively, they reflect similar efforts. Fundamentally, these documents attempt to establish a written educational plan, which identifies the individual student's strengths and needs, as well as setting reasonable goals and objectives and establishing some accountability procedures to evaluate the implementation of this plan. British Columbia's list of what an Individual Education Plan must outline, as indicated in the province's *Special Education Services: A Manual of Policies Procedures and Guidelines*, serves to illustrate the overall breadth and depth of these documents (British Columbia, Ministry of Education, 1995). According to this manual, an IEP should include the following seven components:

1) the present levels of educational achievement/performance of the student;

2) the specific individualized learning outcomes set for that student for that school year, excluding goals that would be normally expected at age-grade level that are prescribed in provincial guidebooks;

3) any required adaptations to educational materials, and instructional and assessment methods designed to accommodate the student's specific learning needs;

4) any support services that are provided to facilitate meeting the student's needs;

5) a description of the place where the educational program is to be provided;

6) the names of all personnel who will be providing the educational program and the support services;

7) the period of time over which the IEP will be in effect and the process for reviewing and evaluating the success of the program inherent in the IEP.

While there are regional differences in what these personal plans should include, the British Columbia example sets the general tone. Some jurisdictions, however, have highlighted additional concerns, for example daily schedules or discussion of transition periods (see below), while others have amalgamated several descriptive factors under larger headings such as 'personal data'. For example, Saskatchewan (1999) requires that a coordinated team be established and transition goals clearly stated in their set individualized plans. These differences often reflect particular provincial/territorial considerations, as well as unique policy evaluations. Although, the diversity of personalized education plans is a phenomenon that deserves mention, the similarity between these initiatives outweighs their disparity. The notion of an individualized plan to justify and guide the education of a student who does not 'fit' the prescribed standard program, is a factor present across Canadian special needs policies. A section of these policies often describes how curricular adaptation will include or integrate the student into the activities that are taking place within the regular classroom.

Inclusion and integration

As we noted earlier, educators in many parts of the world, but particularly in North America, have been preoccupied with the concepts of inclusion and integration; that is, often the focus has been on *where* to offer special needs education service provision, rather than addressing *what to do* and *how to meet* such needs.

In Canada, the trend towards including or integrating all students into regular schools and classrooms has become a focal point of policy directives. Special needs education is fraught with efforts to enshrine that all students are a part of the 'regular' school classroom, and that exceptions to this are rare and sufficiently justified. The Northwest Territories reflect this growing trend in their Departmental Directives when they write:

> Inclusive schooling is more than a method or strategy; it is a way of life that is tied directly to the belief system that values diversity. Inclusive schooling is also a philosophical and practical educational approach, which strives to respond to individual student needs, and is intended to ensure equal access for all students to educational programs offered in regular classroom settings. Inclusive schooling is mandatory within the Northwest Territories school system. [Education Act. Subsection 7(1)]. (Northwest Territories Education, Culture and Employment, 1999b).

The Ministry of Education and Training in Ontario (1996) has recently established an award for exemplary practices in integration, while Prince Edward Island (1998) has just recommended a review of their provincial special education programs in light of the changing philosophy of integration, while Manitoba has just completed such a review (Ministry of Education and Training, 1999). Examples of this sort could be cited across Canada, as the move towards inclusion/integration becomes more lucid in various Ministerial initiatives. As noted, this trend has been ongoing for several years, and as of yet, it has shown little intention of slowing down.

This emphasis on inclusion/integration has led to the initiation of several research projects across the country to begin to evaluate the impact of inclusion (Bunch, Lupart & Brown, 1997; Edmunds, 1998; Lupart, Bunch, & Brown, 1997) and to help prepare teachers-in-training to work in an inclusive classroom (Hutchinson, 1999). More specifically, teachers are not feeling prepared to face the demands inherent in implementing inclusion. For example, Edmunds (*op cit*) examined the perceptions of 183 Nova Scotia classroom teachers towards inclusion and found that, overall, teachers held a strong negative view toward inclusion and were not professionally prepared to teach students with special educational needs. In one effort to redress this dilemma for future teachers, Nancy Hutchinson and her colleagues are engaged in a series of projects to examine the use of 'dilemma cases' to prepare teachers candidates to teach in inclusive classrooms (Hutchinson, *op cit*). In a series of studies, Hutchinson and her colleagues have demonstrated that teacher candidates can adapt their viewpoints and practices regarding how to meet the needs of exceptional learners (Hutchinson, 1996; Hutchinson & Martin, a and b, Forthcoming; Munby & Hutchinson, 1998). Another notable directive that can assist teachers in addressing special needs education service provision is the use of technological adaptations (Sitko & Sitko, 1996).

Technology

The growing number of hardware, software, adaptive devices and other educational and assistive technologies that have entered the market in recent years is testament to an ever-changing world for special educators. In keeping with this growth in technology, there has been an increased push to incorporate its perceived benefits into the education system. The assumption that technology can empower individuals through enhanced communication, mobility and so forth has been taken up by educational decision-makers throughout Canada. Many provinces/territories have developed handbooks and policy guidelines for the incorporation and use of technological aids. Newfoundland and Labrador (1999) for example, have published a document titled *Using Technology to Enhance Students' Differing Abilities*. Other regions such as Ontario have collaboratively invested in computer-based assistance, such as their 'SNOW' program (see, Ontario, 1998b), which provides a Resource Centre for teachers of students with special needs, as well as sections with activities and connections for special needs pupils. Ontario's use of the PEBBLES (Providing Education by Bringing Learning Environments to Students, (Ontario, 1998b) program incorporates robotics technology and video-conferencing in order to connect students in hospital, or at other locations, to the classroom. Although such programs are still novel, they are increasingly being discussed and advocates are arguing in favour of implementing them. The use of technological aides, particularly computer advances, to assist special needs students with access, mobility, communication and learning will continue to evolve along with the innovations that greet the marketplace. One area in which technological assistance has been requested is in the realm of transition periods.

Transition

Particular markers in a student's life have become recognized as significant periods of change and necessary adaptation. Entry into school, the shift between various grade levels and a move onto the world of work or further education are examples of transitional periods that concern educators. The construct of 'transition planning' has been taken up in most regions of the country. Although much of the discussion has centered on directives at the general policy level, the focus on transition periods as significant variables has entered special needs education (Freeze, 1995; Freeze, Frankel, Kueneman, & Mahon, 1995). The Maritime province of Nova Scotia for instance, has initiated a school-to-work transition research project through the Department of Education and Culture (Nova Scotia, 1995).

These sorts of directives, which aim to create meaningful work experiences in order to foster bridges between the worlds of school and work, are seen as particularly relevant for special education students, many of whom will not enter the post-secondary education system. In regards to other transitional periods, provinces such as Alberta have included transition planning as part of the special education program delivery requirements and expectations (Alberta, 1997). For example, in the Alberta program, it is stated that school authorities must include procedures which advise parents of anticipated transition from one level of schooling to the next, termination of any provision of special education services, notification (for parents and community agencies) of the anticipated completion of a special education program at least one year in advance and so forth (Alberta, 1997). Similarly, the province of Ontario requires that 'a Transition Plan ...[must be a] ... part of the Individual Education Plan (IEP) for each exceptional pupil (except for those identified only as gifted)' (Ontario, 1998a). The inclusion of a transition plan as part of the special needs student's overall individual education plan has become a requirement in many provinces/territories. Naturally the transition periods that reach outside of school necessarily include a larger segment of society and this is one area in which the move towards greater community involvement is a key factor. Similarly, the trend towards early identification and intervention is played out during the transition into school and between kindergarten and the primary grades. The move towards active and clearly articulated policies on transition will no doubt create a tendril of further issues and concerns such as the ones just raised.

Summary

The four directives identify: personal education plans; inclusion/integration; technology; transition, reflect identified themes that cross Canadian special needs education. A number of undercurrents, such as those noted above, run through these themes. Regional variation renders any generalised discussion of special education questionable, and for that reason, we have chosen what appear to be the most obvious and consistently identified themes across the country. There are numerous other factors that might have been included in this discussion. However, for brevity's sake, only re-occurring policies were included. The result is perhaps a loosely woven patchwork rather than a tightly knit cover.

Possible Future Trends and Concluding Remarks

Predicting the future of special needs education service provision is probably an exercise in folly, as special education is driven by a combination of political influences, advocacy group pressures, international trends, and, to a lessor degree, evidence from research undertakings. In spite of the interplay of these forces, we suggest that for the immediate term there are five specific themes that will be important in determining special needs education service provision. In addition there are two general trends that we see as salient in the longer term.

First, we anticipate that the current concept of special needs education service provision may be modified to include another option, which is to determine the services that individuals require in order to learn. Two separate influences are emerging that support this conjecture: 1) Educational jurisdictions across the country are continuing to monitor how to fund and provide appropriate services for individuals with special needs (*eg*, Manitoba, Ministry of Education and Training, 1999); 2) Some provinces have changed the manner in which special needs education service provision is funded, moving towards block funding and have already shifted to a modified services-needed model – for example New Brunswick (Crealock & Bachor, *op cit*). Thus, we suggest that there will be a further shift in the manner in which services are provided where the focus is on the support needed to learn effectively, such as in the model suggested by Thomson, Stewart, and Ward (1995) in Scotland. This shift will not mean the elimination of the classification of diagnostic categories for people, but it will result in a change in emphasis to a focus on service provision required as a complement to the former model.

Second, individualized planning will be expanded further to include a wider scope of activities. To some degree this trend is already established. Planning for persons with severe handicapping conditions has been expanded from the academic and behavioral learning goals that typically constitute such plans to focus more broadly on long person-based planning utilizing schematics such as the McGill Action Planning System (Vandercook, York & Forest, 1989).

Third, as long as fiscal constraints remain as paramount considerations for provincial governments, the scope of people providing special education needs service provision will continue to be enlarged. The clearest example of this trend is the emergence of paraprofessionals, although there has been some concern expressed over the role they might play in the classroom (Lam & McQuarrie, 1989). Despite these earlier concerns, we believe paraprofessionals will continue to take an increasing role in special needs education service provision (Jones & Bender, 1993). For example, there were over 6000 'educational assistants' providing support services to individuals with special educational needs in the province of British Columbia as of September, 1998 (Ministry of Education, 1998).

Further, clear guidelines for paraprofessional roles are starting to emerge (National Joint Committee on Learning Disabilities, 1999).

In a similar vein, there will continue to be considerable importance attached to setting standards for professional practice and along with this trend further emphasis on teacher accountability. As noted earlier, there is a presage to review and set standards for professional and ethical practice, such as those recently advanced by the Council for Exceptional Children, that will continue to mark special needs education service provision. These recommendations have yet to be implemented widely across the country. In addition, there will be greater demand for evaluating teacher qualifications as part of this emphasis on standard setting; for example, the province of Ontario is considering introducing mandatory re-certification for teachers ('Harris', 1999). While this requirement would apply to all teachers, if implemented it would have considerable impact on teachers focusing on special needs education service provision. We anticipate that this emphasis on professional standards will increase over the next few years.

The final immediate term trend is a continued focus on quality of life (social inclusion, recreation, personal rights and privileges). As we noted earlier, environments are becoming more accessible and technology is increasingly becoming available to expand the quality of life for all people. This trend has another twist to it, however. Increasingly, medically fragile people are remaining at home and are present in the community and, partly as a consequence, the ethical dilemmas of euthanasia and the right to life have emerged as illustrated in a recent Canadian court case. In the case of *R vs Latimer* (1997), Robert Latimer admitted killing his disabled daughter because he believed she was suffering and would not be able to sustain any quality of life (R *vs* Latimer, 1997; 'Ottawa,' 1997). This, along with the highly publicized case of Jack Kevorkian ('Dr Death', 1999) in the USA has raised the profile of the topic of right to life and quality of life. We believe that this debate will be ongoing for some time.

In a more general sense, with the arrival of the 21st century, the scope and substance of special education in Canada has changed substantially and probably will continue to reform in at least two ways. First, special education no longer applies to school-aged children exclusively. It has been expanded to include services for younger children and to respond to meeting the needs of adults. Second, the substance of special education is being expanded to address a wider mandate of social and economic issues that affect the quality of life of both children and adults with special needs. As noted above, however, this expanded mandate comes in a period of fiscal conservatism, and the impact on social services generally and on service provision for people with various challenges is unknown.

Notes

[1] As of April 1, 1999, Canada added a third territory by dividing the Northwest Territories (NWT) into two independent jurisdictions. The three new Canadian territories are, from west to east, the Yukon, the Northwest Territories and Nunavut. For those readers unfamiliar with the country, the provinces in Canada from east to west are Newfoundland and Labrador, Prince Edward Island, Nova Scotia, New Brunswick, Quebec, Ontario, Manitoba, Saskatchewan, Alberta, and British Columbia.

[2] In Canada, the governing bodies for schools are termed school boards or school districts depending on the province. These elected groups are constituted in a similar manner to Local Education Authorities in Britain. The key difference is that many decisions still are centralized; for example, school-based budgets, for the most part, are set by the district/board but may be the administrative responsibility of the school principal (head-teacher). For ease of reading for international readers, instead of intermixing the various Canadian terms, we will refer to local educational authorities, instead of school boards or school districts.

[3] Learning Assistance support is called by a variety of names across Canada, including Learning Support, Resource Room, Clinical Teacher Support, *etc*. In all cases what is being described is special needs education service provision at the local school level. In most cases, the teacher providing these services are covered by block funding to the school, rather than by having each student designated as having special educational needs. Some students are designated, however.

References

Alberta, Alberta Education (1997), *Guide to Education for Students with Special Needs*, (1999, February 17) available: http://ednet.edc.gov.ab.ca/learning/

Anderson, J and Bachor, D (1998), A Canadian Perspective On Portfolio Use In Student Assessment, *Assessment in Education: Principles, Policy and Practices*, 5, (pp 353-379)

Andrews, J and Lupart, J (Eds) (forthcoming), *The Inclusive Classroom: Educating Exceptional Children*, 2nd ed, Nelson Canada

Bachor, D (forthcoming), Special Education in Canada, in C Reynolds and E

Fletcher-Janzen (Eds), *Encyclopedia of Special Education*, 2nd ed, John Wiley

Bachor, D and Crealock, C (1986), *Instructional strategies for students with special needs*, Prentice-Hall, Canada

Barrier-free school clears path for disabled, (1999, April 15), *The Globe and Mail*, (p A17)

Bunch, G (1994), Canadian perspectives on inclusive education from there to here: The passage to inclusive education, *Exceptionality Education Canada*, 2(1-2), (pp 49-75)

Breakdown in the classroom: Counting the cost of integration, (1997, November 23, part 1 and November 24, part 2), *The Times Colonist*, (p A3)

British Columbia, Ministry of Education, Skills, and Training (1995), *Special Education Services: A Manual of Procedures and Guidelines*, Special Education Branch, Parliament Buildings

British Columbia, Ministry of Education, Skills, and Training (1997), *Review of Learning Assistance Services Report*, (1998, September 17), available: http://www.bced.gov.bc.ca/specialed/las97/aofsec3.htm

British Columbia Ministry of Education, Skills and Training, (1998a), *Headcount Enrollment by Gender, Grade and District/Authority*, Report 1554, School Finance and Capital Planning Branch, Parliament Buildings

British Columbia, Ministry of Education, Skills, and Training (1998b), *Number of Instructional Educational assistants by School District, September 1998*, School Finance and Capital Planning Branch, Parliament Buildings

Bunch G, Lupart, J, Brown, M (1997, April), *Resistance and acceptance: Educator attitudes to inclusion of students with disabilities*, unpublished manuscript, York University

Canadian Charter of Rights and Freedoms (1982), Schedule B of *Canada Act*, 1982 (U.K.) c. 11 (1982)

Crealock, C and Bachor, D (1995), *Instructional strategies for students with special needs*, 2nd ed, Allyn and Bacon

Council of Ministers of Education, Canada (CMEC), (1998), *Report on Education in Canada, 1998*, http://www.cmec.ca/reports:rec98/testeng.htm#chair

'Dr Death' faces up to 25 years for mercy killing, (1999, April 14), *National Post*, (p A1, A15)

Edmunds, A (1999), Classroom Teachers are not Prepared for the Inclusive Classroom, *Exceptionality Education Canada*, 8(2), (pp 27-40)

English now minority tongue, (1998, March 3), *The Globe and Mail*, (p A3)

Freeze, D, (1995), *Promoting Successful Transitions*, Canadian Council for Exceptional Children

Freeze, D R, Frankel, S, Kueneman, R, and Mahon, M (1995), *Passage to employment: A discussion paper*, unpublished manuscript, University of Manitoba

Friend, M, Bursuck, W, and Hutchinson, N (1998), *Including exceptional students: A practical guide for classroom teachers* (Canadian ed), Prentice-Hall, Canada

Hammill, D, Bartel, N, and Bunch, G, (Eds) (1984), *Teaching children with learning and behavior problems* (Canadian ed), Allyn & Bacon

Hardy, M, McLeod, J, Minto, H, Perkins, S, and Quance, W (1971), *Standards for Educators of Exceptional Children*, Crainford

Harris vows to raise bar on teachers, students, (1999, April 20), *National Post*, (p A4)

Hutchinson, N (1996, June), Inclusive education within an inclusive society: Striving for an ideal in Canada, Invited address to the Annual Meeting of the Canadian Association for Educational Psychology and Canadian Society for Studies in Education, St. Catherines, Ontario

Hutchinson, N, (1999), *Teaching exceptional children and adolescents: A Canadian casebook*, Allyn & Bacon

Hutchinson, N, Martin, A, (forthcoming, a), Critical issues and critical reflection, in R Upitis, (Ed), *Who will teach? A case study of changes in teacher education*, Caddo Gap Press

Hutchinson, N, Martin, A, (forthcoming, b), Fostering inclusive beliefs and practices during preservice teacher education through communities of practice, *Teacher Education and Special Education*

Hutchinson, N L and Wong, B (1987), Special Education in Canada, in C Reynolds, and L Mann (Eds), *Encyclopedia of Special Education: a reference for the education of the handicapped and other exceptional children and adults*, Wiley

Munby, H, and Hutchinson, N, (1998), Using experience to prepare teachers for inclusive classrooms: Teacher education and the epistemology of practice, *Teacher Education and Special Education*, 21(2), (pp 75-82)

Kauffman, J, and Hallahan, D, (1995), *The illusion of full inclusion : a comprehensive critique of a current special education bandwagon*, Pro-Ed

Inclusion depends on school culture, (1996, April 11), *The Globe and Mail*, (p A6)

Jones, K, and Bender, W (1993), Utilization of paraprofessionals in special education: A review of the literature, *Remedial and Special Education*, 14(1), (pp 7-14)

Lam, Y, and McQuarrie, N (1989), Paraprofessionals are an administrative time bomb, *Canadian School Executive*, 9(3), (pp 3-6, 12)

Ludlow, B L and Lombardi, T P (1992), Special education in the year 2000: Current trends and future developments, *Education and Treatment of Children*,15 (2), (pp 147-163)

Lupart, J (1996), Moving forward in a time of change, in J Lupart, A McKeough,, and C Yewchuk (Eds), *Schools in Transition: Rethinking Regular and Special Education*, Nelson Canada, (pp 245-270)

Lupart, J and Webber, C (1996), Schools in transition: Issues and prospects. change, in J Lupart, A McKeough, and C Yewchuk (Eds), *Schools in Transition: Rethinking Regular and Special Education*, Nelson Canada, (pp 3-42)

Lupart, J, Bunch, G, and Brown, M (1997), Resistance and Acceptance: Educator attitudes toward inclusion, in G Prater, S Minner, M Islam, D Hawthorne, (Eds), *New Hopes, new horizons: The challenge of diversity in education*, Proceedings from the International Association of Special Education 5th Biennial Conference, Cape Town, South Africa, (pp 325-339)

MacKay, A (1987), The charter of rights and special education: Blessing or curse? *Canadian Journal for Exceptional Children*, 3, (pp 118-127)

MacMillan, D and Hendrick, I (1993), Evolution and legacies, in J Goodlad and T Lovitt (Eds), *Integrating general and special education*, Macmillan, (pp 23-48)

Manitoba, Ministry of Education and Training (1999), *The Manitoba Special Education Review*, (1999, January 28), available: http://www.edu.gov.mb.ca/metks4/instruct/specedu/review/index.html

Manitoba, Ministry of Education and Training (1999), *Early Identification And Education Program (EIEP)*, (1999, January 28), available: http://www.edu.gov.mb.ca/metks4/instruct/regsupp/eiepfin.html

National Joint Committee on Learning Disabilities (1999), Learning disabilities: Use of paraprofessionals, *Learning Disability Quarterly*, 22, (pp 23-30)

New Brunswick, Department of Education (1998), Annual Report, 97-98, (1999, February 16), available: http://www.gov.nb.ca/education/report.pdf

Northwest Territories, Department of Education, Culture, and Employment, *Inclusive Schooling* (1998, March 11), available: http://siksik.learnnet.nt.ca/DOCS/juniorHandbook/InclusiveSchooling.html.

Northwest Territories, Education, Culture and Employment (1999a, February 17), *Towards Excellence: A Report on Education in the Northwest Territories*, http://siksik.learnnet.nt.ca/office/C/4/pro20.htm

Northwest Territories, Education, Culture and Employment (1999b, April 15), *Educating all our children: Departmental directive on inclusive schooling*, available: http://siksik.learnnet.nt.ca/office/D/8/directve.htm

Newfoundland and Labrador, Department of Education (1999), *Using Technology to Enhance Students' Differing Abilities*, (1999, February 16), available: http://www.stemnet.nf.ca/distech/no-frames/online/introduction/index.html

Nova Scotia, Department of Education and Culture (1995), *Nova Scotia School-to-work Transition Research Project*, (1999, February 16), available: http://www.EDnet.ns.ca/educ/program/ssvcs/SCHOWORK.htm

Oderkirk, J (1993), Disabilities among children, *Canadian Social Trends*, Winter, (pp 22-25)

Ontario, Ministry of Education and Training (1994), *Violence-Free Schools Policy*, (1999, April 16), available: http://www.edu.gov.on.ca/eng/document/policy/vfreeng.html

Ontario, Ministry of Education and Training (1996), *Special Education Awards for Exemplary Practice in Integration*, (1999, April 22), available: http://www.edu.gov.on.ca/eng/document/resource/award.html

Ontario, Ministry of Education and Training (1998a), *Minister's Advisory Council on Special Education: Annual Report to the Minister for the Year 1997-98*, (1998, September 30), available: http://www.edu.gov.on.ca/eng/document/reports/report98.html

Ontario, Ministry of Education and Training (1998b), *Update: Special Education*, (1999, February 16), available: http://www.edu.gov.on.ca/eng/document/brochure/update/speced/

Ottawa may consider leniency, (1997, November 7), *The Globe and Mail*, (p A1, A6)

Prince Edward Island, Department of Education (1998), *Summary Report: Review of Special Education*, (1999, February 16), available: http://www.gov.pe.ca/educ/publications/reports/se/review.asp

Prince Edward Island, Department of Education, *Who are the students with special needs?* (1999, April 15), available: http://www.gov.pe.ca/educ/publications/reports/se/whoare.asp

R *v* Latimer, (1997), 1 S.C.R. 217

Reynolds, M (1989), An historical perspective: The delivery of special education to mildly disabled and at-risk students, *Remedial and Special Education*, 10(6), (pp 7-11)

Reynolds, C and Birch, J (1977), *Teaching exceptional children in all America's schools*, The Council for Exceptional Children

Reynolds, M, Wang, M, & Walberg, H (1987), The necessary restructuring of special education, *Exceptional Children*, 53, (pp 391-398)

Saskatchewan, Saskatchewan Education (1999), *Transition planning: Building Bridges*, (1999, February 17), available: http://www.sasked. gov.sk.ca/curr_inst/speced/

Sitko, M and Sitko, C, (Eds) (1996), *Exceptional solutions: Computers and special needs*, Althouse Press

Statistics Canada, (1996), *University degrees granted by field of study, by sex*, http://www.statcan.ca/english/Pgdb/People/Education/educ21.htm

The Council for Exceptional Children (1991), Code of ethics of the council for exceptional children, *Supplement to Teaching Exceptional Children*, 23(2), (pp 1-2)

The Council for Exceptional Children (1997), CEC code of ethics and standards of practice, [Online] available http://www.cec.sped.org/ps/code.htm

The Council for Exceptional Children (1999), CEC international standards for entry into professional practice, [Online] available: http://www.cec.sped.org/ps/ps-entry.htm.

Treherne, D, Dice, T L, Grigg, E E and Sanche, R P (1974), *A matter of principle: Standards governing legislation for services for children with special needs*, Council for Exceptional Children

Thomson, G, Stewart, M E and Ward, K E (1995), Criteria for opening records of needs, Edinburgh: A report to the Scottish Office of Education

Thomson, G, Ward, K, Riddell, S and Dyer, M (1993), Pathways to adulthood for young people with special educational needs, *Issues in Special Education and Rehabilitation*, 8(1), (pp 51-61)

Vandercook, T, York, J and Forest, M (1989), The McGill Action Planning System (MAPS): A strategy for building the vision, *Journal of the Association for Persons with Severe Handicaps*, 14, (pp 205-215)

Wilton, K (1988), Employment and adjustment of school-leavers with mild retarded in New Zealand, *Australia and New Zealand Journal of Development Disabilities*, 14, (pp 235-244)

Winzer, M (1987), History of special education, in M Winzer, S Rogow, and C David (Eds), *Exceptional Education in Canada*, Prentice-Hall, Canada

Winzer, M (1989), *Closing the Gap: Special learners in regular classroom*, Copp Clark

Yukon, Department of Education, *Education*, (1999, February 17), available: http://www.gov.yk.ca/depts/education/

Chapter 10

Special Educational Needs in the West Indies: policy and practice

Gary Hornby, Madge Hall, and Marva L Ribeiro

This chapter will focus on the development of special education and current issues concerning special education services in the major English speaking countries in the West Indies. The countries included are Barbados, Jamaica, Trinidad and Tobago, and the smaller countries making up the Organisation of Eastern Caribbean States (OECS). The three countries which host a campus of the University of the West Indies (UWI), Barbados, Jamaica and Trinidad will be covered in detail followed by a brief comment on the OECS.

Barbados

Background and education system

Barbados is the most easterly country in the West Indies. It is a small island of 166 square miles with a population of around 280,000 people. Barbados was a British colony for over 300 years and gained its independence in 1966. The main components of the economy are sugar cane production, tourism, and a range of manufacturing and service industries relating to its regional location.

Public education in Barbados is compulsory for all children between the ages of five and 16 years. The educational system is structured into four levels: nursery, primary, secondary, and tertiary. Nursery education caters for children between the ages of three and five years who are taught in one of four nursery schools or 50 nursery classes in primary schools. Primary education caters for children between the ages of five and 11 years who are taught at one of 80 government or 16 private primary schools. At the end of primary education pupils sit an 11-plus examination to determine which of the 23 public secondary schools or 12 private secondary schools they will attend. At the end of the secondary level, students sit the Caribbean Examinations Council examinations and can go on to pursue Advanced Level subjects in the sixth forms of four government secondary schools or at the Community College. Tertiary education is provided at four government owned and/or supported institutions: Erdiston Teachers' Training College, Samuel Jackman Prescod Polytechnic, the Barbados Community College, and the University of the West Indies campus at Cave Hill.

Special Education in Barbados

Development

The first example of special education provision in Barbados occurred in the 1950s when some primary schools began to have special classes for children who were experiencing difficulties. These children were taught separately for the 3Rs but were mainstreamed for other subjects. The 1960s saw the opening of two special schools, one privately run for mentally challenged children and one government run for children who are deaf or blind. The 1970s saw the opening of another private special school and two special education units attached to government primary schools, all providing for mentally challenged children. In the 1980s two more government facilities were opened: a children's development centre for children with physical and multiple disabilities; and a centre for pre-vocational training for mentally challenged students aged 13 to 18 years. Also, at this time, an Education Officer for Special Education and a psychologist were employed by the Ministry of Education. In the 1990s three more special education units were opened along with two senior schools for children with moderate learning difficulties at the secondary level and most recently a centre for children with behavioural difficulties. The 1990s has also seen the start of specialist training for teachers of children with special needs being made available in Barbados, initially at the Erdiston Teacher's College and later at the Cave Hill campus of UWI.

Current situation

Government policy on children with special needs in Barbados, as outlined in the most recent white paper (Ministry of Education, 1995), is one of providing for as many children with special needs as possible in mainstream schools while maintaining special schools and units for those with more severe disabilities. Therefore, the majority of children with special needs are in maintained schools. Only children with the most severe disabilities are in special education facilities. From the number of places available at both government and private special facilities it is estimated that children in special schools and units make up around one percent of the overall school population. In contrast, findings from small scale surveys suggest that the proportion of students with special needs in mainstream schools is at least 20 percent.

Special education is currently provided by a variety of government and private education facilities and services. These are outlined below.

Special units: there are five special units attached to government primary schools which cater for mentally challenged children and autistic children who are aged five to 13 years.

Centre for Pre-Vocational Training: this caters for mentally challenged and autistic children aged 13 to 18 years, most of whom have come from the special units.

Special classes within private schools: several private schools have special classes which cater for children who are mentally challenged, dyslexic, or who have moderate learning difficulties.

Special schools: there are three special schools. The School for the Deaf and Blind is a government school which takes in children with severe hearing or visual difficulties. The Learning Centre is a private school which caters for children who are mentally challenged or autistic or who have moderate learning difficulties. The Challenor School is a private school which educates children and young adults who are mentally challenged or autistic or children with multiple disabilities. It also has a workshop in which young adults with disabilities make a variety of products to sell to the public and an independent living centre where four young adults with disabilities live and look after themselves. The Challenor School also runs a small respite care facility for parents to leave their children with special needs for short periods, such as over the weekend, so that they can get a break.

Senior schools: there are three senior schools which cater for secondary age pupils with moderate learning difficulties who are not able to cope with the normal secondary school curriculum.

Education Officer for Special Education: the Education Officer for Special Education is based in the Ministry of Education and has oversight of all government special education schools and units as well as provision for children with special needs in ordinary schools.

Psychologists: Psychologists based in the Ministry of Education conduct assessments of individual children's learning and/or behavioural difficulties and advise teachers and parents.

Children's Development Centre: the Children's Development Centre is part of the Ministry of Health. It is staffed by teachers, therapists, psychologists and paediatricians who can provide a comprehensive assessment of children with special needs. There is an education unit for children with physical and multiple disabilities. There is also a workshop for young mentally challenged adults. An audiologist is available to test children's hearing and, when necessary, fit hearing aids. Physiotherapy, speech therapy and occupational therapy are also available.

Private specialists and organisations: there are several private specialists who work with children with special needs. These include: speech therapists; occupational therapists; physiotherapists; and psychologists. There are also organisations which cater for children with specific special needs, such as the Caribbean Dyslexia Centre.

Support groups: there are support groups for parents of children with various special needs such as autism, as well as several disability organisations, such as the Barbados Council for the Disabled, which provide support and advice as well as advocating for better services and facilities.

Current challenges

There are several factors operating within Barbados which present considerable challenges to the provision of effective education for children with special needs in both mainstream and special schools. These are discussed below.

Concepts of special needs

The first challenge to be addressed is the concept of special needs which is held by many teachers in Barbados. Typically, children with special needs are seen as falling into one of two discreet categories: those in mainstream schools deemed to be in need of remedial help; and those in special schools or units deemed to be in need of special education. Children with significant learning difficulties are referred to as mentally challenged and are typically educated in special schools or units but often without any determination of whether their level of difficulties are moderate, severe or profound. All other children with learning difficulties are regarded as remedial. No distinction is generally made between children who have a specific learning difficulty, such as dyslexia or a speech and language disorder, and those with a general learning difficulty which affects their learning across the curriculum. This creates particular problems in many of the secondary schools where academic subjects are taught and/or remedial teaching is used with students who have general learning difficulties and who should instead follow an alternative curriculum better suited to their needs. There is an urgent need to develop a broadened concept of special needs among Barbadian teachers; in particular, to establish the view that there are several types of disability and a continuum of levels of special need which teachers in both mainstream and special schools are likely to encounter. In addition, teachers must realize that the type and level of special need should determine the curriculum and teaching methods used with such children.

Adequacy of special education facilities

The number of places available in both private and government facilities for mentally-challenged children represents approximately one percent of the entire school population. However, the normal distribution of abilities indicates that around two and a half percent of children will have IQs in the mentally-challenged range. This suggests that there is inadequate provision for mentally challenged children, many of whom remain in mainstream schools or stay home. This is particularly true of those who live in outlying districts. There are also limited facilities for children with learning disabilities (*eg* dyslexia), physical disabilities, multiple disabilities, speech and language difficulties, or emotional and behavioural problems.

Special Education support services

The Children's Development Centre provides a range of part-time clinic-based services including multi-disciplinary assessments, physiotherapy and audiology. Other than this, support services provided by the government for children with special needs are extremely limited. Currently, only one education officer for special education and two psychologists are employed by the Ministry of Education and there are only two speech therapists who are based at the Ministry of Health. There are no itinerant teachers to support children with vision or hearing problems in mainstream schools. There is no specialist service to help teachers cope with children who have emotional or behavioural problems. The limited support for schools makes it difficult for teachers to provide effectively for children with special needs, particularly those in mainstream schools.

Levels of teacher training

Until recently, apart from teachers in the School for the Deaf and Blind who have all trained overseas, the majority of the teachers working in special education had not undergone specialist training. Many of them are currently completing training in special education. However, many of the teachers in private special schools and some in the government facilities have not completed initial teacher training.

The challenge in establishing special education training is therefore to provide courses for both trained and untrained teachers. Another challenge is that teachers in mainstream schools have typically had minimal training in catering for pupils with special needs. However, many primary schools have on their staff a 'remedial' teacher who has completed either a one year full-time training course or short-term training in the remediation of literacy difficulties. The challenge is to provide some training to all practising teachers and more extensive training to at least one resource person in each school, while at the same time expanding the special needs component in initial training courses.

Organisation of the general education system

Barbados has competitive entry to secondary schools by means of an examination, referred to as 'common entrance' or the '11 plus', which is taken at the end of primary schooling. This examination process has an impact on the whole of the education system. It affects the curriculum in primary schools, which tends to focus largely on language, arts and mathematics since these are the subjects assessed in the examination. It also has an impact on the way students with special needs are viewed in primary schools since schools are evaluated by the performance of their students in the common entrance examination. Pupils with special needs are typically seen as detracting from the school's overall performance and are therefore overlooked in many schools.

In addition, placement in secondary schools on the basis of scores on the common entrance examination leads to pupils with learning difficulties being concentrated in the newer secondary schools, all of which have low status in the eyes of the Barbadian public. The funding and organisation of primary schools in Barbados also has a major impact on provision for special needs. A major problem is the non-replacement of staff who are absent, sick or on courses. Since school principals are generally not allowed to bring in substitute teachers, replacements have to be found from within the school. In many schools remedial teachers are being used as substitute teachers for much of the week, preventing them from acting in a remedial capacity with pupils who have special needs. This situation has led to many trained remedial teachers opting to return to ordinary class teaching.

School systems for meeting special needs

Another challenge is presented by the general lack of infrastructure for coping with special needs within mainstream schools. Although some schools have developed their own special needs policy and procedures and are catering effectively for pupils with special needs, in the majority of schools this is not the case. In most schools, mechanisms for identifying children with special needs are inadequate, as are strategies for assessing specific needs, planning individual programmes and for reviewing progress. Also typically lacking are clear procedures for recording and disseminating information about pupils with special needs, for effectively utilizing material and human resources within the school, and for collaborating effectively with parents and other professionals. A critical challenge is therefore one of getting mainstream schools to develop comprehensive policies and effective procedures for meeting special needs.

National policy and procedures for special needs

The lack of school infrastructure for meeting special needs in schools is hardly surprising given the absence of policy and guidance at a national level. Unlike in the UK and USA, there is no Barbadian legislation which specifically sets out policy and procedures for special needs provision in schools. Also lacking are national policy and procedures for identifying special needs, such as in screening young children for vision and hearing difficulties, as well as for the assessment of pupils being considered for transfer to special education facilities.

Sections of the 1995 White Paper on education reform (Ministry of Education) have set out an outline policy for special education, which now needs to be elaborated in order to produce legislation and a set of national procedures for children with special needs.

Salaries and working conditions for teachers

Though the World Bank has provided funding for the construction of several modern primary schools there are still some schools in which two teachers are working with two full classes in one small classroom. Also of concern are conditions at three of the five government special education units, where cramped or unsuitable facilities are in evidence. Another issue is that funding for purchasing material resources for teaching in government schools is minimal. Therefore, the budget for buying additional resources required for pupils with special needs is extremely limited. In addition, teacher aides in the classroom are almost unknown in

Barbados unlike in many western countries in which they are regarded as an essential component of provision for special needs children. Also, teachers generally consider that, in comparison with other occupational groups in Barbados, their salaries are poor. As a result, many teachers attempt to make ends meet by engaging in other activities and teaching is regarded by many others as a stepping stone to a better paid career in the commercial world.

Current initiatives

Edutech 2000

The government of Barbados has just embarked on a massive education sector enhancement project which is to cost $350 million over five years. The project involves several components, including the upgrading of many school buildings; putting computers into all classrooms and giving all schools internet access; promoting a shift from traditional, whole class teaching to a focus on child-centred methods of instruction; as well as the provision of training to facilitate the above components.

As part of the component of the project focussing on upgrading of school buildings, a new and expanded special education unit is currently being built to replace the worst of the five government units. The new unit is to have within it a class specifically for autistic pupils, with reduced pupil-teacher ratio and two teacher-aides. Also, the components focussing on information technology and child-centred approaches are increasing the awareness of the requirements of pupils with special needs and of possible strategies teachers can use with them. In addition, the training component includes a commitment to train teachers from each school in Barbados to act as co-ordinators for special needs work within their schools.

Speech and hearing survey

In a project funded by the Caribbean Development Bank (CDB), screening of all children in government primary schools for speech and hearing difficulties has been carried out over the past two years. The project found that almost 6% of children had hearing problems and around 24% had speech difficulties (Stabler *et al*, 1998). These findings have prompted the government to consider making such screening, and the necessary follow-up, an essential element of the education system.

Awareness of special needs

The CDB also funded a project aimed at raising awareness of children with special needs among teachers in Barbados. During 1997 one-day workshops on special needs education were conducted at all government primary schools which were closed for the day so that all teachers could attend. Similar workshops for secondary schools were conducted during 1999. A handbook for teachers, produced to complement the workshops, was distributed to all teachers in Barbados, including those in private schools (Hornby, 1998).

In addition to the teacher workshops and teachers' handbook the project also involved conducting a series of one-day workshops for parents of children with special needs together with a handbook for parents, which is to be made available through schools, libraries and health clinics (Hornby, 1999).

Training for special needs

In the past two years the elements of a comprehensive training model for special needs have been put in place (Hornby and Neblett-Lashley, 1997). In addition to the one-day school-based workshops referred to above, courses on special needs have been established at the Erdiston Training College and the Cave Hill campus of UWI. The College offers a 150 hour course for teachers working full-time with special needs children and a 50 hour course for teachers in schools with large numbers of special needs pupils. Also, all initial training or in-service training courses at the College include a 15-hour component on special needs. UWI now offers a Masters degree course in special education which is recruiting very well and is to run the training course for learning support co-ordinators, which was referred to above, as well as developing a Bachelors degree course with a specialization in special education.

Review of legislation, policy and procedures

The Barbados Ministry of Education is currently in the process of pro-ducing a policy for children with special needs and is seeking to set this within new education legislation now being drafted. Thus, in the near future, the Ministry intends to provide schools with comprehensive guide-lines about the procedures they must have in place in order to meet the needs of pupils with special needs (Sergeant, 1999).

Jamaica

Background and education system

Jamaica is an island nation in the Caribbean Sea located about 90 miles south of Cuba. It has a length of 146 miles with width varying from 22-51 miles and a total area of 4,244 square miles. Jamaica has a population of approximately 2.5 million persons, and a fairly well diversified economy. Tourism, bauxite and agricultural exports are its main sources of external income.

Enrolment in early childhood, primary and secondary schools numbers 658,931. Of that total 2135, or 0.32 percent, are registered in 11 government-owned and/or government-aided segregated schools catering for children of varied age groups with mental retardation, physical disabilities, visual disabilities, hearing disabilities and multiple handicapping conditions. These students are taught by 250 teachers. The private sector and NGOs also provide various levels of support for 7400 persons in an effort to develop the full potential of persons with special needs. Thirty-four resource rooms or service facilities are located in primary and all age schools (grades 1-9), in different parishes in the island. These facilities were designed as venues for individualized instruction for students with learning difficulties and training sites for college students.

Given the small number of students registered in segregated schools, there is a general understanding that the majority of students with special needs are in mainstream schools. There is good reason for this assumption because, when Lowe and Ragbir (1983) examined 18,269 students or 4.2% of the primary student population, they found that 8.27% of the sample had handicapping conditions. The areas identified were physical, visual, auditory, speech, emotional, learning disabilities and mentally retardation. The category with the largest percentage was learning disabilities. To date there is no evidence suggesting that the situation has changed.

Early childhood education

This programme exposes children within the zero-to-five age range to learning conditions designed to foster development of skills necessary for primary education. There are 4898 teachers employed at this level.

Primary education

This is offered to Grades 1-6 or the 6-11 age group of the primary, primary and junior high, all-age schools and private preparatory schools in the island. The number of teachers employed in public primary schools is approximately 9521. Up to the end of the 1997-98 academic year, promotion from the primary to secondary school was facilitated by either automatic movement in schools offering secondary education or selective placement through the Common Entrance Examination (CEE) or 11+ exam. Historically, places were awarded to less than 50 percent of the entrants due to lack of physical space. Beginning 1998-99, the CEE was replaced by the Grade Six Achievement Tests (GSAT), testing knowledge in science, social studies, mathematics, language arts and communication. It is the culminating test in a national assessment programme designed to monitor how well students at the primary level are doing. In addition to the GSAT, tests are given to children in Grades one, three and four. The GSAT results help in making decisions about which of the six different types of secondary school students attend.

Secondary education

This is provided for students within the age range 12-18 years in Grades 7-13 in junior high, secondary high, comprehensive high, technical high, vocational and agricultural schools. The number of teachers in the 602 public schools offering secondary education is 11,219. The examinations administered at the secondary level include Caribbean Examination Council, Caribbean Advanced Proficiency Examinations, GCSE ordinary and advanced levels and National Vocational Qualifications.

Tertiary education

This level is pursued in 17 publicly-owned institutions including nine teachers colleges, the Edna Manley College for Visual and Performing Arts, the University of Technology and the University of the West Indies, Mona Campus. There are also several private institutions offering tertiary education.

Special Education in Jamaica

Non-Governmental Organizations (NGOs) have been providing educational opportunities for persons with special needs since the early years of the twentieth century and, beginning in the 1970s, governments have articulated the notion of education for all. However, there is no specific legislation relating to the educational needs of persons with exceptionalities. The most recent plans of the Ministry of Education and Culture (MOEC) include the creation of mechanisms for improving and expanding primary education and providing secondary education for all students by the year 2002. Currently, three major projects with funding from the government and bilateral/multilateral sources are part of the process. These projects are the Social Sector Development project, the Primary Education Improvement Project (PEIP) and the Reform of Secondary Education (ROSE) project. The objectives of the school-based projects relate to the improvement of quality, access and equity in education.

The MOEC has a Special Education Unit with a staff complement of six special education officers. These officers work closely with special and mainstream schools as well as NGOs to support students with special needs. The government provides salary for teachers in segregated schools and assists with the general financing of related programmes. For the past five years the MOEC has included in its budget support for the Institute for Excellence in Education. This is an organization that plans and implements programmes for gifted children on a part-time basis.

The MOEC also provides a national braille and large print service in education. The products of this service include teachers' manuals and hundreds of braille and large print primary texts for children with visual impairments.

Mico Teachers College, the largest of its kind in the English-speaking Caribbean, began training teachers to work in the areas of mental retardation, hearing impairment, learning disabilities and physical disabilities in 1976. The area of visual impairment was added in recent years. The government of the Netherlands, in partnership with the Jamaican government, has contributed much to this venture which has provided an initial three year training for persons from most of the Commonwealth countries in the region. The government of the Netherlands also provided financial support for persons pursuing a one-year certificate programme in education for the deaf, which started at the UWI, Mona, in 1971 and was the first teacher training programme in special education in the English-speaking territories. This programme was initiated by a NGO, the Jamaica Association for the Deaf.

In 1986 UWI, Mona Campus, in collaboration with Mico College, introduced a BEd programme in special education with emphasis on aspects of disabilities. In 1994, a BEd with an option on managing learning difficulties began at Mona with the objective to facilitate children experiencing learning difficulties in the mainstream. Several courses are also offered in special education at the graduate level at UWI Mona. UWI has a very dynamic committee for students with special needs which facilitates services such as equipment for students with visual and hearing disabilities and relevant academic support.

Mico also has a Centre for child assessment, research, diagnostic and therapeutic activities. The staff members work with schools and bring students in for short and long term interventions.

There are also several active organizations, including the Combined Disabilities Association of Jamaica (1997), that has recently submitted a draft policy for disabled persons in Jamaica to the government for consideration. The draft policy is framed in the standard rules on the equalization of opportunities published by the United Nations. Eleven major issues, including education, are addressed, and it is the product of a series of national consultations involving persons with and without special needs.

Current concerns

One ongoing concern is the limited number of persons with special needs accessing tertiary level education. At UWI Mona, for example, during the 1994-95 academic year, of the 7695 students registered only 35 indicated that they had special needs. This, and other realities, signal and raise questions about the academic well-being of children with special needs who are in special schools as well as those who are known to be in the mainstream, but are not monitored. Some of the most pronounced issues follow.

Policy

A national policy for persons with special needs is required urgently. Currently, there are only a few legislated items and these relate to access to houses built by the National Housing Trust at a special rate; 5 percent of jobs in the Public sector; and special fares when travelling on the public transport system. One major irony is that although there is unemployment among persons with special needs, they cannot access the jobs allotted because of inadequate qualifications. Furthermore, as mentioned earlier, the draft policy focuses only on persons with disabilities, not on other forms of special needs.

A relevant policy would facilitate identification of the number of students with special needs in the system. In a survey of special needs students in selected mainstream secondary schools in Jamaica, few schools had official records of the presence of special needs students (Hall and Figueroa 1995). However, based on the estimates of guidance counsellors, there were over 900 such students in 32 secondary schools in four parishes alone. As far back as 1991, census data pointed to over 117,000 children, or approximately 18%, in the under 15 age group who have special needs in the categories: hearing, speech, physical disabilities, slowness of learning, and multiple disabilities. A relevant policy would make the school system accountable for reducing inequities in provisions.

Curriculum delivery

Some of the segregated schools use neither the PEIP nor ROSE curriculum. While it is recognized that there are cases when that is justified, the non-use of these special curricula is frequently not justified. Furthermore, many children in the mainstream experiencing learning difficulties are not supported adequately in their efforts to attain grade level requirements. One problem that is common to both special needs and mainstream schools is the inability of some teachers to deliver the curriculum appropriately at the secondary level. In one instance, teachers who have special education training and are working in special schools do not necessarily have the content for the relevant subject areas. In the other case, teachers who are trained to work at the secondary level do not necessarily have the techniques and communication skills necessary to facilitate some learners experiencing difficulties; for example those who are deaf. Either way the situation fosters inequities, and retards the academic progress of many children.

Training

More training is required for professionals and for general awareness regarding the nature and needs of persons with special needs. For example persons should know that a hearing aid does not necessarily allow the user to hear speech with clarity. Currently, in addition to programmes offering certification, trainees enrolled in teachers colleges since 1997-8 are required to pursue a module in special education. This module was designed to create awareness of diversity in the classrooms. The MOEC and NGOs also conduct training session for teachers and parents. During the 1997-8 academic year the first national conference on special education was held.

Physical layout and culture of schools

Several primary and secondary schools are physically hostile to students. Hall and Figueroa (1998) reported that when students were asked their reason for selecting the school they were attending, a popular reason among students with physical disabilities was that it was the only high school with wheelchair access. It is of note that in the expansion and improvement of programmes this aspect is being addressed. Regarding the culture of schools, there are many misconceptions about learning and diversity. It is common practice for teachers to teach to the average child. Consequently those at both ends of the continuum are disadvantaged. The curricula for both primary and secondary levels address multi-level teaching, so possible changes are envisioned. However, an accelerated pace of change is required .

Finally, although there are positive indicators that children with special needs in Jamaica are getting some support, there is much room for improvement. One step in that direction is more collaboration among the NGOs, as well as the MOEC, to better utilize scarce resources. This partnership could facilitate the use of approaches such as whole school management and teaching models, whereby specialists offering a variety of skills rotate within small groups of schools on a weekly basis.

Trinidad and Tobago

Background and the education system

Trinidad, with an area of 1864 square miles, is the southernmost island in the Caribbean and lies only 7 miles from Venezuela in South America. Tobago, an island of 116 square miles, is located 21 miles to the northeast of Trinidad. Trinidad and Tobago has a combined population of 1.3 million people. The main industries are petroleum, sugar, citrus, cocoa and coffee production, as well as tourism in Tobago. Trinidad and Tobago became an independent nation in 1962, and a Republic in 1976.

The system of public education includes pre-primary, primary, secondary and tertiary education. There are 157 registered early childhood education centres, 477 primary schools, 100 government and assisted secondary schools, two technical/vocational institutes, four youth camps, two government schools and more than 12 assisted special schools. Every year 30,000 children (age 11+) write the Common Entrance examination. Over 20,000 of them are placed in secondary schools. Those who do not secure a place attend private secondary schools, post primary centres, or pursue technical/vocational courses at a number of privately run institutions or at the Youth Training and Employment Partnership Programme. Caribbean Examinations Council (CXC) examinations are completed at the end of the secondary level. Some students go on to pursue the Cambridge Advanced Level examinations or attend tertiary level institutions including the local St Augustine Campus of UWI, one of the two Teacher Training Colleges for primary level teachers, or the Technical Institutes. Lately, there are many privately-run organisations which take in students who wish to pursue an associate degree or a degree from a foreign university or college.

Special education in Trinidad and Tobago

As in other parts of the world, special education was started by voluntary philanthropic organisations that responded to the plight of students with special needs who could not attend the regular public schools. The special schools set up received financial subsidies from various government agencies. One of the most significant events in the evolution of special education took place when 'Provision for Special Schools' was enacted in the 1966 Education Act. This supported the establishment of special schools, classes and services, either as separate units or in connection with approved public institutions, and brought special education under the aegis of the Ministry of Education for the first time. In 1979, five special schools were incorporated into the public education system of Trinidad and Tobago. In 1990, a centre for children with emotional and behavioural difficulties was opened in Trinidad and, in 1999, two special schools in Tobago were brought under the jurisdiction of the Ministry of Education.

In 1979 a consultation from the Organisation of American States (Winschell, 1979) recommended the appointment of a Co-ordinator of Special Education in the Ministry of Education. 1980 saw the formation of a Special Education Unit and an Advisory Committee for Special Education. In 1994, the Cabinet accepted an Education Policy Paper (Ministry of Education, 1993) which includes proposals for children with special needs. Also in 1994, the Special Education Unit began the administration of diagnostic tests to teacher-identified students with special needs, to determine whether they needed any special concessions for the Common Entrance examination. In 1998, the Ministry prepared an assessment package for mainstream teachers to help in the identification of children with special needs.

Number of children with special needs in Trinidad and Tobago

A national survey of children with special needs in Trinidad and Tobago (Marge, 1984) reported that 16.1% of the total population age three to 16 years had one of seven categories of disability. A later survey carried out by the Child Guidance Clinic (White Paper, 1993-2003) supported the findings of the Marge Report and further stated that 13.1% of special needs children were attending no school at all, 5.8% were at pre-schools, 5.1% were attending special schools, 6.7% were attending other facilities, while the remaining 67.2% were in primary and secondary schools where there were no special education provisions for them.

Teacher education and training

Between 1987 and 1990 staff from the University of Manitoba conducted a project which aimed to sensitise approximately 1,100 teachers to the needs of children with disabilities in three-week workshops. The two Teacher Training Colleges have included a special education option in their two-year initial training programme for primary school teachers. The teachers at the schools for the deaf and teachers of the visually impaired receive their training at MICO Teachers College in Jamaica.

Since 1989, some teachers have pursued distance education courses in special education organised by Sheffield University. To date 86, teachers have graduated with a Diploma and 47 with a Certificate in Special Education while 22 more teachers are expected to graduate at Diploma level and five at the Certificate level in the year 2000. Sheffield began the MEd in Special and Inclusive Education in 1993 and, to date, 16 teachers have graduated.

In 1996, workshops led by Ministry of Education staff were held at the Learning Resource Centre, one day per week for five weeks, to assist mainstream teachers to use strategies for effective teaching of learners who have special needs.

Support services for Special Needs Education

Special Education Unit: Recently, the Ministry of Education opened a Diagnostic and Prescriptive Services (DPS) Unit. Fourteen special education teachers were assigned to the DPS in order to meet the special needs of children in 477 primary schools spread across eight educational districts.

Services for the Hearing-Impaired: in 1990, the Trinidad and Tobago Association in Aid of the Deaf, formally opened DRETCHI (Diagnostic, Research, Educational and Therapeutic Centre for the Hearing-Impaired). Its purpose is clearly defined in its name with its aim of helping all hearing-impaired children in Trinidad and Tobago to join their hearing counterparts in mainstream schools. 1992 saw the establishment of early intervention services catering to anyone who required such services. The centre is concerned with teaching the deaf to use speech as the main form of communication and it is doing this using the Auditory Verbal approach as far as is possible. The association is responsible for the management of the two special schools for the deaf. There are also some hearing-impaired children attending a primary level special school which caters for children with various categories of special need, under one roof. At the end of primary school many attend the National Centre for Persons with Disabilities which is a rehabilitation centre.

Services for children with mental retardation: the Trinidad and Tobago Association for Retarded Children provides health and social services alongside an educational service for its clients. Health and social services include residential homes, neurological departments, early intervention programmes and parent counselling programmes, while the educational services include day schools and vocational training.

Services for the visually impaired: the Blind Welfare Association is responsible for the School for the Blind. The school prepares some children to enter the mainstream where they are supported by itinerant teachers of the visually-impaired. Another organisation, Persons Associated with Visual Impairment, provides many much-needed services to the visually impaired, such as rehabilitation, outreach seminars, community social groups, white canes, braillers, spectacles and tools for communication at low cost.

Services for the autistic: the Autistic Society of Trinidad and Tobago is an active parent support group with 80 registered families. 37 autistic children are of school age. Of these, 19 are at home, 12 attend special private schools, four attend an integrated private school, two attend regular primary school.

Services for the dyslexic: in 1990 three qualified teachers of children with dyslexia started informal training of teachers who are interested in teaching children with dyslexia. They also provide private tuition for children who need this service.

Services for children with emotional and behavioural disorders: there is only one special school for children with emotional and behavioural problems in Trinidad. It has a staff of qualified special education teachers.

Services for the physically challenged: The Princess Elizabeth Centre for Physically Handicapped Children can accommodate up to 120 children. The Centre is noted for its Scoliosis programme, which is now 24 years old. The Gokool Orthopaedic Workshop is situated on the premises of the Centre and manufactures braces, splints, cervical collars and prostheses. The Centre comprises a nursery school, a primary school, dormitories, workshop, operating theatre and a hospital ward.

Other Services: there are several other private and volunteer organisations and specialists who provide for the special needs of children. There are also groups of parents who form themselves into advocacy groups to seek the best interest of children and adults with special needs.

Current issues

A National Symposium on Special Education was held in Trinidad in 1999. The symposium, which was attended by a wide cross-section of teachers, parents, and personnel from the Ministry of Education, closed with recommendations made in six key areas, which were: policy formulation; teacher education; institutional strengthening; education of community and family on the special needs of students; curriculum enrichment; and the identification and assessment of children with special needs. Ribeiro and Matthews (1999) elaborate on these recommendations. They suggest that policy formulation incorporates definitional issues and implications arising from them; that is, that special needs of students be considered in terms of their functional needs which must be responded to in every classroom, implying that support be available for teachers to facilitate individual learning differences. Teacher education for special needs and institutional strengthening are natural offshoots of such a policy since teachers need training, resources and institutional support if they are to respond appropriately to diversity in their classrooms.

When policies that are implemented have the kind of coherence discussed here, they can become more easily communicated to parents and the community. Support by parents and the community provides one of the most important means for success of any school programme for children with special needs. Identification and assessment must lead to focussing on the functional needs of students and not over-emphasise the particular category of disability. Curriculum enrichment and delivery again depends on how teachers and those planning programmes for children with special needs conceive of their ability to learn and the teacher's ability to teach them. It is believed that curricula for children with special needs are enriched curricula and the strategies used for their delivery are highly rated for effect. This combination results in effective learning as a result of good teaching.

Provision for children with special needs

There are no laws that mandate the assignment of students with disabilities to regular schools with programmes that are adapted to accommodate their needs. All the special schools are primary level. None of the secondary schools has been adequately prepared, in terms of staffing, curriculum and classroom adaptation for children with special needs.

Children from the special schools at the primary level are placed in secondary schools on the same basis as children who attend the regular schools. Some students who are not placed by the Common Entrance examinations attend rehabilitation centres. Others who find difficulty in managing their programmes at the secondary schools sometimes join them. Still others continue their education at the youth camps.

Two junior secondary, one senior secondary comprehensive, and two secondary comprehensive schools, at present, each have one member of staff who was transferred from the schools for the deaf to facilitate hearing-impaired children who were placed at these schools based on performance on the common entrance examination. They are teachers trained to teach at the primary level. They are not subject specialists as required at the secondary level.

Two secondary schools accommodate visually impaired students and their itinerant teachers. One other secondary school has agreed to have students who are physically challenged, using wheel-chairs or prosthesis placed there. This school, with the advocacy of the parent of a physically-challenged, wheel-chair bound student, now has a lift installed to allow such students to use the library, computer room, language lab and other specialised facilities which are situated on the second floor.

Special schools have long waiting lists of school-age children. Regular government and private schools also have long waiting lists. Parents therefore tend to accept the first placement offered to them. Some special needs children are fortunate to find a place in a school where the teachers attend workshops/seminars to learn as much as they can about the teaching/learning of children with specific needs. These children successfully manage in the regular schools. However, many more appear to be only physically present at the schools. The great majority of them are in need of remedial assistance in academic, social, and emotional areas. One must also note the creation of children with special needs by the mere fact of their attendance at some schools.

Summary of major issues

The issues to be faced and resolved in Trinidad and Tobago as they relate to special educational needs are many. They can be summarised as:

- recognition of the need to identify and treat all children with special needs;
- a government policy to mandate equitable education provision for children with special needs;
- adequate special education support services;
- initial teacher education and in-service education and training of the classroom practitioner in special needs education;
- a rethinking of secondary school placement and assessment practices;
- the removal of architectural barriers from all schools;
- recognition for, and appropriate use of, the strengths of teachers brought about by advanced training and experience with special needs children;
- education of the parents and community about the special needs of some learners.

Organisation of Eastern Caribbean States

Several smaller, but mostly independent countries, which are mainly English speaking and members of the Commonwealth, make up what is known as the Organisation of Eastern Caribbean States (OECS). The countries are: Antigua and Barbuda; British Virgin Islands; Dominica; Grenada; Monsterrat; St Kitts-Nevis; St Vincent and the Grenadines; and St Lucia. These islands form a crescent in the Caribbean sea stretching between Puerto Rico in the north to Trinidad in the south. Collectively, their total population is approximately 555,000 persons. The countries are connected by air transport.

The education system of all the countries is organized in four levels, namely early childhood, primary, secondary and tertiary. Primary education is free in all the islands, but there is variation in both quality and quantity. In reference to the Caribbean, the World Bank Report of 1992 stated that there were gaps in the primary level of education for children with special needs because the existing education systems are poorly equipped in terms of resources and programmes.

However, the OECS has specific plans for children with special needs. Evidence of this is seen in the Educational Reform Report that includes 65 strategies and 12 major focus areas for projects (OECS, 1991). In areas dealing with the improvement of both primary and secondary education, for example, the need to be more responsive to the special needs of students, and to provide schooling for the developmentally disabled up to age 15, are underscored.

Traditionally, governments in the OECS have provided financial support in the form of salary payment for teachers working with children who have special needs, rather than having special schools or special classes.

The occurrence of children with special needs in the OECS is estimated at 11,578 or approximately 10% of the 115,787 children enrolled in the five-to-11 age cohort (Bergsma, 1995). However, Bergsma also reported that, of the total estimated, only 1107 have been identified and of those, only 635 are supported in the school system. The major special needs identified are hearing and visual impairments, and mental retardation.

During the period 1978-1994, 80 persons from the OECS received fellowships from the Dutch Government and graduated with certificates and diplomas in special education from Mico Teachers College in Jamaica. In addition, between 1986 and 1994, 14 OECS teachers graduated with a BEd in special education from the UWI/Mico programme. There is, however, a need for more educational support in schools given the estimated number of children and the personnel trained.

Conclusion

Progress is being made regarding services for children with special educational needs in the English-speaking Caribbean but there are still significant gaps in available provision and a need for much more research and development work to be undertaken.

References

Bergsma, S (1995), *Needs assessment in special education*, AIDEnvironment: Donker Curtiusstraat, Amsterdam

Combined Disabilities of Jamaica (1997), *Draft national policy for persons with disabilities*, Government of Jamaica

Hall, W M and Figueroa, M (1995), *Pilot survey of students with special need in secondary schools in Jamaica*, Unpublished report prepared for the Canadian International Development Agency and UWI

Hall, W M and Figueroa, M (1998), Jamaican children with special needs: concerns, realities and possibilities, *Disability and Society*, 13, (2) (pp 269-278)

Hornby, G (1998), *Special Needs in Mainstream Schools: Teachers' Handbook*, Barbados Ministry of Education, (p 28)

Hornby, G (1999), *A Parent's Guide to Special Needs,* Barbados Ministry of Education, (p 30)

Hornby, G and Neblett-Lashley, B (1997), Developing training for teachers of children with special needs in Barbados: Challenges and opportunities, *Journal of Education and Development in the Caribbean*, 1, (2), (pp 163-173)

Lowe, K and Ragbir, F (1983), *Jamaica survey of handicapping conditions in primary schools*, Ministry of Education, Jamaica

Marge, M (1984), *Report of a national survey of handicapped children and youth in Trinidad and Tobago,* Ministry of Education, Trinidad and Tobago

Ministry of Education (1993), *Education Policy Paper, 1993-2003*, Ministry of Education, Trinidad and Tobago

Ministry of Education and Culture (1998), *The National Assessment Programme,* Ministry of Education, Jamaica

Ministry of Education, Youth Affairs and Culture (1995), *Each One Matters: Quality Education for All*, Ministry of Education, Barbados

OECS (1991), *Foundation for the future: OECS Education Reform Strategy*, Organisation of Eastern Caribbean States

Ribeiro, M L and Matthews, D (1999), *Diversity, collaboration and inclusion: Gifted education as a vehicle for school reform*, paper presented at the Fifth Bienniel Cross-Campus Education Conference, University of the West Indies, St Augustine, Trinidad

Stabler, B, Hornby, G, Alleyn, B, Cumberbatch, G, and Sargeant, K (1998), *A national survey of speech and hearing difficulties of primary school children in Barbados*, mimeo

Winschel, J F (1979), *Report on Special Education and Rehabilitation*, Ministry of Education, Trinidad and Tobago

World Bank (1992), *Access, quality and efficiency in Caribbean education: A regional study*, Geneva

Chapter 11

Inter(national) perspectives on Special Needs Education: the case of two countries in Latin America

Dr María Báez

Introduction

International perspectives of special education needs (SEN) have generally focused on the development and implementation of service provision for pupils within local contexts (see for example, Artiles and Hallahan, 1995, Winzer and Mazureck, 1994). Most recently, references relate to experiences of implementing the principles of the Salamanca Statement and Framework for action on Special Needs Education (UNESCO, 1994). This international document promotes the equal participation in education of pupils with SEN, especially in those in early childhood education, girls and young people with disabilities in transition to adulthood. Although the scope for action of the Salamanca Statement (1994) is wide and challenging, countries adhering to this declaration have commenced the move and have indeed made significant progress towards the implementation of more inclusive systems of education (UNESCO, 1997). Subsequently, innovation projects of integration of pupils with SEN into mainstream settings, and the participation in the school system of children at risk of social and educational exclusion, have been set up in countries around the world.

The promotion of more inclusive systems of education has given rise to a globalising discourse of inclusive education which has resulted in a review of special needs education, in terms of much broader social, cultural and political analysis (Báez, 1998). From this perspective, the current discourse of SEN can be examined from a twofold perspective: globally and locally. In this chapter, I will attempt to use this approach to examine the case of two countries of Latin America. In doing so, the choice of the chapter's title, inter(national), reflects this intention. It examines the extent to which global discourses are being used by two countries to generate their own globalising local discourses (Dyson, 1999). Factors which are affecting the production of local inclusive education's discourses have prompted the need to extend the foci of analysis to much larger explanatory accounts on the impact of global changes on special needs education, and this is particularly the case of countries in Latin America (Blanco, 1996).

The chapter provides a general overview of education in Latin America and then it describes special needs education in the region. Secondly, it presents an alternative viewpoint to the traditional description of service provision in Latin American countries. It examines the role of special needs education within the current orientation of education in the region, that is transforming education systems with equity for economic competition. This is followed by an examination of cases of two contrasting countries and their attempt to develop an effective globalising local discourse of integration in the region.

The context

Latin America comprises countries within a range of three sub-continents, North, Central and South America, which have been described as a mosaic of countries and cultures. The analogy makes apparent the wide diversity represented in the cultural, social and political fabric of the three sub-continents. Although, it is fair to say that they share some common cultural elements, it is also fair to acknowledge their strong differences. This, undoubtedly, poses several challenges to any attempt of writing about special needs education in such a wide and diverse continent. This section presents general introductory information. It provides the general framework in which education takes place and hence, the examination of special needs education in two selected countries.

To examine any aspect of educational systems in the region, Latin America's colonial past needs to be borne in mind. This inheritance has had strong influences in attempts to develop a cultural identity or perhaps, from a different viewpoint, to homogenise the apparent diversity through language and religion. Spanish (*Castellano*) is widely spoken in most countries, the main exception being Portuguese in Brazil. These two European languages are the main official languages of Latin America and co-exist with numerous indigenous languages. Most education provision is delivered by using official languages. Literacy indicators have been traditionally measured by means of proficiency in official languages. In addition to other factors, in countries with a wider diversity of ethnic groups, literacy rates tend to be lower. The literacy rate is defined as the population over 15 years old who can read and write. In Chile for example, the ethnic composition is made of 95% of whites and *mestizos*, 3% of indigenous groups and 2% of other groups, mainly immigrants (World Fact Yearbook, 1998). Chile's literacy rate is 95.2% which is comparable to countries in the developed world *eg* 97% in the United States of America and 98% in the United Kingdom (UNESCO, 1998). In comparison, Peru has a much more varied ethnic composition, 45% of indigenous population, 37% of *mestizos*, 15% whites and 3% of other groups (World Fact Yearbook, 1998). Peru's literacy rate is 88.7% (UNESCO, 1998).

With few exceptions, most countries have adopted Catholicism as the official religion. However, an apparent growth of other religious denominations (*eg* the Mormons and other Protestant groups) can be observed, especially in impoverished urban areas in Latin America.

Policies for education in the region

Over the last three decades, the traditional policy emphasis for the education sector in the region was the quantitative expansion of service provision. The passage through education was regarded as providing individuals with tools to increase their life chances. First, it aimed to increase access to basic education and, secondly, to reduce the significant illiteracy rates of the region. This strategy especially targeted the Andean countries. Although some countries did make significant improvements, rapid changes taking place in the world, such as processes of globalisation and the transformation of traditional economies, prompted the need for rapid adjustment to change.

Throughout the 1990s, the main focus of education policy-making has centred on quality issues and the equity of its distribution (Garcia-Huidobro, 1994). However, in a dual system of educational service delivery, with public and private schools, as in most countries of the region, access to quality education is conditioned by the social strata of pupils (Helgo, 1996). The immediate implications of the structural conditions of society in Latin America are that pupils whose parents can afford to enrol them in the semi-private and private sector schools might have better chances to access social mobility through education, to secure a job in their transition to adulthood and ultimately to succeed in life (Puryear,

María Báez

1997). Those who have the public system of schools as their only option might find themselves with fewer opportunities in the future. This viewpoint is reinforced by researchers who have examined factors conditioning social exclusion. Bentley (1997) notices that the geography of poverty has a powerful impact on educational attainment. This social issue has also been identified as affecting education in many countries of Latin America.

Presently, processes of globalisation have geared countries in Latin America, in particular those countries of the Southern Cone, to establish more effective and competitive ways of production. Education is an area which has been identified as having a key role in this transformation. Subsequently, programmes of reform are being developed to support the participation and competitiveness of Latin America in a global context (Avalos, 1996). However, the education systems of Latin America are presently struggling with the growing demands, to rapidly respond to change. The task of implementing educational reforms is challenging and complex. The apparent difficulties of diversifying education according to the demands of modern economies and development trends are issues which are being addressed through a series of important educational programmes which aim to support and develop teachers and learners (UNESCO-OREALC, 1996).

Issues of quality education and the effects on individuals' life chances are particularly important for groups in society whose educational needs differ from the rest of the population, especially for those groups whose special educational needs could place them at risk of social and educational exclusion.

The development of Special Needs Education provision

The traditional service delivery of special needs education in countries of Latin America has been based in the application of a medical model which focuses on 'diagnosis and treatment' of the various disabilities catered for in schools. This approach considers disabilities as 'abnormality or subnormality' in comparison to the able-bodied in society. Subsequently this view reinforces the approach to special needs education to be regarded in a similar way as an illness.

A plausible explanation for the development of a medical approach to special education in Latin America is the prominent role of health professionals on service provision. They have mainly dealt with individuals with disabilities, including those with physical and intellectual disabilities, sensory impairments and multiple and complex disabilities (Bravo, 1977).

Ever since its outset, the delivery of educational services was made on the assumption that pupils with special needs should be trained to develop skills, mostly manual skills, which would prepare and help them in adapting to life in society. Most educational provision, therefore, was made in schools created especially with this purpose, segregated from the mainstream system of schools (Malbrán and McDonagh, 1993). The strong imprint of the medical model of service delivery, unfortunately, has continued and the use of a detailed list of categories of disabilities has remained until the present day in practice and legislation.

In the late 1970s, significant changes started to appear in policies related to issues of special educational needs in some countries of the continent. The strong influences from movements in European countries and the United States of America prompted the adoption of concepts of normalisation which set up the foundations for programmes based on social models. The adoption resulted in a shift of paradigms where society is currently seen as having a prominent role by acknowledging the rights of individuals with disabilities to participate actively and to be educated alongside the able-bodied in mainstream settings. The role of international documents (The JOMTIEM Education for All, (1990) and the Salamanca Statement, UNESCO 1994) have also played a key role in supporting and promoting the recognition of human rights and, in particular, the right to access quality education for all pupils, regardless of their physical disabilities.

Service delivery

It would be inaccurate to identify a common pattern of service delivery in Latin America. This is due to the already mentioned differences in rates and pace of development in countries and, subsequently, the differences on their budget for public expenditure in education. The immediate implications of these differences are apparent on material and human resources across countries; participation in schooling and the effectiveness of the provision; lack of support systems for teachers and learners (Levin & Lockheed, 1993). In general, most service delivery takes place with minimal resources and, in best cases, just adequate to the large number of pupils requiring special provision (Artiles & Hallahan, 1995).

A broad view of current special education services in the public sector of schools comprises at primary age:

- special schools;
- special classes in mainstream schools;
- withdrawal classes in mainstream schools;
- early intervention programmes at pre-school level; and
- projects of integration into mainstream schools.

At secondary level of education SEN provision is very restricted and directed towards the acquisition of manual skills in:

- centres for work training and sheltered workshops;
- day care centres.

Two issues, in terms of service delivery, need to be pointed out. The first refers to the special educational needs of the target population served by these types of provision. There is an increasing number of pupils who are failing to learn in mainstream settings. Although there is no accurate data, in several countries figures have been identified through performance indicators and national assessment systems (*eg* SIMCE tests in Chile). Unfortunately, a large number of these pupils whose needs can be served with additional support within mainstream classes are being considered in need of special education provision (Milicic & Sius, 1995). This raises the issue of appropriately contextualising concepts of special needs education. In this respect, Latin American countries differ greatly from others considered as being more developed where the concept of special needs education has an entirely different meaning, in terms of who needs special support, and when and where and by whom support is provided. The second issue refers to the lack of provision for secondary age pupils within the mainstream system of education. Though some provision is available for secondary age pupils, it takes place in special training centres and the target population is mainly pupils with intellectual and physical disabilities.

Current issues of Special Needs Education

Special education systems have been fully implemented in most countries of Latin America, and provision has been gradually made accessible to more pupils (UNESCO, 1988). Current social and educational policy development in the region has fostered the implementation of integrated service provision to all pupils (UNESCO/OREALC, 1996). However, several issues need to be addressed in order to make this implementation effective. The first refers to (i) understanding and promoting inclusive schooling and (ii) implementing integration programmes (which are developing widely in the region) as the initial step towards more inclusive education systems. Although, the inclusive education discourse is increasingly becoming a global education strategy (Dyson, 1999), the approach taken by Latin American countries is rather contradictory. On the one hand it acknowledges the rights of all citizens to be educated together, and on the other its service delivery is predominantly made through a dated model of categories of disabilities, within inflexible curriculum models for specific categories, and at a more general level, within particular structural conditions of education systems (*eg* highly centralised or highly-devolved systems of administration). These factors might pose risks to the sustainability of integration programmes (Báez, 1999).

It has been mentioned above that special needs education in Latin America developed from a medical model of service delivery. This is an issue which has been identified by service users as a limiting factor. It has been rather difficult to change people's attitudes and practices from one day to another. Though some progress can be observed, schools tend to be more segregating than integrating pupils with SEN. The status of pupils with special educational needs in Chile, for example, is described as follows:

> Children with moderate disabilities are segregated at all levels of the educational system. For instance, children with mild disabilities (*eg* specific learning disabilities or mild mental retardation) are more varied, but they have always tended to be segregated. These children may be enrolled in special education schools segregated from the regular school system or, if they are served in mainstream, their needs are not addressed. Therefore, these students are condemned to academic failure and to drop out of school (Milicic & Sius, 1996, p 169).

In addition, an issue to be born in mind is that schools operate with a shortage of curriculum resources, overcrowding and with barely adequate facilities. Blanco (1996) argues that 'integration conducted under the proper conditions, and with the necessary resources is positive not only for disabled children' (p 80). Thus, questions arise for examination of the extent to which the global discourse of inclusion is constituting somewhat a 'bland' agenda in Latin America. This is by no means an approach in contradiction to the principles of the inclusive education movement. It is rather a critical examination of such discourse, which aims to validate culturally the emergence of local discourses of SEN in the region.

The following section examines the case of two countries, Chile and Peru. By means of basic comparative analysis, it presents an examination of their special needs education and, in particular, their integration programmes.

Both countries have, apparently, very little in common in terms of social, economical and political indicators. However, Chile and Peru have undergone profound structural adjustment as a result of the introduction of Neo-liberal policies. This application has indeed affected the general social system in both countries and it has created and deepened social inequalities. This is relevant to the present analysis, since the education systems in both countries reproduce these inequalities. Most current education policies and social reforms have placed education as a priority area. The current educational policy discourse in both countries focuses on access to quality provision for all pupils, including those with special educational needs. In this framework, special needs education is committed to address issues of social justice and human rights.

The case of Special Needs Education in Chile

With the return of democracy in 1990 a policy for education was enacted to integrate pupils from special education into mainstream schools (Decreto Exento 490/90). During the period of transition to democracy, the Chilean government expressed its commitment to address social inequalities and, in January 1994, a new law was passed, [*Ley de Integración Social de las Personas con Discapacidad, No 19.284*] which concerned the social integration of individuals with disabilities into society. This new legislation promotes the full access and the rights of persons with disabilities to education, labour and social integration. The principles underlined in this law represent a whole different concept and approach to the education of individuals who, in the past, were segregated and or/discriminated against on the basis of their disabilities. In 1998 a Supreme Decree was passed. This decree regulates the practicalities of implementing the Chapter II of Section IV 'Access to Education' mandated by the Law 19.284/1994.

The implementation of this new law has several implications for educational practices. First, it implies a different approach to provision in terms of changing from a traditionally segregated approach to an integrated one. The issue is that, traditionally, the Chilean mainstream educational system has marginalised pupils who do not fit the 'norm'. Secondly, taking into account the traditional status of pupils in special education, the complexity of this type of educational change becomes a major issue for any policy implementation in Chile.

Current principles of Chilean special education

Chilean special education is presently being defined by three fundamental principles:

- a recognition that every individual possesses a potential for cognitive, social and physical development;

- a concept of Human Dignity contained in the Declaration of Human Rights for Individuals with Disability (United Nations General Assembly, 1978);

- an environment in which differences between individuals are recognised and accepted;

A closer examination of these principles suggests that they include a range of concepts, including: normalisation; integration; educatability; organised community participation; integral and integrated provision and family involvement (*Políticas Educacionales, Temas de Gestión*, MINEDUC, 1993).

Concepts and terminology in Chilean special education

In terms of policy, the Ministry of Education uses two terms, 'special' and 'regular' education to identify the type of provision offered to pupils. The former refers to provision outside mainstream schools and the latter refers to provision within mainstream schools, either in municipal, subventioned or private schools.

Special education in Chile is defined in current policies as 'the differentiated method and procedures of delivering the school curriculum' (Special Education Unit, MINEDUC, 1994, *op cit*), which is designed to be flexible, dynamic and to be developed and articulated with the general education system. Special education serves pupils both within the mainstream education system and in special schools. It attempts to provide several options to those pupils who require either a continuous or a temporary special education provision (*ibid*). In 1990, 370 schools provided special education for 31,712 pupils outside the mainstream system.

The terminology used in policies is taken from the aetiology of disability and subsequently the special education curriculum is organised around them. These are:

- 'mental retardation' (mental deficiency);
- visual impairments;
- hearing impairments (profound and partial deafness);
- physical handicap (it refers to the physical disability). It includes cerebral palsy, or peripheral malformations, and amputations;
- language disorders;
- profound deficit in communication (it includes Autism, Dysphasia);
- learning disabilities (it includes pupils with specific learning difficulties *eg* reading, writing, and mathematics which differs from specific learning difficulties catered for within mainstream schools).

From special education to special needs education?

In Chile, the concept of 'special educational needs' which has recently been incorporated in the language of the legislation, refers mainly to pupils who are experiencing 'learning' difficulties (*ibid*). This is defined, in educational policies, as 'pupils who are experiencing a greater difficulty than other pupils of the same age or those who are unable to benefit from services provided in the mainstream classroom' (*ibid*, p 2). The concept of special educational needs does not include multicultural education or 'diversity' which, as stated in the Ministry's policy, should be resolved by using the ordinary resources of the mainstream education system. Pupils from ethnic minorities, and those who have Spanish as a second language, are therefore educated within the mainstream education system by mainstream teachers.

Integration is another concept enshrined in the new policies for special education. This is considered to be the process by which pupils previously educated in segregated settings can be educated in mainstream schools (Manosalva, 1990). Until 1998 integration could take place at three levels: functional, social and physical integration. The Supreme Decree No 1/1998 currently provides four options:

- integration in mainstream classrooms with the required curriculum adaptations to cater for particular SEN of pupils;
- integration in the mainstream classroom with pupils with SEN participating only in those activities which do not require major curriculum adaptations;

- integration in the mainstream classroom with time set aside for withdrawal provision in separate resource rooms;

- integration in special classes or units in mainstream schools and participating socially with pupils in other activities (*eg* meals and trips).

Delivery of special needs education provision

According to the concepts defined in the policies special needs education is then provided in both schools outside the mainstream system and within it as illustrated by the following examples.

Special schools:

These schools provide a differentiated special curriculum for pupils who have learning difficulties, (mild, moderate or severe), a sensory impairment (visual, motor, and hearing impairments), severe difficulties in communication and social relationships (autism, dysphasia and infant psychosis). The range of provision in special schools has similar levels to those mainstream education system. These include the pre-school, primary and post-secondary levels. The entry age in special education can start from age two, after assessment, and pupils can remain in the special education system until age 26.

Special education within mainstream schools:

This aims to serve pupils within their school environment. At pre-school level there is some provision for moderate and severe learning difficulties, in the form of special nursery schools/classes and occasionally support is given in mainstream nursery schools/classes (UNESCO, 1997). Screening and assessment at this level is mainly provided by National Health Service programmes for children under five. These programmes also contain advice for pregnant women, or early screening and prevention (UNESCO, 1988).

Special classes [grupos diferenciales]:

These classes aim to support students who are experiencing difficulties, especially in literacy and numeracy at primary level. In practice, pupils are withdrawn from mainstream classes and attend these support groups or 'special classes' on an alternate basis. Thus, if they attend mainstream classes during the afternoon, they would attend support classes in the morning. Pupils who attend these support classes have been identified and assessed by a specialist team from the Ministry of Education. Most recently, suggestions have been made to teachers by the Ministry of Education to provide in-class support for pupils. However, these suggestions have not been implemented. The argument against them is that classes are overcrowded and pupils would not fully benefit from in-class support (Milicic & Sius, 1995). In 1993, there were 2009 support classes within mainstream schools which served 48,216 pupils.

Integrated projects:

This is another form of special education provision within mainstream schools, though very limited, and enacted by the integration policy 490/90 (Ministerio de Educación, 1990). The rationale for integration is expressed in the policy as follows:

> 'the education system aims to provide the conditions for disabled pupils to develop under conditions of daily assistance as close as possible to the circumstances and ways of life in the society to which they belong'. (Decree 490/90)

Thus, pupils with physical, mental or sensory disabilities can be part of these integration projects within mainstream schools. In 1992, there was a significant number of integration projects within the different types of educational provision.

Table 1
Number of pupils in integrated classes by type of provision

Type of provision	No. of pupils	No. of schools
Special classes	365	24
workshops	534	36
mainstream class	441	197
TOTAL	1340	257

Source: Informes SECREDUC, in MINEDUC 1994

These projects concern integration into mainstream schools. However, as can be seen in Table 1, pupils do not always benefit from the mainstream classes. Some integration projects are being developed in segregated provision within mainstream schools (*eg* special classes).

The decree D E 490/90 constitutes one of the most recent innovations in special education in Chile. It promotes a radical change in approach to provision for pupils in special education. For the first time in official policy documents from the Ministry of Education, 'disability' has been replaced by 'special educational needs'. The implications of using this terminology is not only important in presenting a new wording of the policy, it implies a different concept of special education from the one described in previous official policies. Much emphasis is placed on the adaptation of the educational system to cater for the wide range of special needs of pupils 'in order to ensure real options for learning and social adaptation' (Art. 2 Decreto Exento 490/90, *my translation*).

A further feature of this policy is that it defines special educational needs in broad areas: intellectual, sensory and motor difficulties. There is no longer in its wording a specific terminology of disability, as was previously the case. Contrary to the practice of segregation, this educational policy favours prevention, integration, and personal and social development of pupils with special educational needs. It also promotes the active participation of the family in the process of integrating children into mainstream schools. The policy, though innovative in concept and ideology, is nevertheless vague in the administrative procedures on how the system will ensure provision for integration (Barnard, 1992).

This issue was to be addressed by the recent Supreme Decree 1/1998. Although some improvements are noticed in the spirit of this legislation, an apparent contradiction can be observed. This pertains to the use of categories of disabilities to specify the administration of service provision. The categories have been discussed elsewhere in this chapter, they pertain to a medical rather than a social approach to serve special educational needs.

Chilean special education and the present challenges

Special needs education provision in Chile has been fully implemented for nearly 20 years now, and it has been gradually made accessible to more pupils (Special Education Unit, *op cit*). At present it faces the demands of a fast-growing modern democratic society that has entered the new millennium (Avalos, 1996). The education system is seen as a fundamental part in this process of transformation and accordingly its contribution is required to sustain economic growth by providing a well-qualified work-force. The question arises as to whether special education, with its current status within the system, can be part of this political ideology. From the perspective of the legislation, the right to social integration has been enacted and the active involvement of all citizens is expected to happen. The complexity of social transformation appears to be the main challenge for any successful policy implementation, especially in developing countries (Taka, 1996). Chilean special needs education needs to re-interpret the current discourse of integration. Given the present social situation, the Chilean government is right in its attempt to address social inequalities through education innovation and reforms. However, integration should be channelled towards the creation of a more inclusive system of education: a system which equally addresses rights and needs of pupils with SEN.

The case of Special Needs Education in Peru

The task of examining special needs education in Peru is a challenging one. This is due to the complex economic transformation that the country has been experiencing over the last ten years and the great diversity of needs of the school population. As in Chile, Peru has been affected by processes of globalisation. The education system in this context plays an important role and in a coherent strategy alongside other systems of education in Latin America, the education system in Peru has the prominent task to educate all citizens to take in the development of a modern society, and ultimately, to reduce social inequalities (Sánchez, 1997).

However, two key issues need to be considered. The first refers to the management of a system, which in the case of Peru has over the years envisaged education and the process of schooling from a rather narrow perspective. The main effect of this view is that education has developed in sort of a vacuum without the necessary articulation with other general strategies for development at local, regional and national levels (*ibid*). The second issue refers to the structural conditions in which education takes place. The application of policies of structural adjustment (*eg* 'the Fujishock' in the 1990s) contributed to increased poverty levels and social inequalities. In a spite of the success of processes of economic re-activation in 1994 and 1995, and a high indicator of economic growth (12.9% 1994) this has not been reflected at micro economic levels, with the expected detrimental effects on groups who live at risk of social and educational exclusion.

Public policies of structural adjustment have had a strong impact in education, among others the reduction in the budget for the public system of education. This is seen as a contributing factor of the massive drop-out of pupils in the system in 1991, when school enrolment at primary level was expected to increase by 340,000, yet 115,000 pupils of primary school age did not enrol.

The low quality of public education is another issue which has not been fully addressed by the neo-liberal economic model in place. Instead, the expansion of education provision to recover those pupils who have never enrolled, or who dropped out of the system, became a priority. By 1995 the government claimed that had recovered 90% of those pupils who were out of the education system.

At present, the general education system is making attempts to tackle social issues through education, in particular the importance given to those groups most at risk of educational exclusion, including those with special educational needs.

Current principles of the Special Education System

The special education system was created in 1971 and it is presently defined by two fundamental principles:

- a concept of human rights (it acknowledges that all individuals are equal and therefore, have the same rights – including the right to access education);
- a recognition that every individual has the conditions for personal and social development.

These principles encompass several concepts: normalisation, to create the necessary conditions to access labour and independent living in order to maximise individuals' life chances; integration, by facilitating the incorporation in society of individuals with disabilities; and educability – that is to provide educational opportunities to favour the development process of each individual.

Concepts and terminology

Following the education reform of 1971, special needs education became the remit of the general system of education (D L 19,326). Since its creation in 1971, the National Directorate for Special Education [*Direccion de Educacion Especial*] at the Ministry for Education has played a key role in formulating policies, service delivery and curriculum guidelines for special education in Peru. However, the process of policy making started with a rather humanitarian approach. Its initial purpose was to provide pupils with physical disabilities with an education service and to remove them from the isolation in which most of them were confined (Lineamientos de Políticas de Educación Especial, Ministerio de Educación, 1999). This move promoted an initial recognition of the individual rights of pupils. The aim of providing an educational service was to prepare them for 'the future'.

Although special education provision in Peru initially meant, as expressed in policy documents, to 'integrate' pupils to the mainstream education system, over years of implementing service provision special schools became rather segregated settings. In particular, this was reflected in the long extension of schooling for pupils. Special schools followed an approach primarily centred on pupils' deficit, and as a result teachers in special schools were more concerned with psycho-metric assessment than the original purpose for setting up a special education provision (Lineamientos de Políticas de Educación Especial, Ministerio de Educación, 1999).

Currently, the Ministry of Education is promoting 'integrated education'. It aims to incorporate pupils with special educational needs into mainstream schools. The initiative promotes the enhancement of opportunities for pupils and their families within the context of a 'normalising' school. Accordingly, its purpose it to promote integration and to minimise the isolation between the disabled and the able-bodied. In doing so, the role of the school becomes prominent since it should meet students' individual needs and, ultimately, to facilitate their wider inclusion in society. Change has been introduced in policy documents relating to curriculum guidelines for integrated classes (RM No 016-ED-96) and the organisation of integrated classes (VM No 024-DINEIP-UEE-96) (Lineamientos de Políticas de Educación Especial, Ministerio de Educación, 1999).

From Special Education to Special Needs Education?

The effects of the social and economic transformation of Peru in the 1990s prompted the re-examination of its social institutions, including the education sector. Special education, in particular, was examined in 1992 with the view of discontinuing its practice in isolation of the general system of education. The idea of special education running parallel to mainstream education, with a school population almost forgotten within the system, was considered inappropriate. Taking into account the environmental factors affecting the country in the early 1990s, and its effects on pupils with multiple and complex disability from impoverished income groups, the practice of segregated special education was contributing to widening their chances of greater social exclusion. (Lineamientos de Políticas de Educación Especial, Ministerio de Educación, 1999).

Following the process of examination, the Peruvian Ministry of Education is currently promoting integrated education for pupils with SEN. This approach aims to be in line with principles of normalisation and more up-to-date approaches to special education being encouraged in the region. It has therefore, incorporated in policies the concept of special needs education by stating that present practice should move away from:

- a therapeutic approach based on deficits of pupils towards an approach based on the special educational needs of pupils;
- a segregated special education provision in special schools to an integrated provision in mainstream schools;
- a specific programme based on particular deficits to adapting the curriculum to the special educational needs of individual pupils.
- a medical-psycho-pedagogical approach to an individualised curriculum;
- a special education centred around specific deficits towards in classroom-support with a differentiated curriculum.

The Ministry of Education acknowledges that the task of reforming special education is challenging. However, from an initial expression of commitment to the principles of the Salamanca Statement (UNESCO, 1994) the implementation of some innovation projects of integration have started.

Delivery of Special Needs Education provision

According to the concepts defined in the policies, special needs education is provided in both special schools and within mainstream education settings.

- Special school provision

   As described above, special schools mainly comprises classes where students are served on the basis of categories or deficits. Assessment centres and Early Intervention programmes are also in operation under the responsibility of the special education system.

- Provision within mainstream schools

   This type of provision comprises the implementation of a national integration project. The piloting phase began in 1992 with technical support provided by the UNESCO/OREALC specialist team and funded by DANIDA (Ministerio de Educación, 1995).

A national integration pilot project was set up in four provinces of Peru: Lima, Arequipa, Cajamarca and Ica to run for three years. It was initially implemented in three phases:

Preparatory phase:

This aimed to develop the appropriate conditions and to raise awareness in the school community of the wide diversity of pupils. Throughout this phase, preparations for subsequent phases were made. These comprised training teachers of selected schools on how to cater for pupils with special educational needs. It aimed to build up their confidence on handling diversity and to develop the required skills to differentiate the curriculum. Parents and community members were also included in the preparations. Their participation was considered to be important, since the project aimed to remove barriers and negative attitudes towards pupils with special educational needs. A support team of specialists was a set up to work alongside local co-ordinators and peripatetic support teams.

Implementing the piloting phase of the project:

The experience began by integrating 63 primary age pupils from special schools into mainstream classes. These pupils participated fully in mainstream education. Support was provided mainly within the classroom to both pupils and teachers participating in the pilot experience. The school curriculum was adapted to meet the needs of pupils according to individual differences. Teachers were supported by specialists' teams who came to schools. In doing so, they provided support specifically in topics related to methodology, classroom organisation and the preparation of curriculum resources. Parents were also incorporated at this phase to support the work of teachers in the classroom and at home. Table 2 shows figures of pupils integrated during the national piloting phase.

Table 2
Number of pupils integrated in 1995

Cities	No. of pupils	No. of classes
Lima y Callao	29	24
Arequipa	16	16
Ica	15	15
Cajamarca	18	14
TOTAL	78	65

Source: MINEDUC/DANIDA UNESCO/OREALC (1995).

Consolidating and promoting an integration experience:

This phase had a twofold purpose: a) to ensure continuity and sustainability of the integration experience; and b) to increase the number of pupils being integrated. At this phase, the integration experience was presented to the community emphasising the positive results observed in both pupils and schools.

The ongoing assessment of the national pilot project of integration has provided the Ministry of Education with detailed information of how to extend and to make school integration feasible. Several factors have been identified as playing a key role: legislation and an integration plan; the development in positive attitudes in the school community; willingness of teachers to develop integration projects; opportunities for staff development for integrated education; whole school approach to meet the special educational needs of pupils; managing resources and funding of integration; managing the curriculum; and individual characteristics of pupils.

Peruvian special education and the present challenges

The current experiences of school integration in Peru undoubtedly represent a positive step in terms of educational innovation. In a more long-term benefit, these projects also promote quality education for a sector of the school population. However, the present difficulties facing the general education system inevitably pose integration projects with many challenges.

It has been observed elsewhere in this chapter, that little consideration has been paid to wider issues of quality education by the government as reflected in general social policy-making (Vivar, *et al* 1996). Although, new schools have been opened, there are few indications of providing them with adequate resources, both human and material, in order to cater for the large school population served by these schools. In addition, teachers receive low salaries which adversely affect their general morale and performance.

The government's policy-making process has concentrated on the decentralisation of public services with devolved administration to the private sector. The implementation of such policies into education, as in the case of the Chilean education system, will undoubtedly pose wider challenges to school integration. Evidence from devolving processes of school administration tends to generate wider issues of equity and quality education (Espínola, 1995). In addition this appears to be in contradiction to the principles and the traditional role of education in Peru: free and mandatory education for all (Vivar, *et al, op cit*).

From the perspective of the legislation, the right to social integration has been enacted. However, the complexity of structural adjustment appears to be posing great challenges for any successful policy implementation of mainstreaming. Given the present social situation, the Ministry of Education is right in its attempt to address school integration through school projects. In this respect, the Peruvian experience illustrates how to create conditions and to overcome difficulties. Ultimately, this is especially useful for the countries of the Latin American region in their attempts to contextualise global discourses.

Conclusion

This chapter has presented the current challenges facing special needs education in two Latin American countries. The present analysis has no pretence to be exhaustive; it has rather settled for the examination and the interpretation of the global discourse of inclusion in two local contexts. Special reference has been given to the Chilean and Peruvian education systems, currently struggling with the effects of structural adjustment and much wider environmental, social and political issues.

Although the task of reducing inequalities through education is immense and challenging, efforts towards meeting special educational needs of pupils will continue. The support of international agencies for capacity building (*eg* UNESCO, World Bank and NGOs, among others) to improve the quality of education in Peru and Chile has provided opportunities which other countries in Latin America are taking up.

From an optimistic viewpoint, countries in Latin America are beginning the process of deconstructing/constructing global discourses to facilitate the process of meeting the special educational needs of their pupils.

Acknowledgments

I am specially thankful to Mrs. Mary Galvez Escudero, Director of Special Education at the Ministry of Education, Peru. She agreed to meet me in Lima and provided valuable accounts and reports of the current status of Special Education in her country.

References

Artiles, A and Hallahan, D (1995), *Special Education in Latin America*, Praeger

Avalos, B (1996), Education for Global/Regional Competitiveness: Chilean Policies and Reforms in Secondary Education, *Compare* Vol 26 No2, (pp 217-232)

Baez, M (1999), Developing inclusive education in Chile: public versus private systems, in H Daniels and P Garner, *The World Yearbook of Inclusive Education*, Kogan Page

Baez, M (1998), *Reproduction of Cultural Dependence in Special education Systems of Latin America with Special Reference to Chile*, unpublished Doctoral Thesis, Brunel University

Barnard, A (1992), *The Integration of Children with Special Educational Needs in Metropolitan Santiago*, University of Newcastle

Bentley, (1997), *Learning beyond the classroom*, Routledge

Blanco, R (1996), Integration and Educational Opportunities: A Right for All, *Bulletin 44*, UNESCO/OREALC

Bravo, L (1977), 'La Educacion Especial en Chile', *Revista de Educación*, Vol 27, (pp 21-24)

Dyson, A (1999), Inclusion and Inclusions: theories and discourses in inclusive education, in H Daniels and P Garner, *The World Yearbook of Inclusive Education*, Kogan Page

Espínola, V (1995), *El Impacto de la Decentralización sobre la Educación Gratuita en Chile*, Ponencia presentada en el Seminario Internacional 'La Construcción de Políticas Educativas Locales, Argentina 10-11 Abril 1995

Garcia Huidobro, J E (1994), 'El Programa de las 900 Escuelas' en Gajardo, M (1994) (Ed), *Cooperación Internacional y Desarrollo de la Educación*, Agencia de Cooperación Internacional, Santiago de Chile

Helgo, C (1996), *Chilean social policy reforms form a social mobility perspective*, unpublished Masters Dissertation, The University of Cambridge

Levin, H and Lockheed, M (1993), *Effective Schools in Developing Countries*, Falmer

Malbrán & McDonagh, (1993) Special Education In Ibero-American Countries: Current Situation and Tendencies in P Mittler, R Brouillet and D Harris (Eds) (1993), *World Yearbook of Education: Special Education*, Kogan Page

Manosalva, H (1990), 'Integración: Modelos y Condiciones', in P Araneda and H Ahumada (1990) (Eds), *Integración o Segregación? Guía para integrar a niños discapacitados a la educación regular*, Editorial Interamericana Ltda

Milicic, N and Sius, M P (1995), Children with Learning Disabilities in Chile: Strategies to Facilitate Integration in A Artiles and D Hallahan (1995), *Special Education in Latin America*, Praeger

MINEDUC (1993), *Politicas Educacionales*, Temas de Gestion

MINEDUC (1994), *Special Education Unit*

MINEDUC/Peru (1999), *Lineamientos de Políticas de Educación Especial*

Puryears, J (1997), *La Educación en America Latina. Problemas y Desafíos*, PREAL/CINDE

Sanchez, G (1997), *Gestión Educativa*, Foro Educativo PREAL

Taka, T (1996), *An Evaluation of Community Involvement in the implementation of the Community Junior Secondary School Partnership Policy*, unpublished Doctoral Thesis, The University of Bristol

UNESCO (1994), *The Salamanca Statement and Framework for Action on Special Needs Education*, UNESCO

UNESCO (1997), *First Steps. Stories of Inclusion*, UNESCO

UNESCO World Yearbook (1998), http://unesco.org

UNESCO/OREALC (1995), *Integración de Niños con Necesidades Educativas Especiales a la Escuela Común*, Ministerio de Educación

UNESCO/OREALC (1996), *Bulletin 44*, UNESCO

UNESCO (1988), *Review of Present Situation of Special Education*

Vivar, A et al (1996), *El Ajuste Estructural en el Peru. Una Mirada a las Mujeres*, PREAL

World Fact Yearbook (1998), Internet at :
http://hplus. harvard.edu/alpha/CIAWEB.html

Chapter 12

Contemporary issues and trends in Special Needs Education in Japan

Shimpei Takuma, Toshiro Ochiai and Tetsuya Munekata

Introduction

Children with Special Educational Needs in Special Schools

As some readers may be aware, in June 1998 the Committee on the Rights of the Child presented its observations on the Japanese report (CRC/C/41/Add.1). These observations naturally included some principal subjects of concern regarding children with special needs. The authors believe that subject no. 20 is the key issue we have been facing since a Japanese special education programme was established:

> 'With regard to children with disabilities, the Committee notes with concern, the insufficient measures taken by the State party, notwith-standing the principles laid down in the Fundamental Law for People with Disabilities, 1993, to ensure effective access of these children to education, and to facilitate their full inclusion into society'. (no 20, Principal subjects of concern, CRC/C/15/Add.90).

In fact, according with the School Education Law, 'special schools' are part of the general education system. The authors, however, feel that there might be a public perception that special schools are totally different from ordinary schools as are the children and the teachers in special schools. This perception is strongly based on the categorisation paradigm and remote from the idea that all children might have special educational needs in some settings.

There is another issue that should be mentioned: Japan has been main-taining one of the most expensive special education provisions in the world. Expenditure per student in special schools was about 9,535,000 yen (*ie* more than US$80,000) as of 1996. This expenditure provides exclusively for children in special schools. This is about 11 times higher than that in mainstream schools. In spite of this strong financial support, there have been many struggles and problems with the placement of SEN students in special schools.

Children with Special Educational Needs in mainstream schools

The Japan National Institute of Special Education (NISE) carried out a national survey with classroom teachers on the prevalence of children with learning difficulties, including LD, by means of original teacher questionnaires. As subjects of evaluation, 18,807 students in the 2nd to the 6th grade in elementary schools were selected by random sampling.

Eventually, failing to make clear-cut features of learning disabilities, NISE found that more than 9.45% of the children in the 5th and the 6th grades (11-12 years old) of elementary schools were two years or more behind the expected level of the national curriculum of Japanese language and mathematics. This number probably includes not only children with LD, but also those with learning difficulties resulting from situations such as intellectual disabilities or environmental influences. At any rate, it was revealed that a considerable number of children in regular classes were facing learning difficulties in the school setting (NISE, 1995).

The educational crisis in mainstream schools: school failure

The Japanese mainstream education system is also facing several issues including: long absence; bullying in schools; school violence; suicide; and the breakdown or failure of classrooms and schools.

In February 1998, the Ministry of Education, Science, Sports and Culture – or Monbusho – carried out a nationwide survey about 'Awareness for School' with interviews of about 8,200 students (grades two and five in elementary school, grade two in middle school and grade two in high school), 7,900 parents and 4,100 teachers.

The survey clarified the ratios of students who cannot understand most of school lessons, and students who frequently cannot understand them are 3.4%, 4.8%, 20.3% and 22.8% in grades two and five of elementary school, grade two in middle school and grade two in high school respectively. Add to this the number of children with long absence from schools (more than 50 days a year) and it totals 1.2% of all school-age children, which is in excess of the population of the children in special education units in Japan.

One cannot see the wood for the trees

As described above, every component has issues to be resolved. There have been books and papers published in English regarding the Japanese special education system and its reforms (*eg* Narita and Ohashi, 1993; Tamamura, 1994; Abe, 1998), however, none of those could extend their ideas beyond the special education system itself. Just as the proverb says, 'one cannot see the wood for the trees', the authors add to this: 'especially if one were in the wood'. If we are keen on establishing special needs education in Japan, we need to change the fundamental framework of the 'wood' or the whole Japanese education system rather than 'trees' or existing special education programmes.

In this chapter, we include: the existing special education system and its trends of statistics; the facts regarding integration or inclusion mainly in informal settings; contemporary issues in special needs education in Japan.

The contemporary Japanese special education system

Basic principles for education are provided for in the Constitution of Japan enacted in 1946 and the Fundamental Law of Education enacted in 1947. The Constitution provides for the basic right and duty of the people to receive education as follows: 'All people shall have the right to receive an equal education correspondent to their abilities, as provided by law. Such compulsory education shall be free' (Article 26). The Fundamental Law of education sets forth the basic national aims and principles of education in accordance with the spirit of the Constitution. The Law defines the central aims of education as:

> 'the full development of personality, striving for the rearing of people, sound in mind and body, who shall love truth and justice, esteem the value of the individual, respect labor and have a deep sense of responsibility, and be imbued with an independent spirit, as builders of a peaceful state and society'.

To achieve this aim, the Law sets forth national principles of education such as equal opportunity of education, nine-year compulsory education, co-education, and prohibition against partisan political education.

More specific provisions relating to the school system, educational administration, financial support and other matters are specified in the School Educational Law and many other education laws and regulations which were enacted on the basis of the spirit of the Fundamental Law of Education. The mainstream system comprises: kindergartens; elementary schools; lower secondary schools, and upper secondary schools.

Students with certain disadvantages who cannot be accommodated in mainstream classes in elementary and lower secondary schools are provided with special provision in accordance with the type and degree of their disadvantage either at 'Special Schools' for specific needs, or 'Special Classes' in mainstream elementary or lower secondary schools.

The following categories are defined in the Order for Enforcement of the School Education Law (Article 22-3). The detailed stipulations of this Article are given in the Notification of Elementary and Secondary Education Bureau Director-General, Monbusho. No 309, (6th October 1978).

Education for children with special needs in regular classrooms

There is no legal provision for this. However, team teaching and additional class teachers provide educational support for children with special needs. The support is organised depending on teachers' efforts and decisions. In elementary schools, an average of 2.5 % of all pupils have a special lesson in a break or such activities after school hours. By the year 2000, an additional 17,000 teachers (over the 1990 figure) are to be provided for team teaching on the Sixth Program of Public Compulsory School Provisional Improvement. This is making possible the integration or inclusion of pupils with special needs.

Special education in special classes (full-time)

Special classes in ordinary elementary and lower secondary schools cater for disadvantaged children whose disabilities are not so severe. There are seven types of special classes: for the partially sighted; the hearing impaired; the intellectually disadvantaged; physically disabled; health impaired and physically weak; the speech disordered; the emotionally disturbed.

- Special classes for the *partially sighted* in ordinary elementary and lower secondary schools are provided to improve the visibility condition of the learning environment through special lighting and by the development of various educational materials and equipment, including large print books. In addition to each subject, special therapeutic activities are undertaken, such as guidance for improving sight. Education in special classes for the partially sighted is implemented in close coordination with ordinary classes.

Shimpei Takuma, Toshiro Ochiai and Tetsuya Munekata

- Special classes for the *hearing impaired* in ordinary elementary and lower secondary schools cater for children with comparatively mild hearing difficulties. The contents of instruction in special classes for the hard of hearing centres on language training, as in the case of Schools for the Deaf. There is, however, a difference from the special schools in that language and auditory training is conducted mainly through utilisation of residual hearing.

- Special classes for the *intellectually disadvantaged* in ordinary elementary and lower secondary schools cater for children whose degree of retardation is mild, and who have little problem in social adaptability. Instruction is provided in a small-group setting taking account of individual differences, contriving task-decisions, using instructional materials and equipment, and instructional methods.

At elementary education level, emphasis is placed on acquiring basic life skills and participating in group activities. At lower secondary education level, instruction emphasis is on acquisition of the necessary attitudes and knowledge for vocational and social life-skills for personal independence in the future. Instruction is also given to encourage children to participate in school activities to enrich their experiences.

- Special classes for the *physically disabled* in ordinary elementary and lower secondary schools provide special education depending on the condition of motor dysfunction of each child, referring to the curriculum and educational methods prescribed for schools for the physically disabled. In order to offer effective teaching to enable children to learn with interest, instructional materials and equipment have been developed with auxiliary equipment, such as word processors and electric typewriters, being utilised according to the particular condition of each student.

- Special classes for the *health impaired and physically weak* in ordinary compulsory schools have instruction appropriate to the condition of disease and health of each child. 'Health impaired' means a child who needs medical care and controlled living over a long period due to chronic illness. Restricted living means that, for recovery and improvement of health, much care is required in daily life, in physical activities and diet. In order to provide appropriate education, children who need medical care for less than six months are educated either in special classes, or in ordinary classes with special attention.

- Special classes for the *speech disordered*. Speech disorder includes articulation disorder, voice disorder, disorder of rhythm such as stuttering, and speech and language disorder with a large variety of causes. Some causes are, for example: speech organs are defective, as found in organic disorder; and retardation in mental and physical development. In special classes for the speech disordered, the usual instructional methods applied include play therapy, psychological treatment, and articulation training.

- *Emotionally disturbed* children are classified roughly into two groups. One is those children with uncontrolled or unbalanced expression of emotion, such as selective mutism and problem behaviours. The other is those with very weak emotional attachment and inability to relate appropriately to other individuals, that is, autistic children. Educational placement for children with the former type of emotional disturbance is provided in ordinary classes.

Special education in Special Schools

Schools for the blind

The blind are educated in separate schools, while the partially-sighted received education in various forms because of the diversity of their educational needs which vary with the degree of visual impairment. The majority of schools for the blind have elementary, lower secondary, and upper secondary departments in order to provide education to the visually handicapped consistent with the mainstream. More than half of these schools have kindergarten departments and many schools have dormitories.

The aims and content of each subject in elementary and lower secondary departments are basically the same as those of mainstream schools, except for 'educational therapeutic activities' given to overcome the various difficulties arising from visually impairment. These activities include instruction in orientation, and mobility, tactual discrimination and so on.

In every subject the blind use textbooks in Braille, while the partially-sighted use the textbooks for mainstream children. Textbooks in Braille are translations of standard textbooks with some revisions. The upper secondary department includes a general course and a specialized course. The specialized course includes health-physical therapy, physio-physical therapy, physical therapy, music and a piano-tuning course, each aiming at social independence through vocational education. As an institution of higher education after graduation from the upper secondary department, there is the Tsukuba Technological College for visually and hearing impaired students.

Schools for the deaf

These generally have kindergarten, elementary, lower secondary, and upper secondary departments, though some have only either upper secondary or kindergarten departments. Almost all kindergarten departments of schools for the deaf have their early educational program for three-year-old hearing-impaired infants. In addition to the regular education of an ordinary kindergarten, contents of education include speech and language teaching, auditory training, and communication skill training. Based on education in kindergarten departments and, while trying to improve the language ability acquired already, the emphasis of education in elementary departments is placed on the transition to instruction by subjects.

The contents of education is, in principle, the same as in ordinary 'therapeutic activities'; its main aims of instruction being the development of perceptive ability as the basis of speech and language development; development of ability and attitude using residual hearing; language acquisition; and receptive and expressive language. Lower secondary departments further develop education established in elementary departments. They also provide career guidance after graduation. In some schools for the blind and for the deaf, the number of teachers exceeds the number of pupils, especially because of the sudden decrease of sensory impairment children in recent years.

Schools for the intellectually disadvantaged

These again cover all stages from kindergarten, elementary, lower secondary and upper secondary departments although, at present, few schools have kindergarten departments. The aims and contents of education in elementary departments are to build a healthy body, to acquire basic life skills required for daily living and to develop comprehension and expression of language required for social life.

In lower secondary departments, in addition to providing education in the language required for social life, development of inter-personal relationships and participation in group activities are emphasized. Lower secondary departments also seek to assist the acquisition of working attitudes and experience the joy of work in the form of prevocational education.

In upper departments, the acquisition of necessary knowledge, skills and attitudes for independent vocational living are major objectives. Vocational education in upper secondary departments places emphasis on prevocational education, including such courses as wood craft, metal work, agriculture, gardening, ceramics, cement processing, printing, cooking and sewing. Also, with the cooperation of the community, it provides work-experience training to familiarize students with vocational life.

Schools for the physically disabled

These have elementary, lower secondary and upper secondary departments. Sixteen schools also have kindergarten departments. According to recent statistics, about 70% of children enrolled in these schools suffer from cerebral palsy. Education in kindergarten departments is aimed at the general development of the various aspects of mind and body considered important during infancy.

Particular attention is given to foster self-help skills in daily living, with emphasis on the improvement of motor dysfunction. The contents of teaching in each subject, moral education and special activities in elementary education and special activities in elementary and lower secondary departments, and in each subject, and special activities of upper secondary departments, are basically the same as those of ordinary schools.

In addition, 'educational therapeutic activities' for improving motor function and communication abilities are provided in order to assist the physically disabled to overcome their various difficulties arising from impairments in motor function. Most courses of upper secondary departments are general courses, and such subjects as agriculture, industry and commerce are provided as elective subjects.

Schools for the health impaired

These schools aim not only to achieve the same goal of education of mainstream, elementary, lower secondary and upper secondary schools, but also to provide the instruction necessary for overcoming various difficulties arising from health impairment and physical weakness. Education is carried out in close coordination with medical institutions as appropriate to the condition of the health of each child. Since many of the health impaired and certain physically weak are subjected to restricted school hours and physical activities, special consideration is given to counterbalance delays and blank periods of lessons as much as possible. As many children transfer from an ordinary school to a school for the health impaired and move back again. So, proper instruction in daily living, educational guidance and career guidance are given to all of these students for a smooth transition.

● Ratio of Enrollment in Special Classes

▲ Ratio of Population Exempeted and Postponed from School Education

■ Ratio of Enrollment in Special Schools

◊ Ratio of Population of Children with Long Absence (over 50 days a year)

+ Ratio of Population Enrolled in Part Time Special Class

* Ratio of Population Enrolled in Special Education System

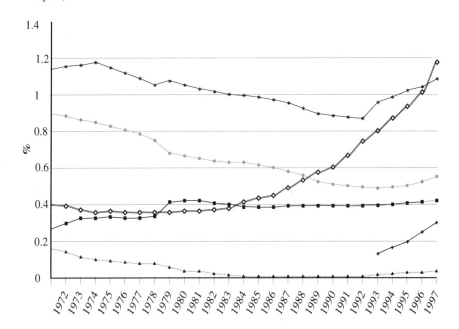

Figure 1. Trends of population enrolled in the special education system and long absence during compulsory education.

Analysis of statistics relating to Special Needs provision

Figure 1 demonstrates the trends of population enrolled in the special education sector, and long absence during compulsory education. There were two big events in special education of Japan. One was the Special Education Act in 1974. It facilitated enrolment of students with disabilities into special schools. Nevertheless, the population and ratio enrolled to special schools and special classes was decreasing until 1993.

For 'Special Education Based on Communities', special classes used to have very important roles. However, students enrolled in special classes also decreased. Some disabled children moved to mainstream classes at elementary and lower secondary schools, but there is no administrative support for children with special needs when they are enrolled in ordinary classes, except part-time special classes since 1993. Instead, the number of school absences, where children are absent from school more than 50 days in a year, are increasing dramatically. From the report of the Committee of Cooperators for the study of maladjustment of school life, 37% of those with school phobia in lower secondary schools, and 23% of primary schools, have some problem of achievement in their schools (Monbusho, 1992). The statistics in 1998 showed an abnormal phenomenon: the population enrolled in special schools, special classes and resource classes in compulsory educational level is smaller that the population of long absence (students who cannot attend school more than 50 days in a year).

Teacher training

Elementary and secondary school teachers in Japan are trained in the universities or junior colleges approved by Monbusho. Most elementary school teachers are trained through four-year courses at national universities. Some are trained at other courses of these universities, as well as at local, public and private universities and junior colleges.

Lower secondary school teachers are trained at national, local public or private universities or junior colleges, while upper secondary school teachers are trained at universities (undergraduate courses) and graduate schools: national, local public and private. In order to become a teacher in an elementary or secondary school, one is required to obtain a teaching certificate awarded by the local board of education under certain conditions.

For each level or type of school, teacher certificates may be classified into three major categories: regular, special and temporary. Special certificates are intended to attract working people to the teaching profession. Therefore they are granted to those who are working in sectors other than the teaching profession and who have specialized knowledge and techniques. Temporary certificates are granted to those who are not qualified for a regular certificate. They are issued when an adequate number of teachers holding a regular certificate are not available for the teaching profession.

The regular certificate is sub-divided into three classes, advanced, the first and the second. Teachers holding an advanced class certificate have earned a master's degree (or its equivalent of 30 credits, obtained by a period of study lasting one year or more on an advanced university course). In addition to these basic qualifications, required numbers of credits for teaching specialized subjects is prescribed by law and other relevant regulations for each teaching certificate class. Teachers who have served for a predetermined number of years with good records can obtain higher class certificates by earning additional credits. Those holding a first or second class certificate have earned a bachelor's degree. In addition, for the lower and upper secondary school levels, each type of certificate is further divided into several categories according to the kinds of subjects to be taught.

Most local education committees have already implemented a special education needs course for all newly appointed teachers. Over the past two years, all university/college students on teacher training courses should have care experience with children with SEN, or aged persons for a minimum of one week.

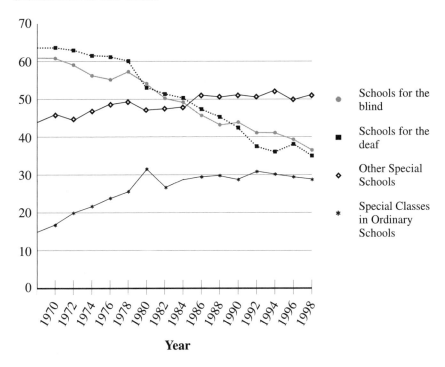

Figure 2. Population of the teachers who have licences in special education (1970-1998).

Facts on integration or inclusion in Japan

Educational provision

It is very difficult to explain integration in Japan. There is no phrase such as integration in the public education system. However, there is in fact integration in Japan. There is data to show how many disabled students are enrolled in Japanese private universities and colleges. 1,363 students with physical disabilities, 105 blind students, 189 deaf students and five deaf-blind students were enrolled in 164 private universities and colleges in 1987. They were provided financial and technical support for examination and usual school life. Research on deaf students in universities and colleges in 1988 showed that 39.4% of them had not enrolled in schools for the deaf. The same data showed there were 25 blind students, four of whom were educated in ordinary high schools within the mainstream system (Association of Study on Issues of Disabled Students, 1990).

Concept

In total, 1.2% of all school-aged children in compulsory education are allocated special education provision. However, it was estimated that 3.69% of all school-age children had special educational needs in 1967 (Monbusho, 1967). This means that over three quarters of the population with special educational needs are in mainstream schools.

However, there was no administrative assistance for children with special educational needs in ordinary schools in most places in Japan before 1993. It was left mainly to the teachers' or schools' discretion and effort. The resource room system was organized from 1993 as a national policy. However, part-time special class systems and total integration have already been implemented in some cities in Japan, one of them since 1978. It would be rather difficult to say whether Japanese special education has a policy of integration or not. However, if we use the category of 'integration' according to the definition of Denmark (Jorgensen, 1979), we can find 'integration' as an informal feature in Japan.

Brief history

In the early twelfth century, disabled people, especially the blind, entered the Blind Buddhist priesthood, but little is known of this issue until modern times. There were guilds for the blind, established in the 14th century, as well as guilds for musicians and practitioners of Oriental clinics (acupuncture and moxibustion) of the blind.

In parallel, like most countries which initiated special education as a separate system, Japan promoted the Kyoto Blind-Deaf School which was established in 1878 as the first 'public' special school in Japan. In 1923, a decree was promulgated for schools for the blind and for the deaf, but attendance was still not compulsory, but thereafter the local government assumed responsibility for maintaining and developing schools for the blind and for the deaf. By 1944, the total population in schools for the blind was 5,956 with 8,421 in schools for the deaf. This is more than today's population of the schools for the blind and for the deaf. The education for the blind and for the deaf became compulsory from 1948, and was extended to nine years in 1956.

The rise in the compulsory school attendance rate brought about the development of a teaching system to address special needs. Since 1890, special classes for children who had difficulty in following classwork were established in some of the elementary schools but, from the beginning of the Japan-China War through to the end of the Second World War in 1945, there was some contraction.

After 1945, the educational system was restarted and reformed on the report of the US Mission on Education and legislation for the compulsory education of children with special needs was proposed. In 1947, the School Educational Law was promulgated and noted, 'Schools for the blind, for the deaf and for the otherwise handicapped, aim at providing the enrolled students the education equivalent to that of ordinary kindergarten, elementary school, lower secondary school or upper secondary school, as well as providing them with the necessary knowledge and skill to make up for the disadvantages'. In 1956, the Law Governing Special Measures for the Improvement and Maintenance of Public Special Schools for Children with Mental or Physical Disadvantage as well as Health was put to effect, resulting in an increase in establishment of special schools.

In 1978, a notable research effort regarding integration was published by NISE (Koyanagi *et al*, 1978). Problems they found for developing an integrated education system were:

- systematization of an itinerant teacher plan; and

- establishment of an organization for the supply of special materials and devices to the children.

It was not until 1979 that complete implementation of compulsory education was achieved. On one hand, the aim of the policy was mainly for ensuring the opportunity of education for all disadvantaged children including those with multiple disabilities. On the other hand, parents were forced to put their children in special schools despite the fact there there was no administrative assistance for children with educational needs in the ordinary school in most places before 1993. It was mainly left to individual teachers' or schools' discretion and effort. Only from 1999 have special needs resource rooms been a national policy. However, the part-time special class system and total integration has already been implemented in some cities in Japan, especially in the Kansai area, since 1978. The part-time special class system began in 1993 as a national system.

Functions of integration in Japan

Integration of location

There are several types of integration systems in Japan. In big cities we find so-called 'Mini Special Schools'. The typical structure of these schools is an L shaped school building. Disabled children visit ordinary classrooms with special teachers from a mini Special School and join in classroom activities. In addition non-disabled children visit a play room or have lessons in their gymnasium. It can be said that a 'Special Class System' is also one of 'locational integration' systems. Such sub-schemes are located within the ordinary elementary or lower secondary education schools. This is not, however, a nationwide system.

Large or middle size cities have teacher aid systems when children with special educational needs are placed in regular classrooms at elementary and secondary schools. They have assistants to take care of attending various needs including both facilities and meals.

Social integration

Special Schools have sharing activities programmes which provide as much opportunity as possible for disadvantaged children to participate in educational activities with children in ordinary schools, develop sociability, and build up desirable interpersonal relationships.

The sharing activities programme between ordinary and special schools is implemented by individual schools with different ideas and designs as appropriate to the actual circumstances of the school and the community. Very often it is implemented through school events, such as field days and club activities. Such joint activity programmes are expected to contribute to the education not only of disadvantaged children but also of mainstream children.

Through close relationships with each other, it is expected that all children will develop a feeling of comradeship, and will not just have sympathy for themselves but for society as a whole, leading to the spirit of respect for human rights. This programme was organised as activities between schools. Furthermore, disabled children in special schools visit ordinary classrooms with a special class teacher. This idea has been extended to activities between schools and counties to build up 'special education based on communities' (Monbusho, 1991, p 32).

Functional integration

Integration is implemented in ordinary classrooms through a team teaching approach. Administratively it is not a system for special education, but some schools use it for functional integration based on the Principal's decision. Usually a team teaching system is organised depending on the subject, for example, for language, arithmetic, music, physical education or homemaking courses. The curriculum is founded on children's needs and is developed by two teachers. This system has been well developed in the Kansai area of Japan since 1978. Recently, some educational boards have implemented open curriculum systems in schools which have flexible educational arrangements different to the traditional system.

Structure of integration in Japan

Mini special schools

Ordinary schools with mini special schools are like twin schools, sharing school grounds and facilities as in the Figure 3.

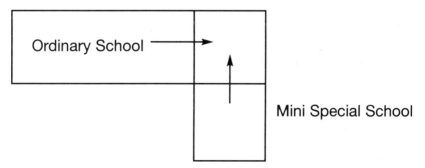

Figure 3. Function of mini special schools system.

Special class rooms

Disabled children allocated to special classes may sometimes attend ordinary classes depending upon the needs as illustrated in Figure 4.

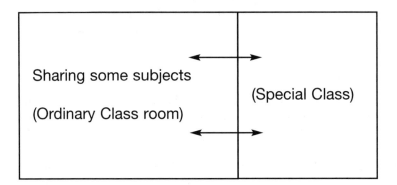

Figure 4. Function of Special Class in Elementary and Secondary School.

Part-time special classes inside and outside of the school

This is illustrated in Figure 5.

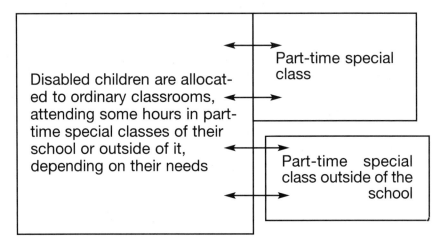

Figure 5. Function of part-time special classes.

Team Teaching

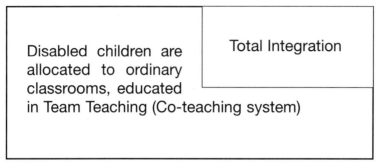

Figure 6. Team teaching.

Policy and administrative procedure for Special Needs in Japan

Compulsory education was introduced for severely and profoundly disabled children in 1979. For mildly disadvantaged children, special classes were established in ordinary elementary and lower secondary schools as described above. In 1978, the Tujimura Report proposed an educational programme for children with partial sight, hearing impairment, intellectual disabilities (including slow learners) and physical disabilities and health impairment. However, it took 15 years for the implementation of part-time special classes as part of the formal education system. This has been partly due to a period of research conducted since 1979 to examine the issue of social integration. Through this activity Monbusho nominates 'mainstream' schools for prospects and studies how to achieve integration and community activities. Other studies related to joint activities between special and mainstream schools and providing additional financial and human resource. Subsequently the Ministry published a booklet almost every year to disseminate findings and introduce outcomes in respect of cooperative practice.

The part-time special class has been a distinctive feature of innovation in this field in Japan, and was implemented in 1993. In principle, it is for students with moderate disabilities allocated to mainstream classrooms with periods in special classes depending upon their needs. They attend general subjects in ordinary classrooms and receive specialized training in special classes to overcome their disabilities and improve their general life skills.

Contemporary issues in Special Needs education in Japan

Impact of Advisory Panel's Report on the Improvement and Promotion of Japanese Special Education

On 19 September 1997, the Advisory Panel's Report on the Improvement and Promotion of Japanese Special Education was released. The Panel, established to conduct research regarding contemporary issues in special education, reflected upon the fundamental policy issues identified by the Central Council for Education on 12 September 1996. Three main issues of the panel's first report were:

• enrichment in the upper secondary department of special schools, such as establishing more classes for severely and multiple-disabled students and starting homebound education in the department;

• establishment of curriculum-based exchange activities (Ko-ryu Kyoiku) among disabled students and non-disabled peers; and

• enhancing educational counselling for disadvantaged children from a very early age as a new role for special schools.

A second report was concerned with two major fields, the improvement in curriculum and the enrichment in the profession of teachers. The first included reconstructing the contents of 'Educational Therapeutic Activities' to put more emphasis on the importance of doing independent activities. The second contained the following aims:

• to increase the number of special education certified teachers, to consider a comprehensive certification for special education rather than specific single disability domain certification;

• to try to improve in-service training on special education not only for special education teachers but also for ordinary school teachers;

• it also recommended preparing the system for the 'Kaigo-taiken' law which mandates teacher training students to have at least one opportunity to study work for the aged or the disabled.

The newly revised standard of the national curriculum consequently reflected these trends.

Key points of newly revised standards

Faced with rapid social changes including internationalization, the growth of an information-oriented society and the development of science and technology, Japan has been developing educational reforms for the new era. In the field of elementary and secondary education, various types of reform have been attempted for cultivating a 'zest for living' of each individual child including those with SEN. Consequently the 'National Curriculum Standards Reform for Kindergarten, Elementary School, Lower and Upper Secondary School and Schools for the Visually Disabled, the Hearing Impaired and the Otherwise Disabled' was officially announced in March 1999, and were to be put into effect from the next school year. Related professional development and opportunities for teachers in special education were also announced.

Some key points from the newly revised standard of National Curriculum in Japan are worthy of mention. There are three major changes. The first one is Koryu-Kyoiku [interchange or joint activities]: at all education levels from kindergarten, through elementary, lower secondary and upper secondary and they are to have joint activities with children with special educational needs or the elderly. Now all non-disabled children should have joint activities with children with special educational needs, or the elderly, in their communities.

The second change is as follows: some subjects, the so called Sogo-Teki na Gakushu no Jikan [school hour/s for comprehensive subjects or integrated subjects], these are non-categorical subjects, which the teacher can arrange subjects on children's needs.

The third change is in teacher education, so that all students who want to become teachers have to learn about students with special needs and have practice with them as a compulsory element of their training.

Responding to a highly information-oriented society - new horizons for special education technology in Japan

Responding to a highly information-oriented society, there would be no exclusions for the children with special needs. We should help them to prepare to live in such a society. In the educational reforms, for example, 'information study' was selected as an option for children with intellectual handicap. The use of 'Assistive Technology' has been encouraged. Some related books were published for school teachers and practitioners. There are well thought through examples for the use of Assistive Technology in AAC settings. In the reformed standards, in educational-therapeutic education, Assistive Technologies will be considered as main communication tools and no longer as auxiliary or supplementary aids.

CEC, the Center for Educational Computing, has published reports regarding use of the Internet in schools including special schools. According to the survey of the Monbusho (1998), more than 20% of special schools have been connected to the Internet since March 1998, twice as much as in the previous year. All special schools will be linked to the Internet by the end of 2001.

In the field of educational research, the Japan Society for Educational Technology conducted the first research conference on Special Education Technology on 29 July 1998. There were 15 presentations at the conference. A few advanced multimedia-related projects have started. ISDN-based TV was used for enhancing homebound education of the severely physically disabled as well as for establishing interactions among students who were located separately. Regarding use of the technology, it will be necessary to develop accessible devices and media for the needs of individual children. Unfortunately, we do not have sufficient resources presently; we have to keep moving forward to enrich the infrastructure by fitting and developing resource centres.

Conclusion

There is a difference in the historical process between special education in Japan and other industrialized countries. It can be said that today's model of special education was established in the 1960s. The model of disabilities was the medical model and the purpose of special education was mainly remedial education.

However, in the late 1970s, the movement of integration or inclusion became dominant and added the idea of advocacy and the general principle of non-discrimination. Such arrangements promote enrolment to the special education system. The Special Education Act of 1979 in Japan provided wider opportunities for introducing severely disabled children into school education. There was no arrangement for slightly disabled children until 1993, when a resource room system was implemented. There has been little research in special education concerning integration and education for slightly disabled children. In the 1990s, inclusive education was started in some countries, adding to remedial educational techniques. Such arrangements promoted enrolment.

An idea has been put forward that special schools be reconstructed as Special Resource Centres, especially for the blind (eg the Commission on the System of Special Education of the Japan Association of Special Education, 1993-1999).

The authors believe there is an urgent need for the strengthening of the law against discrimination in respect of special education. In spite of increasing the cost of education for disabled children, we do not find increasing school attendance in the special education system. Educational placement implemented by the education board is by law. However, it is impossible to place children in the special education system without the parents' agreement. The UN Committee on the Rights of the Child was concerned that legislation does not protect children from discrimination as defined by the Convention, and was especially concerned that the situation of Japanese education is not moving sufficiently towards integration or inclusion.

The review of the present situation in Special Needs Education (UNESCO 1995) showed that educational reform was carried out for special education. However, it is necessary to analyze the situation of Japanese special education scientifically and objectively in terms of the local context and not only taking advantage of international trends for ideas.

References

Abe, Y (1998), Special education reform in Japan, *European Journal of Special Needs Education*, 13, 1, (pp 86-97)

Association of study on issues of disabled students (1990), *Sogo-daigaku ni okeru Shogai-gakusei no Arikata no Kiso-Kenkyu [Basic Research on Situation and Perspectives of Disabled Students' Life in Universities]*, Tokyo, Taga-shupan

Committee on The Right Consideration of Reports Submitted by States CRC/C/15/Add 90 Jun-98, UNICEF

Government Headquarter on Promoting Development of Policies for the Disabled (1995), *Shogai-sha Puran – Nomaraizeishon 7-kanen Senryaku [The Plan for the Disabled – A 7-year Action Plan for Normalization]*, Tokyo

Hori, M (1994), *Shogai-ji-Kyoiku no Paradaimu Henkan [Paradigm Conversion of Education for Handicapped Children – Theoretical Approach toward Integration]*, Tokyo, Akashi-shoten

Ito, R (1998), *Zen-Hokatu Kyoiku no Shiso [Ideology of Inclusive Education]*, Tokyo, Akashi-shoten, (Revised version of Ito's *Shogai-ji Kyiku no Shiso [Ideology of Education for Disabled Children]* in 1972)

IPA: Information-technology Promotion Agency and CEC: Center for Educational Computing (1998), *Intaneto wo Riyo shita Jugyo Jisen Jirei II [Case reports of Classroom Applications on Using the Internet II]*, Tokyo

Japan Association of Educational Technology (1998), *Tokushu-Kyoiku ni okeru Kyoiku-kogaku no Atarashi Tenkai [New Horizon of Special Education Technology]*, Research Report of JET Conferences, JET98-4

Koyanagi, K, Hara, Y, Yamanashi, M and Watai, H (1974), 'Hutu-gakkyu ni Okeru Hitori no Zen-mo-ji to Sono Kyoiku' ['Education of Totally Blind Children in a Regular Classroom'], *Research Bulletin of the National Institute of Special Education*, 1, (pp 167-176)

Jorgensen, I (1979), *Special Education In Denmark*, Copenhagen

Mogi, T (1994), 'Current Issues on the Human Rights of Persons With Disabilities', *Japanese Journal of Studies on Disability and Handicap*, 22, 2, (pp 5-11)

Monbusho (1967), *Jido-Seito no Shinshin Shogai no Jo-kyo [Situation of Disabled Pupils/Students – Nation-wide Survey of Disabled Children]*, Tokyo

Monbusho (1992), *Gakko Futekio Taisaku Chosa Kenkyu Kyoryoku-sha Kaigi Hokoku-Sho [Report of The Advisory Panels on Treatment of Maladjustment of School Life]*, Tokyo

Monbusho (1992), *Outline of Education in Japan*, Tokyo

Monbusho (1995), *Tokushu-Kyoiku Shiryo [Special Education Statistics]*, Tokyo

Monbusho (1999), *Mo-Gakko Ro-Gakko oyobi Yogo-Gakko Yochi-bu Kyoiku-Yoryo-An Sho-gakubu Chu-gakubu Gakushu Shido-Yoryo-an Kotobu Gakushu-Shido Yoryo-An [National Curriculum Standards for Kindergarten, Elementary School, Lower and Upper Secondary School and Schools for the Visually Disabled, the Hearing Impaired and the Otherwise Disabled]*, Tokyo

Monbusho (1997), *Kyoiku-Kaikaku puroguramu [Program for Educational Reform]*, Tokyo

Monbusho (1994), *1994 – A Graphic Presentation*, Tokyo

Monbusho (1997), *To Encourage Zest for Living – Special Education in Japan*, Tokyo

Monbusho (1998), *Gakko ni okeru Joho-Kyoiku no Jittai-to ni Kansuru Chosa Kekka [National survey on Information Education or Educational Computing in Schools]*, Tokyo

Nakano, Y, and Kato, Y (1967), *Waga-Kuni Tokushu-Kyoiku no Seiritu [Foundation of Japanese Special Education]*, Tokyo, Toho-shobo

Narita, S, and Ohashi, T (1993), *Asia Regional Study of Children with Special Educational Needs – Japan Case Study*, Washington, The World Bank

Ochiai, T (1997), 'Atarashi Kyoshi-Zo Inkurujon ni Yosete [My expectations for a teacher in new era – regarding inclusion]', *Jinken to Kyoiku [Human rights and Education]*, 26, (pp 82-91)

Ochiai, T. (1998), Shogai-ji wo Shiten ni Ireta Kyoiku-Kaikaku he – *Kyoiku e no Michi* Saramanka Sengen wo Yomu [Toward General Education Reforms including Children with Disabilities', in the book *Way to Inclusive Education*], edited by Editorial Board of Kyoiku e no michi [Way to Inclusive Education], (pp 15-33), Tokyo, Advantage Server

Otsutake, I (1929), *Nihon Shomin Kyoiku-shi [History of Private Education for the People]*, Tokyo, Meguro-shoten

Special Education Division, Elementary and Secondary Education Bureau, Monbusho (1999), *Tokushu-Kyoiku Shiryo Heisei 10 Nendo [Special Education Statistics in 1998 fiscal-year]*, Tokyo

Taniai, S (1989), *Charenji Suru Mo-jin no Rekishi [A History of the Blind who Made Challenges]*, Tokyo, Kozue

The National Institute of Special Education: NISE (1995), *Tokubetu Kenkyu Hokoku-sho: Kyouka-Gakushu ni Tokui na Kon-nan wo Shimesu Jido-Seito no Ruikei-ka to Shido-ho no Kenkyu [Report of Special Research Project: Subtype and Intervention Research on Pupils and Students with Learning Difficulties in Specific Academic Skills]*, Yokosuka

Tamamura, K (1994), 'Problems and Issues of Special Education in Japan', *Japanese Journal of Studies on Disability and Handicap*, 22, 2, (pp 27-33)

The Central Council for Education (1996), *21-Seki wo Tenbo shita Wagakuni no Kyoiku no Arikata ni tuite [The model for Japanese education in the perspective of the 21st Century (The 1st Report)]*, Tokyo

The Central Council for Education (1997), *21-Seiki wo Tenbo shita Wagakuni no Kyoiku no Arikata ni tuie [The model for Japanese education in the perspective of the 21st Century (The 2nd Report)]*, Tokyo

The Advisory Panel on Improvement and Empowerment of Special Education, Monbusho (1997), *Tokushu-Kyoiku no Kaizen Jujitu ni tuite [Improvement and Empowerment of Special Education, the 1st and the 2nd Reports of the Panel]*, Tokyo

The Advisory Panel on Promoting Information Education through Elementary and Secondary Schools for Responding to the Information-Oriented Society, Monbusho (1997), *Taikei-Teki na Joho-Kyoiku no Jishi ni Mukete – Dai Ichi-ji Hokoku [Toward Developing and Enforcing Consistent and Systematic Information Education – the First Report of the Panel]*, Tokyo

The Advisory Panel on Promoting Information Education through Elementary and Secondary Schools for Responding to the Information-Oriented Society, Monbusho (1998), *Joho-Ka no Shinten ni Taio Shita Kyoiku Kankyo no Jitugen ni Mukete – Saishu Hokoku [Toward Building Appropriate Infrastructure in Education for Responding to the Information-Oriented Society – the Final Report of the Panel]*, Tokyo

The Commission on the System of Special Education, Japan Association of Special Education (1995), 'Nihon Tokushu-Kyoiku-gakkai Shogai-ji Kyoiku Shisutemu Kenkyu Iin-kai Kenkyu-seika Hokoku(I) [Report of the Commission on the System of Special Education Japan(I)]', *The Japanese Journal of Special Education*,33, 3, (pp 75-76)

The Commission on the System of Special Education, Japan Association of Special Education (1995), 'Nihon Tokushu-Kyoiku-gakkai Shogai-ji Kyoiku Shisutemu Kenkyu I-In-Kai Kenkyu-seika Hokoku(II) [Report of the Commission on the System of Special Education Japan(II)]', *The Japanese Journal of Special Education*, 33, 3, (pp 77-81)

The Commission on the System of Special Education, Japan Association of Special Education (1995), 'Nihon Tokushu-Kyoiku-gakkai Shogai-ji Kyoiku Shisutemu Kenkyu I-In-Kai Kenkyu-seika Hokoku(III) [Report of the Commission on the System of Special Education Japan(III)]', *The Japanese Journal of Special Education*, 33, 3, (pp 83-86)

The Commission on the System of Special Education, Japan Association of Special Education (1996), 'Nihon Tokushu-Kyoiku-gakkai Shogai-ji Kyoiku Shisutemu Kenkyu I-In-Kai Kenkyu-seika Hokoku(IV) [Report of the Commission on the System of Special Education Japan(IV)]', *The Japanese Journal of Special Education*, 33, 4, (pp 75-79)

The Commission on the System of Special Education, Japan Association of Special Education (1996), 'Nihon Tokushu-Kyoiku-gakkai Shogai-ji Kyoiku Shisutemu Kenkyu I-In-Kai Kenkyu-seika Hokoku(V) [Report of the Commission on the System of Special Education Japan(V)]', *The Japanese Journal of Special Education*, 33, 4, (pp 81-84)

The Commission on the System of Special Education, Japan Association of Special Education (1996), 'Nihon Tokushu-Kyoiku-gakkai Shogai-ji Kyoiku Shisutemu Kenkyu I-In-Kai Kenkyu-seika Hokoku(VI) [Report of the Commission on the System of Special Education Japan(VI)]', *The Japanese Journal of Special Education*, 34, 2, (pp 81-86)

The Commission on the System of Special Education, Japan Association of Special Education (1998), 'Nihon Tokushu-Kyoiku-gakkai Shogai-ji Kyoiku Shisutemu Kenkyu I-In-Kai Kenkyu-seika Hokoku(VII) [Report of the Commission on the System of Special Education Japan(VII)]', *The Japanese Journal of Special Education*, 36, 3, (pp 51-62)

The Commission on the System of Special Education, Japan Association of Special Education (1998), 'Nihon Tokushu-Kyoiku-gakkai Shogai-ji Kyoiku Shisutemu Kenkyu I-In-Kai Kenkyu-seika Hokoku(VIII) [Report of the Commission on the System of Special Education Japan(VIII)]', *The Japanese Journal of Special Education*, 36, 3, (pp 63-65)

The Commission on the System of Special Education, Japan Association of Special Education (1998), 'Nihon Tokushu-Kyoiku-gakkai Shogai-ji Kyoiku Shisutemu Kenkyu I-In-Kai Kenkyu-seika Hokoku(IX) [Report of the Commission on the System of Special Education Japan(IX)]', *The Japanese Journal of Special Education*, 36, 3, (pp 66-71)

The Commission on the System of Special Education, Japan Association of Special Education (1999), 'Nihon Tokushu-Kyoiku-gakkai Shogai-ji Kyoiku Shisutemu Kenkyu I-In-Kai Kenkyu-seika Hokoku(X) [Report of the Commission on the System of Special Education Japan(X)]', *The Japanese Journal of Special Education*, 36, 5, (pp 143-153)

The Commission on the System of Special Education, Japan Association of Special Education (1999), 'Nihon Tokushu-Kyoiku-gakkai Shogai-ji Kyoiku Shisutemu Kenkyu I-In-Kai Kenkyu-seika Hokoku(XI) [Report of the Commission on the System of Special Education Japan(XI)]', *The Japanese Journal of Special Education*, 36, 5, (pp 154-164)

The Curriculum Council (1998), *Yochi-En Sho-Gakko Chu-Gakko Koto-Gakko Mo-Gakko Ro-Gakko oyobi Yogo-Gakko no Kyoiku-Katei no Kijun no Kaizen ni tuite [Final Report: National Curriculum Standards Reform for Kindergarten, Elementary School, Lower and Upper Secondary School and Schools for the Visually Disabled, the Hearing Impaired and the Otherwise Disabled]*, Tokyo

The United Nations Children's Fund (1989), *The Convention on the Rights of the Child*, http://www.unicef.org/crc/text.htm

Tujimura Report (1978), *Keido Shin-shin Shogai-Ji ni Taisuru Gakko Kyoiku no Arikata [Needed services in school education for the children with less special educational needs than categorized by conventional law]*, Tokyo, Monbusho

Chapter 13

Key issues in Special Educational Needs in New Zealand

Dorothy Howie

This chapter first explores the positioning of a child with special educational needs within New Zealand education legislation, from the perspective of 'Positioning Theory'. This theoretical development has arisen from a new paradigm in psychology, (Harré and van Langenhove, 1999) and is increasingly being applied to the study of persons with special educational needs (Howie, 1999a). It considers the ways in which persons are positioned and position themselves, within discourse. Issues of agency and power are central in the dynamic and interactive process of positioning. The author worked with Harré and associates in Oxford in considering the positioning of children with special educational needs.

The chapter then discusses several other key issues of international interest. These are the moves to inclusion, changing paradigms in teaching approaches and, finally, addressing cultural challenges.

The positioning of children with special educational needs within New Zealand education legislation

The 'person' status of a child with special educational needs

New Zealand ratified the United Nations Convention on the Rights of the Child in 1993. This document confers person status on the child, as does the 1990 New Zealand Bill of Rights. Under the New Zealand Bill of Rights, 'every person' has freedom from discrimination 'on the ground of race, ethnic or national origins, sex, marital status, or religious or ethical belief' (Section 19). A further right to the observance of the principles of natural justice (Section 27) is of importance to our discussion, and that these rights appear to include the child, under the rubric of 'every person' seems clear from Section 29, which states 'Except where the provisions of this Bill of Rights otherwise provide, the provisions of this Bill of Rights apply, as far as practicable, for the benefit of all natural persons'.

A leading New Zealand lawyer, Rodney Harrison, in his paper to the 1993 Conference on Education and Law concerning the duties and accountability of School Boards of Trustees, stressed that Boards need to comply with the principles of natural justice in relation to students' rights. One of the principles cited was the right to a procedurally fair hearing, which has obvious implications for students facing exclusion or rejection from a school environment.

Further, although the New Zealand Human Rights Act (1993) does include age as a prohibited grounds of discrimination, this reference to age appears to be primarily for the benefit of persons 16 years of age and over (Section 34, i). There is a danger if this allows for a lack of concern relating to negative discrimination against children.

There has been a notable shift in the terminology used in key education legislation, from that of the 1964 Education Act 'unable to be educated' (Section 111, Clause 4b) leading to widespread labelling of children as 'ineducable', to the careful use in the 1989 Education Act of the term 'person' for children, and the phrase 'people who have special educational needs' (Section 8). This suggests that the child is available for positioning, as a human person, with at least some of the key rights which that personhood confers.

The voice of the child

A central issue in positive positioning is the extent to which a child has a voice (Howie, 1999b). One should consider whether the legislation confers the moral right to have a voice, and to act with power within an active and subject role, rather than to remain positioned within a passive and 'object of service provision' role, characterised by protection and paternalism.

In the United Nations Convention on the Rights of the Child, 1989, the child is viewed as having a right to a voice in all matters affecting the child. Article 12 states the responsibility of our country, as a signatory, to 'assure to the child who is capable of forming his or her own views the right to express those views freely in all matters affecting the child, the views of the child being given due weight in accordance with the age and maturity of the child'.

One of the strongest demonstrations of the right to a voice for persons with a disability within the New Zealand legislation is found in the 1988 Protection of Personal and Property Rights Act. It was influenced by wide consultation with advocacy and self advocacy groups, and in particular by Sir Justice Beattie's paper on advocacy and the attainment of the rights of persons with intellectual handicap. He advised in that paper that any guardian order should 'extend no further than the proved evidence of dysfunction' (Beattie, 1976, p 34) and also stressed the important role that the guardian should have in fostering decision-making skills, stating, 'In effect, a guardian would act as a good parent would, not be overprotective, and help the ward to stand on his own feet' (*ibid*, p 35).

In line with such aims, the Act places the onus on the Court for provision of evidence of incapacity to have a voice before someone can speak for the person with a disability. The Act assumes the moral right to make a decision, and uses as a criteria the skill to communicate, in deciding if a person needs to have another speak for them. The Act would be even better if evidence of incapacity, in spite of training and opportunity to practice the skills, was required. The Act is strong in the unique and important requirement that, even if speaking on behalf of the client, the welfare guardian has the duty at all times to 'encourage the person to develop and exercise such capacity as that person has to understand the nature and foresee the consequences of decisions relating to the personal care and welfare of that person, and communicate such decisions' Section 18, Clause 3.

Another unique and benchmark New Zealand Act, the 1989 Children, Young Persons and their Families Act, does have clear statements about the moral right of the child to a voice, although caveats of age, maturity, and cultural appropriateness are stated. Section 11 of Part I of the Act states very clearly that there is a duty on the Court and Counsel to encourage and assist the child or young person to participate in proceedings. In Part II of the Act there appears to be a strong attempt to recognise the direct voice of the child and give the child or young person agency, for example, in the unique provision for the Judge in the Family Court to both require others in the court to withdraw while the child or young person gives evidence in private, and to confer in private with the child or young person (Section 167). At the end of this part of the Act, there is a strong statement about the right of the child or young person to make representation.

The New Zealand 1989 Education Act, although progressive and forward looking in many aspects pertaining to the rights of students with special educational needs, is clearly inadequate in terms of giving the child a voice. In an important section of the Act concerning right to reconsideration of the decision made about a child's special educational provision, only the parent is given the right to require the result to be sent to an arbitrator (Section 10). In another very important section on suspension, and contrary to the principles of natural justice by which school Boards of Trustees should proceed (Harrison, 1993, p 72), the student was given no clear right to present a defence. It is encouraging to note that in the revisiting of the suspension and expulsion requirements in the 1998 Education Amendment (No 2) Act, the student is given a clear voice. Section 17b states 'if a student has been suspended, the student, the student's parents, and their representatives are entitled to attend at least one meeting of the Board and speak at that meeting, and to have their views considered by the Board before it decides whether to lift or extend the suspension or expel the student'.

The 1989 Education Act Section 97, which did allow for student representation on the Board of Trustees, has subsequently been reversed.

The whole philosophy of the 1989 Education Act places the child in an object position, as the recipient of both services and decisions made for such service provision. The dependent nonagentive position is particularly noticeable in the section which confers on the student a right to guidance and counselling. The 'student's parents are told of matters that, in the principal's opinion ... are preventing and slowing the student's progress', (Section 77,b). There is no mention of student involvement in any decision-making about receipt of guidance and counselling. Again, it is encouraging to note that in the more recent 1998 Education Amendment (No 2) Act, in relation to suspension and expulsion, the Act states 'When a student is stood down or suspended from a state school, the principal must take all reasonable steps to ensure that the student has the guidance and counselling that are reasonable and practicable in all the circumstances of the stand-down or suspension' (Section 17a). This confers on the student a more agentive role.

As an example of the very paternalistic tone of the 1989 Education Act, it is noted that the Act uses the phrase 'may require the child or other person *to be produced*', (writer's emphasis) in Section 10 on the parent's right to the reconsideration of the special education direction. This is a clear statement of an object non-agentive position for the child.

A small glimmer of acknowledgement that the child plays a key role as a partner in the learning process comes in relation to the School Charter. The Charter should be developed in consultation with parents 'and any other person it thinks fit' (Section 61, Clause 3, c). This, presumably, would allow for consultation with students. Clearly, if a partnership model is to work, this needs to include an obligation to also consult with students. This partnership with students is affirmed later in the section on the effects of the charter, which states that 'the school, and its *students* (writer's emphasis) and community, achieve the aims and objectives of the Charter' (Section 64b). If the students have this responsibility to achieve Charter aims, they should have the related right to be partners in developing those aims, and will probably achieve aims more effectively if viewing themselves as active agents and partners in the whole process.

England also fails to give students a voice within its education legislation, but the 1994 Code of Practice (DfE), which arose to give clear guidance on special educational needs following the 1993 Education Act, has strong statements concerning the necessity to involve the child's voice and ascertain the students' viewpoint, as unique from that of the parent. This commitment to pupil voice is mirrored in all subsequent key policy documents on special educational needs.

In contrast, although in New Zealand in the 1980s there was considerable attention drawn to the need for self-advocacy by persons with intellectual disabilities (Howie and Cuming, 1986; Howie, 1987; Bramley and Elkins, 1988), and strong moves towards consumer voice in health accountability areas relating to disability, the present discourse around special educational needs in New Zealand stresses parental voice but makes little mention of student voice.

A clear exception to this comes in the Ministry of Education IEP Guidelines for Special Education 2000 (1998). Here, students are given a key role as a team member in the IEP process. This possibly reflects the input of Charlotte Thomson, whose study with Christine Rowan (1995) of IEPs in New Zealand schools found that there was a low level of recorded attendance of parent, class teachers and students at IEP meetings, and in the focus group discussions carried out as part of that study both teachers and parents identified the need to involve the student more. Ballard also draws attention to this issue of pupil voice in recent international publications (Ballard, 1997, Ballard and Macdonald 1998, and Ballard 1999).

The right to education for all children

A key legal issue is the right to education for all children, irrespective of disability. The New Zealand 1989 Education Act is a landmark act, conferring an unambiguous right to education for all children and the placement on the State of an obligation to provide this right. Section 3 states 'every person who is not a foreign student is entitled to free enrolment and free education at any state school during the period beginning on the child's 5th birthday and ending on the Ist day of January after the person's 19th birthday'. This contrasts vividly with the 1964 Act provision that a child may be exempted from enrolment (and frequently was, Howie, 1980, Sleek and Howie, 1987) on the grounds that 'the child is unable to attend school regularly or is unable to be educated by reason of physical or mental handicap' (1964 Education Act, Section III, Clause 4b).

The requirements of the State are similarly sharply contrasted in the two Acts. In Section 9 of the 1989 Act the Secretary has a responsibility, stated as a 'shall' in contrast to the 'may' of the 1964 Act, to work in agreement with the parent to ensure provision for a child with special educational needs. The 1989 Act states 'the Secretary shall – (a) Agree with the person's parents that the person should be enrolled, or direct them to enrol the person, at a particular state school, special school, special class, or special clinic' (1989 Education Act, Section 9, Clause 1). This requirement is followed by explicitly spelled out rights of reconsideration on parental request, as commented on by Judge Williams in a landmark hearing (Maddever, as cited by Harrison, 1993, p 92).

This contrasts starkly with the 1964 Act which stated 'it shall be the duty of the parent of every child who has attained the age of seven years and is of school age and is suffering from disability of body and mind of such magnitude as to require special education to take steps to provide efficient and suitable education for the child' (1964 Education Act, Section 115, Clause 1).

Schools are also required to ensure, within their School Charters, that equitable outcomes are assured for all children irrespective of ability or disability. A goal must be included in all charters as follows 'To enhance learning by ensuring that the school's policies and practices seek to achieve equitable outcomes for students of both sexes; for rural and urban students; for students from all religious, ethnic, cultural, social, family and class backgrounds and for all students, irrespective of their ability or disability'. (Department of Education, 1989, p 10).

These philosophical changes, focusing on the right to education for all children, and the state's responsibility in delivering this, are very clear and have been followed up by continuing efforts to find ways to deliver provision in an equitable and efficient way. Some of these efforts, known to the writer, were the Special Education Policy Implementation Team (SEPIT) which carried out an intensive period of consultation, ending in a detailed report (Ministry of Education, 1994). Following on Mitchell's (1992a) paper, *Contesting Constestability in Special Education: A Critical Analysis of Special Education Policies in New Zealand*, presented to a conference on social justice and dilemmas relating to disability in Education, at the University of Queensland, Mitchell and Ryba were contracted by the Ministry of Education to review the criteria for admission to special educational facilities and allocation of discretionary resources. This involved consultation and was finally reported on in 1994 (Mitchell and Ryba, 1994).

Howie, who was concerned about media reports of rejection of children with special educational needs from their local schools, and had been an advocate for the new 1989 education legislation, approached the Ministry of Education concerning the carrying out of a sensitive study on accountability. Only the first small phase was funded; it involved consultation with a small selected sample of key policy makers, service providers and parents, and resulted in a confidential unpublished draft report (Howie and Westera, 1994).

A major new policy development was eventually finalised, following the Ministry's developmental work on special education from 1995, called Special Education 2000. Its aims, as spelled out by the chief Ministry officers heading the policy implementation, Davies and Prangnell, are 'to improve educational opportunities and outcomes for children with special educational needs in the early childhood and school sectors, to ensure there is a clear, consistent and predictable resourcing framework for special education; and to provide equitable resourcing for those with similar needs irrespective of school setting or geographic location' (Davies and Prangnell, 1999). These developments clearly relate to providing equitable education for all children, and research is currently underway, contracted to several independent, such as university, research teams, to evaluate the effectiveness of the policy changes.

In the writer's view, there are currently two major threats to this right to education, and an equitable service provision. The first relates to the caveats at present in the human rights legislation. The New Zealand 1993 Human Rights Act spells out a moral right to education, in that it prohibits discrimination on the grounds of disability (1993 Human Rights Act, Section 34). This prohibition is spelled out in more detail later as follows 'it shall be unlawful for an educational establishment ... to refuse or fail to admit a person as a pupil or student; or ... to exclude a person as a pupil or a student or subject him or her to any other detriment, - by reason of any of the prohibited grounds of discrimination' (1993 Human Rights Act, Section 57). However, Section 60 of that Act sets out exceptions available to schools, on the grounds that the 'person requires special services or facilities that in the circumstances cannot reasonably be made available... where the person's disability is such that there would be a risk of harm to that person or to others, including the risk of infecting others with an illness, if that person were to be admitted to an educational establishment and it is not reasonable to take that risk'. The provision under Section 60 (3) limits the power of this second clause by stating 'Nothing in subsection (2) of this section shall apply if the person in charge of the educational establishment could, without unreasonable disruption, take reasonable measures to reduce the risk to a normal level'.

In commenting on these aspects of the 1993 Human Rights Act in their report on Human Rights and Special Needs Education, the Human Rights Commission (1996) stated that section 57 would apply where any school was refusing to accept a student because of their disability, a school attaching more onerous conditions on the admission of a student with a disability, a school denying access to benefits or services normally provided because of a student's disability, and a school excluding a child, that is expelling or suspending or treating them detrimentally because of their disability. The Human Rights Commission writer then goes on to explain Section 60 as follows 'If a complaint were received in any of these situations it would have to be tested against the *defences* available to the school under section 60' (Human Rights Commission, 1996, p 7).

When this issue was discussed by the writer with a member of the Human Rights Commission, and the concern expressed that the caveats to rights ran counter to the whole philosophy of the 1989 Education Act, it was pointed out that the 1989 Act would have precedent, in that a late section in the Human Rights Act states 'Except as expressly provided in this Act, nothing in this Act shall limit or affect the provisions of any other Act or regulation' (1993 Human Rights Act, Section 160).

This, unfortunately, is not spelled out in the Human Rights Commission Report. As pointed out by an advocate within the New Zealand Society for Persons with Intellectual Handicap, the Human Rights Commission is the body to determine the extent to which such requirements are 'unreasonable' (1993 Human Rights Act, section 93) so that the onus of proof to the Human Rights Commission that an action is not discriminatory is on an education body such as a school (Sue Gates, personal communication). To the writer's knowledge, the rulings within section 60 have still not been tested.

The Human Rights Commission in their 1996 report suggest that it is 'able to be involved in investigating and conciliating cases where educational establishments (for example Boards of Trustees) are refusing to admit students, or admitting them on less favourable terms because of their disability' (p 14). The Commission is also required to draw to the attention of Government any Act, regulation, government policy or administrative practice which may conflict with the unlawful discrimination provisions of the Act or infringe its spirit or intention. It detailed at that time a 'Consistency 2000' exercise which had the possibility of showing where the Ministry of Education policies and practices may be in conflict with the Human Rights act.

A second main factor endangering the rights to education for children with special educational needs is the legal provision for enrolment schemes, as allowed for in the 1991 Education Amendment Act. This Amendment Act came into being in parallel with economic changes which related to school choice policies and greater emphasis on the market.

There is some indication that schools have been using the provisions of the 1991 Education Amendment Act for enrolment schemes to develop such schemes which discourage attendance at their schools of children with special educational needs. Mitchell cited some indications of this negative use of enrolment schemes in relation to children with special educational needs and noted 'According to a legal opinion obtained by the IHC, the [education] Amendment Act does constitute a limitation on the right of enrolment in Section 3 of the Education Act 1989 but does not derogate from the equal enrolment right given by section 8' (Mitchell, 1992b, p 34). Knight (1993, p 115) also noted the growing concern that some schools were operating discriminatory enrolment practices.

Further, it was of concern that the Ministry of Education appeared to have had no requirement in terms of approving enrolment schemes, as reported by Mitchell (1992b, p 34), up until late 1998. That seemed diametrically opposed to the philosophy of rights underpinning the 1989 Education Act, and it is hoped that tighter Ministry monitoring of enrolment schemes, under the provisions of the 1998 Education Amendment (No. 2) Act, section 11, will lead to a closer alignment of practice with philosophy. This Amendment Act requires approval from the Ministry of

Education (the Secretary) for both embarking on the development of an enrolment scheme, and approval of the scheme itself. The Board of a school, when developing a scheme, has to ensure that students can 'attend a school of their choice...when developing, adopting, amending and implementing an enrolment scheme' (Section 11 B 2). The nature and effect of the scheme has to be made publicly available by the Board of the school, and reviewed annually. Also, the Secretary has the power, under this Act, to direct the Board to enrol a person, when the interests of a particular student justifies this action (Section 11 N).

Both of these concerns relate to the impacts of New Zealand's move towards a more market philosophy of competition and choice, on the right to education for children with special educational needs. This move occurred in the late 1980s, with each school becoming 'an independent, competitive, self-managed "education provider" under a Board of Trustees' (Ballard, 1996, p 39).

That competition and choice may have similar negative consequences for children with special educational needs in New Zealand as those noted in Britain (Ball, Bowe and Gold, 1993), seems likely. The 1994 OECD Report, *A Matter of Choice,* in commenting on these market developments in New Zealand stated 'perhaps the most radical aspect in international terms is the independence given to school boards in terms of identifying and, where necessary, selecting, their client markets' (p 73).

Further, by 1994 there was growing concern at how school suspension and expulsion figures were skyrocketing. The 3511 suspensions and 30 expulsions in the January to June 1994 period represented a 22% increase over the same period for 1993 (figures provided by Commission for Children, 1994). Ballard (1997) notes that in 1995 the Ministry of Education had to give official notice to all Boards of Trustees and school principles reminding them that they must not exclude children with disabilities.

It is hoped that the strengthening of provisions for children with special educational needs through the Education 2000 initiative, the related training of teachers to deal with learning and behaviour problems, the tightening of Ministry of Education controls over enrolment schemes, and the new provisions of the 1998 Education Amendment (No 2) Act relating to suspension and exclusion, including the right of the Secretary to make rules regulating the practice and procedures to be followed by School Boards in relation to suspension and exclusion (Section 8), will guard against school rejection of children with special educational needs. However, the relationship of SEN philosophy and provision to wider socio-economic issues, including poverty and market philosophy, warrant far greater attention (Dyson, 1997; Mittler, 1999).

Moves towards inclusion

In discussing development of the new Special Education 2000 policy, Davies and Prangnell (1999) point out that 'the passage of the 1987 Education Act ... gave legislative commitment to the right of every child to enrol in a regular school' (p 4). The 1989 Education Act states that 'Except as provided in this part of this Act, people who have special educational needs (whether because of disability or otherwise) have the same rights to enrol and receive education at state schools as people who do not' (Section 8).

Davies and Prangnell see the Special Education 2000 policy as needing to maintain a genuine choice of education setting for all students, but identify the tension between 'the policy objective of the Special Education grant and the present reality of "magnet" schools' (Davies and Prangnell, 1999, p 17). They state, 'the policy aims to assist in developing a culture that encourages all schools to meet the full range of student needs, and to accept all students from the local community' (*ibid*, p 17-18). They also identify the difficulties 'around gaining a consensus from specialists, parents and schools about the needs of individual students' (*ibid*, p 18).

Ballard (1996) in discussing inclusive education in New Zealand, reminds us that 'New Zealand has evolved a dual regular and "special" education system, much like that in Western industrial democracies, and significantly influenced by research, theory and legislation from Britain and America ...' (*ibid*, p 33). The present writer suggests that the following may be forces in New Zealand which will facilitate a way ahead in which 'education and special education are seen not only in simple individualistic terms, but in the wider perspective of enlightened and socially-oriented self-interest' (Corbett and Norwich, 1997, p 386). These are :

1   The New Zealand education legislation spells out the right to education in the regular school with much greater clarity and force than does the English legislation. The British 1993 Education Act continues to list the caveats or conditions found in the Warnock report concerning right to attendance at a regular school, as follows 'unless that is incompatible with the wishes of his parent' (Section 160, (1) ... and that it is 'compatible with – (a) his receiving the special educational provision which his learning difficulty calls for, (b) the provision of efficient education for the children with whom he will be educated, and (c) the

Dorothy Howie

efficient use of resources' (Section 160 (2). It should be noted that these are similar to those listed as caveats or exceptions in section 60 of the New Zealand 1993 Human Rights Act, and the writer urges that New Zealand continues its positive leadership on this rights issue and considers the withdrawal of these caveats.

2 The history of parent leadership in progressive policy development for special educational needs in New Zealand has been very strong, initially for any provision (such as in the key early role played by the then Intellectually Handicapped Children's Society), then for changes in the rights to education for all children, moving to parental partnership, and then more recently to integration (Brown, 1990, 1994).

Further, some of the parents playing key roles in pointing the way for policy development have a dual responsibility, both as a parent of a person with a special educational need, and as a key professional in the field. A leading research body in the field of special educational needs, The Donald Beasley Institute, under the direction of Anne Bray, carries out exemplary research, particularly in terms of partnership with parents, which can inform policy development, and it has a strong underpinning philosophy of inclusion.

3 The pride which New Zealand can feel in its teaching and learning practices, with initiatives fostering the highest standards in the teaching process (such as Clay's 1985 internationally used Reading Recovery Programme); an early and enlightened commitment within teacher training to the Vygotskian theoretical approach, suggesting the importance of heterogeneous learning environments, and the socio-cultural nature of learning; and the current instructional discourse surrounding the teacher training provision for all teachers under the Education 2000 provisions, whether in regular schools, attached special education units or in special schools; should maximise the chances of the needs of all children being met within a truly inclusive system.

Changing paradigms for teaching approaches in special educational needs

The very recent new policy development, Special Education 2000, has a strong component of staff training as part of the funding and provision for Resource Teachers in 'learning and behaviour'. As spelled out by Davies and Prangnell (*op cit*) these teachers 'constitute a new class of special education teacher. The 730 teachers work across a cluster of schools with students (and teachers of students) who have moderate learning and/or behaviour difficulties' (p 11). These resource teachers have been provided with a training course costing $11 million, at both undergraduate and graduate level. The course has been developed by a consortium of three Universities (Auckland, Waikato and Victoria) 'to meet the learning and behaviour needs of students in the classroom' (p 13). This provision, which will support teachers across regular schools and special education provisions, is further supplemented by professional development for all teachers. 'Between July 1998 and June 2000 all schools will have the opportunity to participate in a special education professional development programme. This initiative is an integral part of the implementation of Special Education 2000. It is the first time that professional development in special education has been available to all schools ... It is to be focused on the needs of each school as identified by an analysis of needs' (*ibid*, p 14).

Clearly, such professional support and training will strengthen the possibility of schools meeting the needs of all students, within an inclusive ethos. However, as pointed out by Thomson (1998) many resource teachers continue to work in withdrawal situations in the 'extra pair of hands' model. Rarely do they work at a class or school systems level. Teacher aids are usually 'attached' to identified individual students. These patterns of practice will not disappear overnight. Indeed, we are likely to be operating in a dual paradigm system for some time to come (*ibid*, p 9).

Moore, Brown, Thomson, Glynn, Macfarlane, Timperly and Anderson (1999) discuss the changing paradigms underpinning the professional training being provided for the new Special Education 2000 initiatives. They contrast a 'functional limitations paradigm, on classification and remediation, and an ecological paradigm, which posits that the primary problems facing people with disabilities can best be understood and addressed within the social and learning context in which the problems occur' (p 1). They see the task of educators working within the latter paradigm as altering, adapting and improving educational organisations and environments to meet the needs of all students. This, they point out, ties in with the current New Zealand requirement for schools to identify barriers to learning and to put in place adaptations to remove them.

In their paper, these key leaders in the provision of training for the new teachers in learning and behaviour contrast a behavioural approach with that of individual-based psychometric assessment, stating: 'Knowledge of specific environmental antecedent and consequent variables has proved to be a better predictor of behaviour change than has the individual-based psychometric assessment approach' (Moore *et al*, 1999, p 3), with an examination of the ecological context essential. What seems missing in this analysis of current paradigm thinking in special education is an appreciation of what many current theorists have to say about the learning process and learning in context from a more cognitive perspective. One of the writers of the paper, Brown, does point out elsewhere (Brown, 1998) that 'the approach we use must be collegial and the orientation must be towards problem solving' (*ibid*, p 11).

As early as 1979, Brown and French wrote a detailed paper called *The Zone of Potential Development: Implications for Intelligence in the Year 2000*. In that paper, they followed a brief critique of psychometric testing, the paradigm referred to above. They then outlined an alternative, strongly based on Vygotskian theoretical ideas of interpersonal and intrapersonal learning, and the zone of proximal or next development, in order to discuss learning and everyday thinking. They made a plea 'to expand our basic theories of psychology so that they can go beyond the cognitive capabilities of the elite...' (p 270)... 'we need to develop an understanding of the cognitive demands of everyday life based on a theory of cognition that includes a consideration of more than academic intelligence' (p 269).

New Zealand appears to be aware of and making moves to minimise a psychometric testing approach, particularly in relation to its multi-cultural population needs (personal communication). It has also established, as part of its National Curriculum framework, a requirement for the teaching of problem solving skills.

It is now possible within New Zealand to train in and deliver internationally-recognised programmes for cognitive enhancement, including Feuerstein's (Feuerstein, Rand, Hoffman and Miller, 1980) Instrumental Enrichment programme (Howie, in press). It would be helpful to recognise that the Feuerstein theory, assessment and intervention programmes operationalise the Vygotskian theoretical emphasis on human mediation (Kozulin, 1998).

They also provide a theoretical framework for the type of analysis of real-life problem solving advocated by Brown and French (1979). The programme is now applied as a whole school approach, with particular emphasis on the infusion to all classroom and real-life learning; it is used widely internationally and, particularly in multi-cultural contexts, for the enhancement of learning, particularly for children with special educational needs; and it has been extensively evaluated in a variety of New Zealand educational settings, including with Maori adolescents and their teachers (Howie, Thickpenny, Leaf and Absolum, 1985; Thickpenny and Howie, 1990; Howie, Richards and Pirihi, 1993.)

The important roles of Vygotsky and Feuerstein in this paradigm change have been noted by a recent key British writer in special educational needs, Professor Norwich, at the Institute of Education, the University of London. He and his colleague state, in commenting on paradigm change and tensions in Britain:

'There have been influences from a more socialised form of developmental psychology which has been driven by social constructionist assumptions that learning has to be seen in a social-historical context and involves the internalisation of the interpersonal. Vygotsky has been rediscovered as the source of this social critique of individual cognitive learning and development ... These ideas have awakened interest in group and interactive approaches to assessment and teaching methods in professional educational psychology. This can be seen in the interest in assisted or dynamic assessment associated with using Vygotsky's notion of the zone of proximal development and Feuerstein's theory of mediated learning experience ... However, the systematic development of assessment procedures based on these principles has not emerged, partly from conceptual confusion and also because of pressures from the changing service context.'

(Corbett and Norwich, 1997, p 381)

With recent visits to New Zealand of leaders in the cognitive enhancement fields of such eminence as Professor Feuerstein (1997) and Professor Robert Sternberg (1998), and the opportunity to develop new paradigm approaches to assessment and learning in the New Zealand context, conceptual confusions should be overcome and there be an openness to such new paradigm approaches.

The cultural challenge

New Zealand is a multicultural country and strong efforts are being made in all key cultural groups to provide for culturally appropriate educational services. However, this section will focus on the bi-cultural initiatives as an example of the ways in which a partnership process can develop. The discussion will draw heavily on a paper presented by Macfarlane (1998), called *Culture Counts in Special Education*, and another by Glynn and Macfarlane (1999) called *Developing National Special Education Initiatives – making Culture Count*.

A bicultural partnership in New Zealand has firm foundations in thĕ Treaty of Waitangi, and is considered widely as a supreme value which should inform policy development and organisational provision. Austin (1994) raises important issues of the ownership and power over knowledge, and children themselves as 'taonga' [treasure], as part of the discourse about children in law. The slowness of the state school system to honour this partnership treaty in terms of its provisions was reflected in the high proportion of Maori children in special education facilities in the early years of special education provision (Wilton, 1980), and the growing number of Maori experiencing behaviour difficulties in the 1990s (Macfarlane, 1998).

Some early moves had been made, in the early 1980s, by the New Zealand Society for Intellectual Handicap to encourage culturally appropriate and Maori-led services for its clients, and even in a video programme on self-advocacy developed by Howie for that body, a partnership process was used to determine content appropriate to both Maori and non-Maori clients. The Special Education Service also took a lead, in the early 1990s, under Ross Wilson's leadership, in partnership with Maori elders, to develop a Policy for Tangata Whenua (Maori). In more recent developments as part of the Maori school development, there have been instances of development of inclusive practices (Bevan-Brown, 1994, cited by Ballard, 1996).

Glynn and Macfarlane (1999) describe the process whereby, under the new Special Education 2000 initiative, those providing the training for the new teaching and support initiatives would be prepared appropriately in terms of Maori cultural perspectives on learning and behavioural difficulties. As reported in their paper, the Resource Teachers in Learning and Behaviour Team Programme Developers 'sought the advice of a wide reference group of Maori educators and Kaumatua [Maori elders] in debating the content and delivery of the programme. The team is accountable also to members of the Specialist Education Service Runanganui, which comprises Kaumatua representing tribes within each SES area' (*ibid*, p 2).

In several Hui [Maori meetings] 'Kaumatua expressed the wish that the programme would do justice to the Maori perspectives on learning and teaching, and would respect the wairua [spirit] of all Maori students' (*ibid*, p 2). The Maori educators and Kaumatua from the SES Runanganui 'have had considerable and early input into the design and delivery of this course' (*ibid*, p 6). Macfarlane (1998) outlines, in discussing the issues and concerns about the way in which resource teachers of learning and behaviour should develop professionally, the more holistic and Maori world view outlined by Durie, involving the Taha Wairua (spiritual side), the Taha Tinana (physical side), Taha Hinegnaro (thoughts and feelings) and Taha Whanua (the family).

Conclusions

The issues covered all appear to have an element of partnership in them. The new developments with Education 2000 reflect a desire to take seriously the government's responsibility, under the UN Convention on the Rights of the Child, to share responsibilities with parents, including to 'render appropriate assistance to parents and legal guardians in the performance of their child-rearing responsibilities and shall ensure the development of institutions, facilities and services for the care of children' (Article 18) and 'recognise the right of the child to education' (Article 28).

The need to ensure equal rights for all children within the current market-led education system, regardless of special educational need, ethnic background, and socio-economic background, remains an ongoing key issue of concern. The new training provisions for resource Teachers in Learning and Behaviour are an example of partnership under the Treaty of Waitangi. Partnership with parents has been a recognised value in New Zealand for some time. But partnership with pupils requires further concerted attention and effort, both in legislation and in practice.

References

Austin, G (1994), *Stories the Law Tells Us*, Victoria University Press

Ball, S, Bowe, R and Gold, A (1993), Special educational needs in a new context: Micropolitics, money and education for all, in R Slee (Ed.) *Is there a Desk with my Name on it?* Falmer

Ball, S J, Bowe, R and Gewirtz, S (1994), Market forces and parental choice: Self-interest and competitive advantage in education, S Tomlinson (Ed.) *Educational Reform and its Consequences,* IPPR/Rivers Oram

Ballard, K (1996), Inclusive education in New Zealand: Culture, context and ideology, *Cambridge Journal of Education*, 26, (pp 33-45)

Ballard, K (1997), Researching disability and inclusive education: Participation, construction and interpretation, *International Journal of Inclusive Education*, 1, (pp 243-256)

Ballard, K and Macdonald, T (1998), New Zealand: Inclusive school, inclusive philosophy? in T Booth and M Ainscow (Eds), *From Them to Us: An International Study of Inclusion in Education,* Routledge

Ballard, K (1999), *Inclusive Education: International Voices on Disability and Justice*, Falmer

Beattie, Sir Justice D S (1976), *Advocacy and Attainment of the Rights of the Intellectually Handicapped,* The Research Foundation of the New Zealand Society for the Intellectually Handicapped

Bevan-Brown, J (1994), Intellectual disability: A Maori perspective, in K Ballard (Ed.) *Disability, Family, Whanau and Society*, Dunmore Press

Bramley, J and Elkins, J (1988), Some issues in the development of self-advocacy among persons with intellectual disabilities, *Australia and New Zealand Journal of Developmental Disabilities*, 14, (pp 147-157)

British Education Act 1993, HMSO

Brown, A and French, L A (1979), The Zone of Potential development: Implications for intelligence testing in the year 2000, *Intelligence*, 3, (pp 255-273)

Brown, C (1990), Fight for children left for the crows, *Dominion Sunday Times*, 29 April (p 10)

Brown, C (1994), Parents and professionals: Future directions, in K Ballard (Ed.), *Disability, Family, Whanau and Society*, Dunmore Press

Brown, D (1998), *An Educational Model and Professional Development for Resource Teachers*, paper presented to 28th Annual Conference of the Australian Teacher Education Association

Children, Young Persons and their Families Act 1989, Government Printer, (NZ)

Clay, M M (1985), *The Early Detection of Reading Difficulties (3rd edition)*, Heinemann

Corbett, J and Norwich, B (1997), Special needs and client rights: The changing social and political context of special educational research, *British Educational Research Journal*, 23 (pp 379-389)

Davies, T and Prangnell, A (1999), *Special Education 2000 – A National Framework,* paper presented to Special Education 2000 – Research Conference

Department of Education (1989), *The Charter Framework,* Department of

Education

DfE, (1994), *The Code of Practice for the Identification and Assessment of Special Educational Needs*, HMSO

Dyson, A (1997), Social and educational disadvantage: Reconnecting special needs education, *British Journal of Special Education*, 24, (pp 152-157)

Education Act 1964, Government Printer, (NZ)

Education Act 1989, Government Printer, (NZ)

Education Amendment Act 1991, Government Printer, (NZ)

Education Amenment Act (No 2) 1998, Government Printer, (NZ)

Feuerstein, R, Rand, Y, Hoffman, M and Miller, R (1980), *Instrumental Enrichment*, University Park Press

Feuerstein, R (1997), *All Children Can Learn*, Keynote Address to Conference on Teaching for Intelligence, Auckland

Glynn, T and Macfarlane, A (1999), *Developing National Special Education Initiatives – Making Culture Count,* paper presented to Special Education 2000 Research Conference

Harré, R and van Langenhove, L (1999), *Positive Positioning*, Blackwell

Harrison, R (1993), Powers, duties and accountability of School Boards of Trustees in Legal Research Foundation (Ed.), *Education and the Law in New Zealand*, Legal Research Foundation

Howie, D (1980), Suggested changes in education legislation relating to the needs of the mentally retarded, *Mental Handicap in New Zealand*, 5, (pp 6-14)

Howie, D R, Cuming, J M and Raynes, N V (1984), Development of tools to facilitiate participation by retarded persons in residential evaluation procedures, *British Journal of Mental Subnormality*, 30, (pp 92-93)

Howie, D R, Thickpenny, J P, Leaf, C A and Absolum, M A (1985), The piloting of 'Instrumental Enrichment' in New Zealand with eight mildly retarded children, *Australia and New Zealand Journal of Developmental Disabilities*, 11, (pp 3 - 6)

Howie, D R and Cuming, J (1986), *Self-Advocacy by Mentally Retarded Persons: A New Zealand Study*, New Zealand Institute of Mental Retardation

Howie, D R (1987), Retarded person's self-advocacy in monitoring procedures: Dissemination data, *Mental Handicap in New Zealand*, 11, (pp 22-26)

Howie, D R, Richards, R and Pirihi, H (1993), Teaching thinking skills to Maori adolescents, *International Journal of Cognitive Education and Mediated Learning*, 3, (pp 70-91)

Howie, D R and Westera, J (1994), Confidential Phase One Draft Report: Accountability for Students with Special Educational Needs, University of Auckland

Howie, D (1999a), Models and morals: Meanings and underpinning the scientific study of special educational needs, *International Journal of Disability, Development and Education*, 46, (pp 9-24)

Howie, D (1999b), Preparing for positive positioning, in R Harré and L van Langenhove (Eds), *Positioning Theory*, Blackwell

Howie, D R (in press), *Thinking about the Teaching of Thinking*, New Zealand Council for Educational Research

Human Rights Act 1993, Government Printer, (NZ)

Human Rights Commission (1996), *Human Rights and Special Needs Education*, Human Rights Commission, (NZ)

Knight, R (1993), Access to education: School zoning, entitlement and eligibility to enrol children with special needs, in Legal Research Foundation (Ed.), *Education and the Law in New Zealand*, Legal Research Foundation

Kozulin, A (1998), *Psychological Tools: A Sociocultural Approach to Education*, Harvard

Macfarlane, A H (1998), *Piki Ake Te Tikanga: Culture Counts in Special Education*, paper presented to 28th Annual Conference of Australian Teacher Education Association

Ministry of Education (1994), *Final Report of the Policy Implementation Team on Delivering Special Education*, (SEPIT), Ministry of Education

Ministry of Education (1998), *The IEP Guidelines: Planning for Students with Special Educational Needs, Special Education 2000*, Ministry of Education

Mitchell, D (1992a), *Contesting Contestability in Special Education: A Critical Analysis of Special Education Policies in New Zealand*, paper presented to the invitational conference on Social Justice and Dilemmas Disability in Education, University of Queensland

Mitchell, D R (1992b), *Special Education: Whose Responsibility?* Keynote address to 1991 NZARE Conference

Mitchell, D and Ryba, K (1994), *Students with Education Support Needs: Review of Criteria for Admission to Special Education Facilities and for the Allocation of Discretionary Resources*, School of Education, University of Waikato

Mittler, P (1999), Equal opportunities – for whom? *British Journal of Special Education*, 26, (pp 3-7)

Moore, D W, Brown, D, Thomon, C, Glynn, T, Macfarlane, A, Timperley, H and Anderson, A (1999), *Learning and Behaviour – Connecting Theory and Practice,* in Paper presented to Special Education 2000 – Research Conference

New Zealand Bill of Rights 1990, Government Printer

OECD (1994), *A Matter of Choice*, OECD

Protection of Personal and Property Rights Act 1998, Government Printer, (NZ)

Sleek, D and Howie, D (1987), Legislation, rights and advocacy, in N Singh and D Mitchell (Eds), *Special Education for New Zealand's Exceptional Children*, Dunmore Press

Sternberg, R J (1998), *Successful Intelligence*, Keynote address to Conference on Successful Intelligence, Aukland

Thickpenny, J P and Howie, D R (1990), Teaching thinking skills to deaf adolescents: The implementation and evaluation of instrumental enrichment, *International Journal of Cognitive Education and Mediated Learning*, 1, (pp 193-209)

Thomson, C and Rowan, C (1995), *Individual Education Plans in New Zealand Schools*, Wellington College of Education

Thomson, C (1998), *Inclusion and Professional Development for Resource Teachers*, paper presented to 28th Annual Conference of Australian Teacher Education Association

United Nations (1989), *Convention on the Rights of the Child*, United Nations

Wilton, K (1980), Research on special education in New Zealand, *The State of the Art Papers*, NZARE/Delta

Chapter 14

The enhancement of cognitive development in a disadvantaged community: KwaZulu Natal, South Africa

Belle Wallace and Harvey B Adams

Introduction

The following chapter outlines the salient findings of an action research project which took place in Black schools in KwaZulu Natal (South Africa) between 1985 and 1998. Although the action research project was located in KwaZulu Natal, it is important to stress that the educational conditions prevalent in that province are replicated in the majority of the other nine provinces. However, the writers claim that the general findings and the final recommendations are universally relevant to any discussion of special educational needs in a wide variety of social, economic and political situations especially in situations of extreme disadvantage.

The writers established the Curriculum Development Unit (CDU) at the University of Natal (Pietermaritzburg) in 1985 with the main aim of undertaking research, teaching and community service activities in low socio-economic, high unemployment areas to help teachers maximise the extent to which all pupils develop their potential. In this context, it could be argued that the level of endemic and chronic under-achievement of the vast majority of learners places them in the category of 'children with special educational needs'.

It is important to stress at the beginning of this chapter that the writers do not work within a framework of *cultural deficit*. Nor do they propose that any one culture has a definable and favourable set of 'strengths' in the realm of learning strategies. However, they do suggest that *all* learners require the development of a range of comprehensive and universally applicable cognitive 'tools' which they can use to focus and direct their learning *in any context* whether that be within an informal cultural context or a relevant, formal school context. Under certain conditions of socio/educational disadvantage and cultural deprivation, the essential cognitive 'tools' which facilitate formal school learning are under-developed.

Background to the project

KwaZulu Natal consists mainly of rural, subsistence farming and low socio-economic urban settlements. The total school enrolment is currently estimated at 1.5 million, but is rapidly rising, with only 67% of the school-age population actually attending school. Moreover recent surveys suggest that 53% of the entire KwaZulu Natal population is under 15 years of age.

The current levels of school dropout, repeating of classes and the failure rate in the Senior School Certificate examination taken at 17+ years, all indicate considerable underachievement amongst Black learners. From figures indicated by Edusource (1992), it can be deduced that only 25% of Zulu learners reach Grade 12 (the current school leaving age). Of these, approximately 39% obtain a Senior School Certificate (that is 9.8% of the cohort) and 2.5% of the cohort obtain a level of matriculation which would enable them to apply for university entrance. Of those, few can afford to proceed to university and almost all who do are 'under-prepared' and fail their first year of tertiary education. Universities have, in consequence, established 'bridging' courses and 'student support services'.

> 'However, many of these 'bridging' courses attempt to prepare students for a university curriculum that is firmly embedded in a Western paradigm. Few such courses attempt to analyse the students' needs from their own perspective and few address the need to develop students' thinking skills. Most universities are concerned with bridging gaps in content from their own perspective; fitting students to engage in the university curricula rather than attempting to match the university curricula to the students' needs. The argument frequently used is that if the universities changed their curricula, then "standards" would fall. Those "standards" are often content bound and immutable and consequently have a rigidifying effect on the school system especially at secondary level'.   (Wallace and Adams,1993a, p 45)

The South African government has announced its intention of developing an outcomes-based (*ie* process-based) system of education (OBE) which will be developed and implemented in all schools by 2005. The new system will implement revised, culturally appropriate curricula. However, to date there has been no change in secondary curricula which would impact on the situation outlined above. Changes in the first three years of schooling have statutarily been implemented but the nine provinces have generally failed to supply appropriate books to schools and teacher preparation for change has been inadequate.

Although recently there has been a large increase in funding for education from central government, there is an acute shortage of funds provincially to pay for sufficient fully-trained teachers. Classes are large, although it is difficult to obtain documented figures for current class sizes. Furthermore, within the lessons themselves lie further causes of underachievement since, although the learners' home language is Zulu, English is used as the medium of instruction for all subjects beyond the third year of primary schooling. Therefore, any inadequacies in the teaching and learning of English compound the difficulties experienced by pupils in the learning of other school subjects.

Many teachers themselves have only a basic command of English and an equally basic understanding of their subject matter. Consequently, the large classes with a wide range of pupil ability cause difficulties which most teachers attempt to solve by means of a rigid and didactic teaching style aimed at promoting the 'recitation script' of whole class chanting and rote learning. Many rural parents speak no English at all, yet most Zulu parents want their children to be taught in English: they see it as the international language and as a key to open the doors to high status occupations.

The traditional Zulu culture (like many other African cultures) promotes deep respect for senior members of the community and for those in authority. Young people are not encouraged to question their elders and it is considered impolite to push oneself forward as an individual. Social cohesion is strong and consciousness of one's place in the society is both implicitly and explicitly encouraged. Teachers usually encourage and expect compliance and conformity and although the government has banned the use of corporal punishment, it is still extensively used in many areas as a form of deterrent when learners are 'cheeky' enough to ask questions.

With regard to traditional attitudes and values in general, there is often widespread conflict between teachers and their students and between parents and their children. In semi-urban and rural areas, many parents work away from home for long periods and the 'care-giver' is a grandparent who lives even closer to the old traditions and thus, the gap in the mediation of life values and goals between learner and adult is even greater than it is in urban areas.

Two key issues arise from the conditions outlined above: the importance of language in cognitive development as well as positive self-concept.

The importance of language in cognitive development

Maker and Schiever (1989) discuss the extensive research which clearly indicates the feeling of powerlessness learners develop when they begin to feel alienated from their own language and culture, or when parents can no longer communicate effectively with their children because the latter speak a different language. When new words are used in school learning, with no equivalent words in the child's home language, the problems of alienation are exacerbated.

Zappia (in *ibid*) emphasises the importance for all learners of acquiring basic interpersonal skills, which initially rely heavily on visual cues and take approximately two years to develop. As this basic language is used and extended, cognitive academic language develops with semantic and functional meaning. Cognitively undemanding language communication requires only the knowledge, understanding and language processes of mainly pronunciation, vocabulary and grammar patterns. Cognitively demanding communication, however, requires the skills of analysis, synthesis and evaluation, with the appropriate language processes of semantic and functional meaning.

All children *have language* but Cummins (1983) argues that learners are empowered or disabled by the degree to which: pupils' home language is incorporated into school language and learning; learners' community values are incorporated into school activities; teaching first promotes and then extends the active use of learners' language; and, scholars' cultural strengths are recognised and fostered.

As stated above, learners in school learn in their second language and the prevailing paradigm of teaching methodology is 'teacher talks and pupils listen'. Vast amounts of content are provided for learners to memorise and the language used to convey that content is acquired through drill of grammar patterns.

Although the current government has pledged to change this situation, and is trying to initiate growth towards an outcomes-based curriculum, it is the writers' considered opinion that teachers who are largely untrained in a process-based teaching and learning style will not have had the experience, and hence will not have acquired the essential skills, needed to implement the necessary methodological changes. When teachers have always used the 'recitation script' style of whole class drill, it is very difficult to transform the paradigm to one of creative, analytical or evaluative thinking with students working in groups and being encouraged to interact creatively and to think for themselves.

To compound the depth of the problem, Vygotsky maintains that intellectual development is not just the acquiring of experience, it is the result of social transaction of meaning which occurs mainly through language which is the fundamental vehicle of education (Bruner, 1985). He stresses the vital importance of mediation of the child's learning experience. Capable tutors (parents and teachers) initiate the child by structuring activities so that the child gradually gains mastery (Cole, 1985). The learner internalises the concept and thus gains conscious control over his/her actions, which can then be used as tools for further learning. The tutor performs the function of providing scaffolding for the learning task until the learner becomes independent. The new higher concepts transform the meaning of the lower thus it becomes possible to reflect on past experience in order to interpret the new (Bruner, *op cit*).

Leontev and Luria, Vygotsky's students, are quoted as saying:

'The process of social intercourse and specifically its most systematized form, the teaching process, forms the development of the child, creates new mental formations and develops higher processes of mental life... The assimilation of general human experience in the teaching process is the most important specifically human form of mental development in ontogenesis. This deeply significant proposition defines an essentially new approach to the most important theoretical problem of psychology, the challenge of actively developing the mind...'   (Foreman and Cazden, 1985 p 323)

Since language is the main vehicle for the process of mediation of meaning, learners who are rote learning in their second language through the 'drill and remember' method will not experience the mediation necessary for them to fully (if at all) develop vital cognitive tools which enable them to make sense of their school learning.

Vygotsky also stresses the importance of cultural transmission in the intentional mediation of the learner's experience. The dominant culture in South Africa has been a White Western culture and Black culture was harshly and systematically repressed. The culture of Black learners was mediated in a fragmented way with divisions inevitably arising between the values of home and school.

This situation was (and still is) exacerbated by the wide division between the home culture of rural children and the school culture. Pupils in schools have always used texts that have been decidedly White Western in orientation with characters, stories and incidents which excluded their own cultural literature and history. Where the process of cultural mediation is inadequate then the learner fails to develop a positive sense of self which is essential for cognitive and affective learning.

The importance of positive self-concept and internal locus of control on cognitive development

Goleman (1996) argues that emotional intelligence is a necessary requisite for the efficient development of all other forms of intelligent and creative functioning. He maintains that emotional intelligence can be taught and is open to constant modification through mediation and personal reflection. He defines emotional intelligence as the ability to think positively about the self, the ability to motivate the self, to delay gratification and to persist despite frustrations.

The grounding for the development of these abilities resides essentially in the mediation the child receives through the family and the school. In conditions of cultural repression, grinding poverty, high unemployment, fragmented families, mediation for passivity, oppressive school (and often family) discipline, and inadequate language for school learning, many pupils acquire the syndrome of 'learned helplessness'. They see themselves as helpless in a very powerful world, imprisoned by their home and school circumstances rather than empowered by them.

Rotter (1966) maintains that for children to develop a positive self-image and a sense that they have some control over their own lives and their powers of decision-making, they need to experience and perceive positive relationships between their actions and the outcomes of their own behaviour. When this happens, they gradually develop an internal locus of control whereby they feel motivated to achieve and are more able to persist to task completion.

Rotter's premise is complemented and extended by Bandura's Social Learning Theory (1971,1977), and its precursor the Observational Learning Theory (Bandura and Walker, 1963), which assumes that learning involves a three-way relationship between the environment, personal factors and behaviour (which includes the learner's own cognitive processes). The relationship between each of these three relationships is bi-directional. For example, membership of differing social classes may activate differential social treatments, leading to varying influences upon self-concept which in turn influence perception of events and consequent actions. Bandura refers to this as reciprocal determinism.

In Social Learning Theory, there are three components of learning.

- modelled behaviours which may be live, verbal or symbolic. The characteristics of a model stimulus (observed behaviour of parents, peers, teachers, or instructions, television, film *etc*), is that it is so organised that the learner can extract and act upon information conveyed, without needing to act overtly. The learner needs to believe in and accept the adult model as positively reinforcing;

- consequences of behaviour which might be direct reinforcement, vicarious reinforcement, or self-reinforcement whereby the learner has self-prescribed standards of behaviour, has reinforcing events under her/his control and is able to act as her/his own reinforcing agent;

- the learner's cognitive processes *ie* the ability to code and store transitory experiences in symbolic form and represent future consequences in thought and language. These cognitive processes include attention, retention, motor production (*ie* some form of behavioural output), and motivational processes.

Bandura (1982) emphasises that the acquisition of complex skills and abilities depend upon two additional components. These are, perceived self-efficacy *ie* the learner is convinced that s/he can successfully execute the behaviour required to produce a particular outcome, and the capability for self-observation, self-judgement and self-response. A positive sense of the self together with an internal locus of control are pre-requisites for successful task commitment.

However, although cognitive development can be irreversibly impaired as a result of hereditary or organic factors, other writers (Feuerstein, 1979, 1980; Campione, 1982; Brown and Ferrara, 1985) show that cognitive and affective underfunctioning resulting from insufficient mediation can be remedied by appropriate intervention. With this premise, the authors began an intervention programme in KwaZulu Natal which aimed to remediate and uplift the capacities of learners to learn more effectively. It was not within the capacity of the writers to intervene and alter curricula, but the overall aim was to empower the learners so that they could better cope with both the demands of school learning and of the general environment.

The 'Thinking Actively in a Social Context: TASC' action research project

While accepting the theoretical tenets of Vygotsky and Bandura as forming the base of their work, the writers also embraced the theories of

Sternberg's (1985) Triarchic Theory of Intelligence, and Borkowski's (1985) General Model of Intelligence. Therefore it is necessary to outline the major points of these two researchers.

Sternberg proposes that intelligence consists of three inter-related aspects:

- the *contextual* sub-theory in which intelligence is viewed as mental activity directed towards the purposeful adaptation to and the selection and shaping of real world environments relevant to one's life. There are clear implications in this for cross-cultural differences in cognition and hence the need for culturally relevant courses in the development of cognition;

- the *experiential* sub-theory which proposes that performance on any task is an indication of intelligence only to the extent that it requires, first, the ability to deal with novel tasks and, secondly, the ability to automatize the processing of information together with the development of thinking and problem-solving behaviours;

- the *componential* sub-theory in which the mechanism of information processing is specified. These include the meta-components which are the executive processes used to plan, monitor and evaluate one's strategy for solving problems; the performance components which are used to carry out instructions of the meta-components for solving problems, and the knowledge acquisition components which are used to learn how to solve problems in the first place. All three kinds of components are interactive and need to be trained in tandem.

Borkowski (1985) elaborates a general model of intelligence first proposed by Campione and Brown (1978). The model distinguishes between the *architectural* system, that is the biologically, genetically-based properties necessary for processing information such as memory span, retention of stimulus traces and speed of encoding and decoding information; and the *executive* system, that is the environmentally learned components that guide problem-solving, such as long term knowledge and its retrieval, Piagetian schemes, control processes and metacognition. In common with Sternberg (1986) he stresses the importance of metacognition in the development of pupils' successful learning and discusses three perspectives: a) metacognition as one component of intelligence interacting with other components throughout life; b) metacognition as the process which promotes the generalisation of thinking strategies; and, c) metacognition as a possible link between intelligence, self-knowledge and regulation.

304

With the body of theoretical knowledge in place, under the broad aim of the CDU, and in the light of the perceived needs of pupils, an initial pilot project was launched in 1986 to develop a course to teach problem-solving and thinking skills to 30 pupils in grade 10, *ie* the third year of high school. The focus was on developing higher levels of thinking and problem-solving amongst disadvantaged under-achieving pupils who were approaching their grade 12 school leaving examinations. The project was started at this point in order to try and equip senior pupils with the skills they needed to obtain the matriculation standard necessary for entry into university.

The aims of TASC at the outset were: to improve general attitudes to school and levels of achievement and motivation for learning, thereby opening doors for increased life opportunities; to improve scholars' self-concept and inner locus of control by helping them to tackle for themselves problems at home, at school or elsewhere which inhibited their learning; to equip students for decision-making and leadership roles in the community and in the work place and also for their future roles as citizens in a society that was undergoing rapid and profound change; and to help disadvantaged young people to adopt roles in society for which few role models existed in the older generation.

The developmental stages of the initial pilot project were monitored intensively, discussed and evaluated by all the participants: the pupils, their teachers, two senior educational psychologists and the researchers. There is not the space to report the detail of that discussion here but it revealed the need for a much more intensive and extensive project which was to last until 1998. The remainder of this chapter is a summation of the 12-year project.

Revised and extended TASC framework

A series of pilot projects were carried out with the same intensity of monitoring, discussion and evaluation, and the aims of TASC were revised and extended. It is important to note, however, that although the TASC model was designed by Adams and Wallace (Adams, 1985, 1986; Adams and Wallace, 1988; Wallace and Adams,1987, 1988), their essential belief is that teachers and learners should play a major role in the development of any course purporting to meet their needs. Consequently, TASC was open to the pragmatic, evaluative reflection of teacher and learner throughout the stages of its development and the proposed model is intended to be used as a framework for the guidance of curriculum developers and teachers in designing their own courses in problem-solving in the light of their specific experiences and the needs of themselves and their pupils.

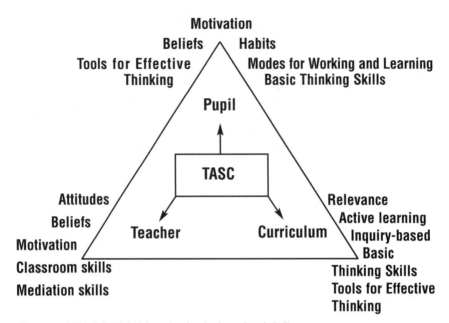

Figure. 1 TASC Thinking Actively in a Social Context
The Overall Aims of TASC

Extended and overall aims of TASC

The general aims of TASC with regard to the pupils remained the same but the pilot projects revealed the need for additional and extensive training in understanding the need for perseverance, accuracy and reflection as opposed to impulsivity; and for training in truly participatory and co-operative, as well as independent, modes of working.

Most importantly, a number of key 'Tools for Effective Thinking' were identified and embedded in the problem-solving procedure (outlined below). In addition many learners had under-developed basic skills and concepts, such as the ability to compare and contrast using simple criteria of 'same and different', and the ability to communicate using the words 'first, next, then, finally'. (This problem was eventually tackled at the primary level of schooling through an intensive language and thinking programme. See the Addendum below.)

The general aim for teachers was to improve their effectiveness as facilitators of children's 'learning how to learn'. The objectives included developing teachers' abilities to establish a democratic and co-operative climate within their classrooms; use interactive classroom skills; provide 'cognitive scaffolding' including modelling and mediation of learners' experiences; extend their knowledge of subject content and of principles.

As far as the curriculum was concerned, there were short and long term aims. The short term aim was to modify existing syllabuses in order to begin to make incremental changes and the long term aim was to reconstruct the curriculum and rewrite syllabuses in order to achieve the general aims for teachers and pupils.

The objectives for such a syllabus included the need to make the curriculum relevant to pupils' past, present and anticipated needs and experiences; the need to include enquiry-based, active learning experiences; and the need to include experiences specifically designed to develop and strengthen cognitive resources and strategies.

Teaching principles of TASC

Through a series of workshops, the teaching principles evolved from teachers' and learners' reflective discussions of their needs.

- *Adopt a model of the problem-solving process and teach this:*

  A problem situation is defined as one in which a person or persons have a goal which cannot be achieved because of an obstacle or obstacles. As Jackson (1975) puts it: *Problem = Objective + Obstacle.* Students are given training in the identification and formulation of problems which are relevant to themselves.

- *Identify a set of specific skills and strategies and give training in these:*

  As with the training of any skill, one can lay down a sequence of events *viz*: demonstrate, analyse and label sub-skills and improve these by means of external feedback, build the sub-skills into complex skills and improve these to the point of automization of use. This has implications for the manner in which skills are taught and begs the issue of which skills are to be selected. Here TASC has taken a pragmatic approach, whereby in the pilot courses, a set of skills were selected then modified and extended. For example, as the set of skills became more specific it became evident that there was a need for basic skills, such as comparisons and analogies, and complex skills, such as working backwards from a goal or means-end analysis. It is also important to stress here that the skills and the contexts in which the skills are embedded need to be culturally relevant to the learner. For example, in our case there were major differences between urban and rural children.

- *Develop a vocabulary*

  If learners are to engage in reflection on their own performance and discussion of their thought processes then they need a suitable vocabulary. For example, 'Evaluate' could be replaced by 'How well did our solution work?' This discussion is essential in order to internalise the problem-solving process and the thinking skills.

- *Give ample practice in both the skills and the strategies*

  Wherever possible, learners' own problems should form the basis of their initial learning. Their own experiences should be the starting points for their analysis and development of more effective cognitive functioning.

- *Give attention to the motivational aspects of problem-solving*

  Many disadvantaged learners turn away from tackling problems out of a sense of learned helplessness. They perceive themselves as 'incapable' and as victims in a world where others are powerful and they are powerless. Learners need to develop a positive self-concept and an internal locus of control: they need to learn how to resolve conflict between the dominant and less dominant value systems. It is therefore essential to ensure early successes and to provide constant positive reinforcement so that learners feel empowered as successful problem-solvers.

- *The progression of teaching is from modelling by the teacher to guided activity for the learner and eventually to autonomous action by the learner*

  The teacher must be sensitive to the rate of learning and to the development of learners' confidence, gradually removing his/her intervention (scaffolding) as the student gains mastery.

- *Every effort must be made to enable the learner to transfer skills and strategies*

  This involves employing all skills in as wide a range of contexts as possible and getting the pupils to explicitly identify links with syllabus and out of school contexts.

- *The emphasis is upon co-operative learning in small groups*

  This enhances the opportunity for participation by each individual. The emphasis is also upon verbal communication which encourages confidence and develops language and thinking skills.

- *Teachers should encourage pupils' self-monitoring and self-evaluation*

  This includes the ability to learn from errors and partial failures as well as successes. Feedback from the teacher is essential and pupils should be guided not only in the assessment of the end result of the problem-solving process but also on the problem-solving process itself.

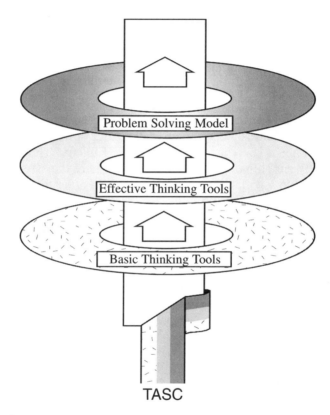

Figure. 2 TASC Thinking Actively in a Social Context
The TASC Three-tier Model

The TASC working model

The TASC framework coincides to a certain extent with a number of thinking skills programmes. However, most of these programmes were designed as extra-curricular activities and the intention of TASC was to provide a framework which would bring about the multiple objectives outlined above. The writers took a pragmatic and eclectic approach and surveyed the research and projects available with regard to the development of thinking and problem-solving skills. The authors acknowledge the influence of these researchers and, together with their own findings (Adams and Wallace, 1988), have drawn up a systemic and holistic framework for the development of effective learning across the curriculum, and outside school.

As is mentioned above, from the base of an initial course to teach problem-solving, it was necessary to extend the pilot project into a much more intensive and extensive project. It is not within the scope of this chapter to justify each stage of its development and only the final TASC working model is presented here.

The original problem-solving model was extended and a selection of core thinking tools was incorporated on the basis of their usefulness and frequency of need. These are called 'Tools for Effective Thinking'. Then a range of 'Basic Thinking Skills' were identified as the essential cognitive building blocks which need to be in place in order for the Tools for Effective Thinking to develop fully.

However, although the TASC working model developed from the top down *ie* from diagnosing the needs of senior learners to diagnosing the needs of primary learners, this chapter will present the range of Basic Thinking Skills first, followed by the Tools for Effective Thinking embedded in the TASC Problem-Solving Model. It must be stressed here that no model for the development of thinking and problem-solving can be completely exhaustive and teachers trained and skilled in using a thinking skills approach across the curriculum could identify many skills as they identify learners' needs. Below we give an illustrative sample. (See Wallace and Adams (1993b) for a fuller list of examples).

Knowledge   Attitudes/Motivation   Metacognition   Skills & Process

Figure 3. TASC Thinking Actively in a Social Context
Basic Thinking categories

TASC Basic Thinking Skills

The TASC Basic Thinking Skills integrate knowledge, attitudes and motivation, metacognition, and skills and processes so that the learner is regarded in a holistic way as a dynamic thinking and feeling person. Indeed the development of cognition and emotion are inextricably interrelated. Also some of the skills fall into more than one category since data must be accurately processed at the receiving, processing and output stages of learning.

Knowledge includes the acquisition of verbal labels and concepts, and relevant information about ideas, objects, events and people. With regard to attitudinal and motivational factors these include being purposeful, optimistic and interacting actively with the environment; avoiding impulsive responses; recognising the need for systematic exploration; being willing to work co-operatively or independently as the occasion demands. Metacognition at all stages of learning is essential if what is being learned is to be retained as a working repertoire of cognitive tools and this involves being aware of the existence, incongruity or incompletion of a problem; selecting appropriate cognitive resources and strategies, monitoring solutions and being sensitive to feedback.

The Skills and Processes can be sub-divided into:

- *Gathering and Organising Incoming Information:* for example, being precise and accurate when necessary; considering more than one source of information simultaneously; Developing spatial and temporal concepts; deciding which features of an object remain constant even when changes occur,

- *Using Gathered Information to Identify and Solve Problems:* for example, relating new data to previous experiences and distinguishing between relevant and irrelevant information; selecting mode of representation, such as symbols, diagrams, drawings, keywords, flowcharts *etc*; analysing and synthesising ideas; and using logical evidence to prove things and defend opinions;

- *Communicating with Co-learners and Communicating Outcomes:* which means avoiding ego-centric communication; thinking things through before beginning to communicate; selecting mode for communication; being an active listener;

- *Learning from Experience:* this involves comparing new experiences with previous ones; considering other circumstances in which the

Fig. 4 TASC Thinking Actively in a Social Context
Detail of the Problem-solving Framework and selected Tools for Effective Thinking

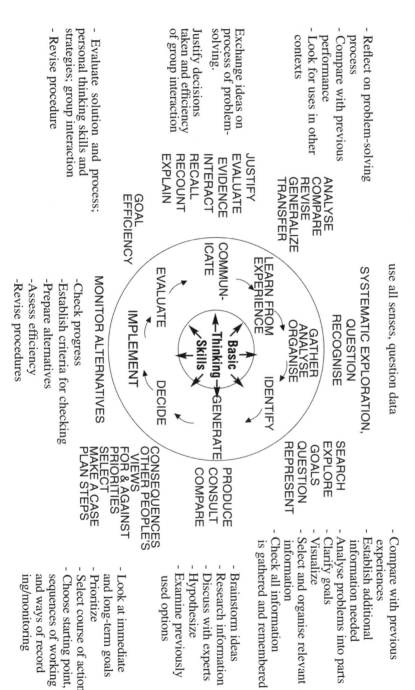

information, outcome or insight might apply; deriving rules and principles from experiences; hypothesizing and predicting about related problems and issues.

TASC Tools for Effective Thinking and the TASC Problem-Solving Model

The diagram in Figure 4 provides a summary of the key thinking skills terminology used throughout the TASC problem-solving procedure, although this terminology needs to be simplified according to the stage of development of the learner.

As we mentioned above, the Basic Thinking Skills lay the foundation for the Tools for Effective Thinking which in turn are embedded in the Problem-Solving Model. However, there can be no clear delineation between the stages of developing cognition from basic thinking skills to advanced problem-solving and some skills re-occur at each level in a more complex form.

The skills need to be embedded in a relevant content in a culturally appropriate context which is determined by the stage of the learners' development. For example, the skill of 'comparison' occurs at an early stage of cognitive development in the comparison of number, while at a more advanced stage of development the learner might compare ideas among characters in a novel. At an early stage of cognitive development, a learner might be analysing 'smallest' and 'biggest', while at a later stage of development a learner might be prioritising ideas. The writers argue, however, that every learner needs experience and consolidation of appropriate basic thinking skills in order that higher level thinking skills can be developed.

The TASC Tools for Effective Thinking are amplified with the TASC Problem-Solving Model as sequenced below:

- *Gather, analyse and organise information:* At this first stage, the Tools for Effective Thinking require the student to recognise that a problem exists in the first place and then to systematically explore and question all the data.

- *Identify the real, rather than the perceived or imagined, problem:* Here the pupil is required to search for and explore further information, make comparisons with previous experiences and establish what additional information is needed; analyse the problem into parts, establish goals and select relevant information and then to check and represent gathered information clearly.

- *Generate ideas about tentative solutions:* At this stage, the Tools for Effective Thinking require the learner to: produce ideas by brainstorming, consult other people, analyse previously-used options, research further information and hypothesise new alternatives.

- *Decide on a possible solution:* Before making a decision, the learner is encouraged to: look at the immediate, mid- and long-term consequences; consult other people about their opinions; establish priorities in order to select a course of action; make a case for the course of action chosen; and then plan a starting point, sequence of working and ways of recording and monitoring.

- *Implement a course of action:* Whilst carrying out a decision, the student is taught how to monitor progress and efficiency and is encouraged to consider alternative procedures if necessary.

- *Evaluate the extent to which the goals have been achieved and whether the process was efficient:* While learners are encouraged to reflect on their thinking strategies at every stage of the problem-solving procedure, now the requirement is for a summative assessment of the effectiveness of the whole procedure, including the effectiveness of skills and strategies used and the quality of group interaction.

- *Communicate ideas and experiences so that ideas are clarified and shared:* Whilst the learners are communicating in their small working group at all stages in the problem-solving procedure, they are now required to share with the larger group, justifying decisions taken and evaluating the evidence on which they were based. This involves recalling thoughts and actions and explaining succinctly to others.

- *Learn from experience is a summative metacognitive stage and is crucial to the whole problem-solving learning experience:* The students are encouraged to compare their present performance with previous performances, analysing strengths and weaknesses. They are helped to generalise what has been learned in order to effect transfer to new situations. Then with each subsequent problem-solving situation, learners are asked to recall previous experiences which will help them in the current situation.

Conclusion

The TASC framework has been developed in a context where the majority of learners are severely disadvantaged with regard to their efficient cognitive development. We strongly insist that learners are *under*-developed and we have not worked from a framework of cognitive deficit. Teachers and pupils worked alongside the authors contributing their own ideas and evaluating the outcomes of pilot and trialling projects. We worked intensively in a metacognitively reflective and cyclic action research mode rather than a statistical data collection mode and we would claim that we worked within a 'thinking actively in a social context' paradigm in order to develop and refine TASC.

Due to the escalating violence and instability arising from the political situation in which pupils were often protesting and boycotting schools, a large part (although not all) of our developmental work was concentrated in four residential schools in the then apartheid-designated Black homeland of KwaZulu. The pupils in these residential schools had been selected on the basis of relatively high achievement in their normal day schools and were part of an upliftment programme although none of the teachers had received any additional training or resources. In addition, residential, vacation TASC courses were held in the University of Natal for mixed ability pupils and their teachers.

After all courses, pupils' evaluation included comments of which the following are typical:

> 'For the first time I believe in myself and I believe that I belong in my own country... I now believe that I can learn and take my place in society... I never thought that I could be a problem-solver, I always thought that other people would have to solve my problems for me... I now know that I am not stupid. The skills I have learned this week I can use all my life... Even though I am a girl, I am a good learner and I can do something worthwhile with my life. TASC has improved my brain'.

With regard to the development of the teachers, the authors always modelled a variety of teaching techniques and then the teachers tried to put the techniques into practice with the authors' classroom support. Teachers reported growth in their understanding of interactive, mediating teaching methods and gradually became more skilled in handling group work and open questioning.

In follow-up meetings after the vacation courses, teachers and pupils were continuing to use TASC methods and both pupils and teachers reported and demonstrated an overall improvement in attitudes to school and in levels of attainment.

In the four residential schools, where our work was highly concentrated, the follow-up feedback was very similar to the above and we were also able to monitor the matriculation results which were the highest for all Black schools in the province. It was also possible to monitor the progress of some of the pupils through university and at 'reunion' meetings on refresher TASC courses, students reported their success and also reported setting up study groups in which they taught TASC skills to the other students.

In final summary, the underlying rationale of the whole project was developed from a number of assumptions: thinking skills can be systematically developed, thus enabling all pupils to become increasingly more efficient in 'learning how to learn'. An information-processing approach was adopted based on current research of how children best learn and the framework of thinking skills is designed so that teachers and learners can incorporate issues and problems which are identified by the pupils themselves since learning best occurs when learners begin with their own cultural experiences. It is not possible to arrive at an exhaustive list of thinking and problem-solving skills which need to be internalised and automated but those incorporated in the TASC model coincide well with Sternberg's and Borkowski's metacognitive approach. There is a major emphasis within the TASC paradigm upon developing motivation, instilling a sense of self-worth, establishing an internal locus of control, and cultivating an image of the self as an increasingly efficient learner and problem-solver.

Whilst the TASC model was developed in conditions of prolonged political unrest and widespread violence in which our work was often disrupted and fragmented, our claim is that there are good grounds for believing that the TASC approach has the possibility of achieving significant changes in learners' capacity to benefit from their schooling while also developing their confidence to solve life problems. As always in education, much will depend upon the capacity of administrators and teachers to cope with the adjustments that would be required should a TASC approach be adopted. However, the adoption of TASC can be incremental with, teachers and learners gradually introducing and mastering skills and techniques.

References and Bibliography

Adams, H B (1985), The teaching of general problem-solving strategies, *Developing Cognitive Strategies in Young Children*, SAALED Conference Proceedings, October 1985), University of Durban-Westville, SA

Adams, H B (1986), Teaching general problem-solving strategies in the classroom, *Gifted Education International*, 4, 2, (pp 84-89)

Adams, H B and Wallace, B (1988), The assessment and development of potential of high school pupils in the Third World context of KwaZulu Natal (Part 3) Developing higher order thinking skills and problem-solving strategies in a cooperative learning environment, *Gifted Education International*, 5, 3, (pp 132-137)

Bandura, A (1971), *Social Learning Theory*, Prentice Hall, N J

Bandura, A (1982), Self-efficacy mechanism in human agency, *American Psychologist*, 37, (pp 122-147)

Bandura, A and Walker, R H (1963), *Social Learning Theory and personality development*, Prentice Hall, NY

Blagg, N (1986), *Somerset Thinking Skills Course: Awareness Details*, Somerset County Council, U K

Borkowski, J E (1985), Signs of Intelligence: strategy generalization and metacognition. in Yussen, R S (Ed), *The growth of reflective thought in children*, Academic, N Y

Borkowski, J E and Cavanaugh, J C (1979), Maintenance and generalization of skills and strategies by the retarded, in Ellis, N R (Ed), *Handbook of Mental Deficiency (2nd ed)*, Lawrence Erlbaum, N Y

Brown, A L and Ferrara, R A (1985), Diagnosing zones of proximal development, in J V Wertsch, *Culture, Communication and Cognition: Vygotskian Perspectives*, Cambridge University Press, N Y

Bruner, J (1985), Vygotsky: A Historical and Conceptual Perspective, in J V Wertsch, *Culture, Communication and Cognition: Vygotskian Perspectives*, Cambridge University Press, N Y

Campione, J C and Brown, A L (1978), Toward a theory of intelligence: Contributions from research with retarded children, *Intelligence*, 2, (pp 279-304)

Campione, J C and Brown, A L (1982), Mental retardation and intelligence, in R J Sternberg, *Handbook of Human Intelligence*, Cambridge University Press, N Y

Chipman, S F, Segal, J W and Glaser, R (Eds) (1985), *Thinking and Learning Skills-Vol 2 Research and Open Questions*, Lawrence Erlbaum, N J

Cole, M, Gay, J, Glick, J and Sharp, D W (1971), *The Cultural Context of Learning and Thinking*, Basic Books, N Y

Cole, M (1985), The zone of proximal development: Where culture and cognition create each other, in J V Wertsch, *Culture, Communication and Cognition: Vygotskian Perspectives*, Cambridge University Press, N Y

Cummins, J (1983), *Heritage language education: A literature review*, Ministry of Education, Toronto

Cummins, J (1986), Empowering minority students: A framework for intervention, *Harvard Educational Review*, 56, (pp 18-36)

De Bono, E (1976), *Teaching Thinking*, Temple Smith, London

Dostal, E and Vergani, V (1984), *Future Perspectives on South African Education*, Occasional Paper, 4, Institute for Future Research, University of Stellenbosch, S A

Edusource, (1992), *Edusource Data News*, Education Foundation, S A

Feuerstein, R and Shalom, H (1986), The Learning Potential Assessment Device, in B W Richards (Ed), *Proceedings of the First Congress of the International Association for the Scientific Study of Mental Deficiency*, Michael Jackson, U K

Feuerstein, R et al (1979), *The Dynamic Assessment of Retarded Performers: The Learning Potential Assessment Device, Theory, Instruments and Techniques*, University Park Press, Baltimore

Feuerstein, R et al (1980), *Instrumental Enrichment: An Intervention Programme for Cognitive Modifiability*, University Park Press, Baltimore

Flavell, J H (1979), Metacognition and cognitive monitoring: A new area of cognitive-development enquiry, *American Psychologist*, 34, (pp 906-011)

Flavell, J H (1985), (2nd ed), *Cognitive Development*, Prentice Hall, N J

Foreman, E A and Cazden, C B (1985), Exploring Vygotskian perspectives in education, in J V Wertsch, *Culture, Communication and Cognition: Vygotskian Perspectives*, Cambridge University Press, N Y

Frankenstein, C (1979), *They Think Again: Restoring Cognitive Abilities through Teaching*, Van Rostrand Reinhold co

Freire, P (1972), *Pedagogy of the Oppressed*, Penguin, U K

Goleman, D (1996) *Emotional Intelligence*, London, Bloomsbury

Hanson, J (1987), *Oxford Skills Programme*, Oxfordshire County Council, UK

Jackson, K F (1975), *The Art of Solving Problems*, Bulmershe College of Education, U K

Link, F R (1981), Instrumental enrichment: the classroom perspective, *Educational Forum*, May, (pp 425-428)

Link, F R (1985), Instrumental enrichment: a strategy for cognitive and academic improvement, in F R Link (Ed), *Essays on the Intellect*, ASCD, 1985, (pp 89-106)

Maker, J C and Schiever, S W (1989), *Critical Issues in Gifted Education*, 2, Pro Ed Texas, U S A

Rotter, J B (1966), Generalised expectancies for internal versus external control of reinforcement, *Psychological Monographs 609*

Salovey, P and Mayer, J D (1990), Emotional Intelligence, *Imagination, Cognition and Personality 9*

Segal, J W, Chipman, S F and Glaser, R (Eds) (1985), *Thinking and Learning Skills: Vol 1 Relating Instruction to Research*, Lawrence Erlbaum, N J

Siegler, R S and Richard, D D (1982), The development of intelligence, in R J Sternberg, *Handbook of Human Intelligence*, Cambridge University Press, U K

Sternberg, R J (1983), Criteria for intelligence skills training, *Educational Researcher*, 12, 6

Sternberg, R J (1985), *Beyond IQ: A Triarchic Theory of Human Intelligence*, Cambridge University Press, N Y

Sternberg, R J (1986), *Intelligence Applied: Understanding and Increasing your Intellectual Skills*, Harcourt, Brace, Jovanovich, San Diego

Vygotsky, L S (1978), *Mind in Society. The Development of Higher Psychological Processes*, (Edited and translated by Cole, W *et al*), Harvard University Press, M A,

Vos, A J (1986), Aspects of Education in KwaZulu Natal, *Paedomenia*, 13, 2, Journal of the Faculty of Education, University of Zululand, S A

Wallace, B and Adams, H B (1987), Assessment and development of potential of high school pupils in the Third World context of KwaZulu Natal (Part 1), *Gifted Education International*, 5,1, (pp 6-10)

Wallace, B and Adams, H B (1988), Assessment and development of potential of high school pupils in the Third World context of KwaZulu Natal (Part 2), *Gifted Education International*, 5, 2, (pp 72-79)

Wallace, B and Adams, H B (1993a) (Eds), *Worldwide Perspectives on the Gifted Disadvantaged*, AB Academic Publishers, U K

Wallace, B and Adams, H B (1993b), *TASC Thinking Actively in a Social Context*, A B Aacademic Publishers, U K

Wallace, B and Adams, H B (1993a) (Eds), *Worldwide Perspectives on the Gifted Disadvantaged*, AB Academic Publishers, U K

Wertsch, J V (1985), Introduction, in J V Wertsch, *Culture, Communication and Cognition: Vygotskian Perspectives*, Cambridge University Press, U K

Wertsch, J V (1985), Adult-child interactions as a source of self-regulation in children, in S R Yussen (Ed), *The Growth of Reflective Thinking in Children*, Academic, N Y

Wertsch, J V and Addison Stone, C (1985), The concept of internalisation in Vygotsky's account of the genesis of higher mental functions, in J V Wertsch, *Culture, Communication and Cognition: Vygotskian Perspectives*, Cambridge University Press, N Y

Addendum

For readers wishing to see the practical application of the TASC approach, the teaching principles and thinking and problem-solving skills have been used to design and write a series of second language texts which systematically develop cognition and metacognition. The language series is written in English (grade1 to grade 12) together with readers for teachers and learners in South Africa. The series is called *Language in my World*. The first three grades are published and available from Juta Educational Publishers, PO Box 14373, Kenwyn 7790, Cape Town, South Africa.

Index

L

language disorders, 53, 83, 105, 208, 238, 256

Latin America, **229**

Latvia, 73

learning difficulties, 11, 20, 21, 22, 40, 53, 54, 60, 71, 76, 79, 83, 92, 101, 104, 106, 108, 119, 120, 189, 206, 207, 208, 209, 210, 214, 216, 217, 218, 223, 238, 239, 252, *273*, 286

learning disabled, 159

learning support assistants, 29, 42, 47

LEONARDO, 73

LINGUA, 71

Lithuania, 73

Luxembourg, 81

M

Maastricht Treaty (1992), 72, *88*

Macedonia, 118

mainstreaming, *32*, 77, 82, 83, 248

market system, 32

medical model, 12, 17, 18, 77, 93, 108, 109, 164, 232, 233, 235, 270

memory, 133, 152, 304

mentally handicapped, 91, 121, 123, 126, 128, 129, 130, 131, 132, 133, 134, 135, 136, 137, 138, 139, 140, 141, 142, 144, 145, 146, 147, 148, 149, 150

mentally retarded/mental retardation, *89, 120, 151*, 214, 216, **222**, 226, 235, 238, *294, 317*

N

Netherlands, 82, 85, **121**, 154, 216

networks, 12, 69, 71, 72, 73, 118

New Zealand, 13, *88, 204,* **276**
    Education Acts (1964, 1989), 277, 278, 279, 280, 281, 283, 284, 286, *294*
    Education Amendment Act (1991), 284, *294*
    Maoris, 289, 291, 292, *293, 294*
    School Charters, 279, 281
    Special Education 2000, 280, 282, 286, 287, 288, 291, 293, 294, 295, 296

normalisation, 68, 69, *88, 89, 120,* 129, 233, 237, 243, 245

Norway, 91

O

Organisation of Eastern Caribbean States (OECS), 205, 225, 226, *227*
    Education Reform Report (1991), *227*

P

parental choice, 19, 25, *33*, 86, *292*

parents, 15, 18, 21, 23, 24, 25, 26, 27, 29, 31, *33, 35*, 52, 54, 56, 60, 61, 62, 63, 65, 66, 70, 78, 79, 81, 82, 86, 97, 100, 159, 160, 182, 185, 190, 195, 207, 208, 211, 213, 218, 222, 223, 224, 225, *227,* 230, 231, 246, 252, 264, 271, 278, 279, 280, 281, 282, 286, 287, 292, *293,* 299, 300, 301, 303

Parent's Charter, 31

peer relations, 162, 165, *174*

NOTES

NOTES

NOTES